CONGRESSMAN ABRAHAM LINCOLN

CONGRESSMAN

ABRAHAM

LINCOLN

DONALD W. RIDDLE

GREENWOOD PRESS, PUBLISHERS
WESTPORT, CONNECTICUT

Library of Congress Cataloging in Publication Data

Riddle, Donald Wayne, 1894–
   Congressman Abraham Lincoln.

   Reprint of the ed. published by University of
Illinois Press, Urbana.
   Bibliography: p.
   Includes index.
   1. Lincoln, Abraham, Pres. U.S., 1809–1865—Political
career before 1861. 2. United States—Politics and
government—1845–1861. 3. Presidents—United States—
Biography. I. Title.
[E457.4.R5 1979]   973.6'092'4   79-11614
ISBN 0-8371-9307-9

First published in 1957 by the University of Illinois Press,
Urbana

Reprinted by permission of the University of Illinois Press

Reprinted in 1979 by Greenwood Press, Inc.
51 Riverside Avenue, Westport, CT 06880

Printed in the United States of America

10 9 8 7 6 5 4 3 2 1

PREFACE

This book has been written to serve two purposes: to further the understanding of Abraham Lincoln and to aid Lincoln's biographers.

To understand Lincoln it is necessary to study him in the full context of the historical situations which occurred during his career, and I have attempted to do this. His Congressional term was served at a time of transition in the growth of the United States and in a transition period in his own life. Western expansion, the Mexican War, the administrative policies of President Polk, the changing political party alignments, the inevitable crises in territorial organization as a result of the Mexican War, and the rapidly heightening tension of the slavery issue need to be depicted in order to understand Lincoln's action in relation to them. When this is done it is possible to perceive not only what he did but the reasons for his acts and statements. Value judgments are inescapable. A critical study of background and response will further the understanding of Lincoln.

A detailed study of the limited subject of Lincoln's Congressional career can be of assistance to Lincoln biographers. The source materials for the life of Lincoln are so enormous in volume that no one can read all of them. It is questionable whether one can cover all the manuscripts. For my limited subject I have utilized all known and available materials in manuscripts, newspapers, and official records. I have quoted sources extensively, believing that the reader is best served by his own inspection of sources which bring him into contemporaneous relationship with the subject matter. It is my hope that this full coverage of extant sources for the limited period will make it unnecessary for Lincoln biographers to repeat the task.

It is pertinent to point out, in this connection, that in quoting sources I have exhibited content, spelling, and punctuation literally. I have refrained from changing spelling and punctuation to conform to modern usage, and from indicating deviations by (sic).

The impulse for the writing of this book is the observation made by my late colleague, Professor James G. Randall (in his article, "Has the Lincoln Theme Been Exhausted?") that Lincoln's Congressional career had not been thoroughly investigated. I trust that this field is now covered.

The preparation of this book has involved work in the following libraries, and I take this occasion to offer my thanks to these institutions and to the members of their staffs who have so effectively helped me: the Libraries of Harvard University, the Libraries of the University of Illinois at Urbana and the Chicago Undergraduate Division, the Newberry Library, the Libraries of the University of Chicago, the Illinois State Historical Library and the Abraham Lincoln Association in Springfield, the Library of the Chicago Historical Society, the Indiana State Historical Library, the Indianapolis Public Library, the Library of the Lincoln National Life Foundation of Fort Wayne, Indiana, the Library of the Ohio State Archaeological and Historical Society, the Rockford Public Library, the Library of Congress, the National Archives, the Archives of the Department of State, and the Archives of the Department of the Interior. I am obliged, too, to Mrs. H. H. Kean, of Terre Haute, Indiana, for her kind permission to use manuscripts of her grandfather, Richard W. Thompson.

Of the many scholars who have been of assistance to me none has done more than the late Dr. Harry E. Pratt. Both he and Mrs. Pratt were untiring in placing source materials before me, and both have been helpful in counsel and encouragement.

Dr. Pratt read my typescript and enabled me to correct errors.

My wife has worked with me in every aspect of the preparation of this book except its actual composition.

If the book serves to fulfill the two purposes for which it has been written I shall be more than rewarded for the effort involved in its writing.

Donald W. Riddle

THE UNIVERSITY OF ILLINOIS
CHICAGO UNDERGRADUATE DIVISION
FEBRUARY 6, 1957

CONTENTS

1

THE LONE WHIG FROM ILLINOIS

"As you are all so anxious for me to distinguish myself, I have concluded to do so, before long."

So wrote Congressman Abraham Lincoln to William Herndon, his law partner, not quite two weeks after reaching Washington as a member of the Thirtieth Congress.

He began to distinguish himself nine days later by presenting his Spot Resolutions, a series of highly invidious questions designed to make party political capital of the Mexican War issue.

Less than two weeks after offering his Spot Resolutions he distinguished himself again: he voted "Aye" on the Ashmun amendment which stigmatized the Mexican War as "unnecessarily and unconstitutionally begun by the President."

Then, a little over a month after he took his seat, Congressman Lincoln made a full-length speech in the House. This speech was doubtless what he had in mind in his bantering remark to Herndon. Entitled "The War With Mexico," it followed the Whig party's view. It was severely critical of the war policy of the Polk administration, caustic in its references to the President, and negative in its attitude toward the war.

The distinction which Lincoln achieved was by no means what, presumably, he had expected. The Washington correspondent of the Baltimore *Patriot* referred to the Spot Resolutions with approval; his complimentary reference to Lincoln was copied in the Whig newspapers in Illinois. But from the first reference to Lincoln's activity in Congress which appeared in the Chicago *Democrat*, a chorus of opposition resounded throughout Illinois. The Spot Resolutions were denounced, his vote on the Ashmun amendment was indignantly characterized as not in accord with the views of his constituents and as unworthy of them and of Illinois. His speech on the war was denounced as craven and unpatriotic.

Most of the few Whig newspapers of the state, especially those which Lincoln could control, defended him and his course of action, but his three conspicuous acts concerning the war were unpopular even among fellow Whigs of his own congressional district. Herndon feared for his political future. Another law associate, Usher F. Linder, broke with him in regard to the war issue. His most faithful friend and loyal supporter, Dr. A. G. Henry, pointed out an area of fundamental disagreement and warned Lincoln of the probable consequences of extreme antiwar opposition. Some Whig newspapers were silent; one, the Alton *Telegraph*, was in opposition to Lincoln's course. The sobriquet, "Spotty," was coined and applied to him; it stuck to Lincoln throughout his political life in Illinois, recurred in the Lincoln-Douglas debates, and plagued him when he was a candidate for the Presidency. Newspaper squibs gibed him not only in his own state but in Indiana, Kentucky, and Missouri.

Worse came in the Congressional election of 1848. The Seventh Congressional District, which Lincoln represented, had for years been the one certain Whig stronghold in Illinois. Until Lincoln distinguished himself it was assumed that the Whig nominee for Congress in that district was certain to be elected. Lincoln's vote, when he was the candidate in 1846, was by far the largest polled by a Whig up to that time. No Democrat had ever been elected to Congress in the Seventh District. But in 1848 the Whig stronghold was lost to the Democrats. The election was decided upon the Mexican War issue. An unusual number of returned soldiers voted, and a veteran of the war was elected. The Whig defeat was directly charged to Lincoln's three acts as Congressman.

Moreover, when Lincoln campaigned for Taylor in Illinois in the Presidential canvass of 1848 he was roughly handled—

heckled with aspersions of his acts as Congressman, derisively called "Spotty," and denounced as unpatriotic and unrepresentative of the people. Whether he was "used up" in this brief speaking tour on Taylor's behalf, as the Democratic press asserted, or retired from the field for reasons more gratifying to himself, it is a fact that Lincoln did little for his party in his own state in the elections of 1848.

Indeed, Lincoln's unpopularity, the result of his record as Congressman, placed him in political eclipse. Albert T. Bledsoe, a Springfield friend and fellow Whig, said later that Lincoln's unpopularity at the end of his term in Congress was so great that he could not have been elected to any office, not even Justice of the Peace or constable. Lincoln spoke the plain truth, when he was mentioned as a possible candidate for Congress in 1850, that any one of several other Whigs could be elected as easily as he. As is well known, Lincoln rationalized his eclipse as a voluntary retirement from politics until his interest was revived by the repeal of the Missouri Compromise in the Kansas-Nebraska Act. The fact was that though Lincoln was retired from politics he never lost his ambition for office. He became a candidate as soon as he could rehabilitate himself and find an issue.

When Lincoln returned to Springfield from his one term in Congress he was a repudiated politician, not highly valued by some of the influential leaders of his party. He had sought an appointive office commensurate with his ability and worth, but it had gone to another. He was appreciated by President Taylor, who offered him appointment as Governor of the Oregon Territory, but in an egregious example of maladroitness a cabinet secretary offered him the post of secretary of that territory, a $1,500 job suited to the talents of a party hack, and, assuming Lincoln's acceptance, sent him the commission for the minor position.

Lincoln had failed to get the only appointive office which would suit his plans and aspirations. He could not win an elective office. The 1,500 Whig majority in his Congressional district had been changed to a Democratic plurality. He faced the prospect of some years of obscurity until he could live down his unpopularity and the reasons for it.

This unhappy situation existed despite the fact that Lincoln had demonstrated praiseworthy industry and much better than average ability in his one Congressional term. He was a faithful party man. He missed few roll calls, and never "skulked" a vote on touchy issues. He served well and conspicuously in his committee assignments. He participated actively in debate. In two of his formal speeches he made an excellent presentation of his party's case. He made an effective appeal for his party's candidate for the Presidency. He made lasting friendships with a number of his colleagues. He learned much of inestimable value to him in his subsequent political career.

Why did Lincoln, in his single term in Congress, come short of success? What errors of judgment did he make—wrong judgments of party policy, failure to make correct estimates of the views of his constituents, mistakes in the evaluation of colleagues and of party leaders? Why did he fail to secure the appointive office which he sought, and why was that office given to a man who, in Lincoln's opinion, was, of all Illinois Whigs, the least deserving? How can the series of blunders in the Oregon appointment be explained? And what elements of personal character did Lincoln have to enable him to accept failure and rebuff in good humor, with no diminution in his loyal support of his party and its leaders—even of those responsible for his own ill treatment—without complaint and without recrimination? How are we to understand his patient waiting? What issue did he ultimately seize upon to get back into the race for office? If answers to these questions can assuredly be found there is reward in studying the career of Congressman Lincoln.

Patient waiting was no new trait of character in Lincoln. Getting elected to Congress required its full exercise. Lincoln actively sought nomination for Congress as early as 1843, but circumstances delayed his election until 1846. Circumstances delayed, but it was Lincoln's own astuteness and patience which found the way and the means to his ultimate success.[1]

In the one dependable Whig Congressional district in Illinois there were three Whig leaders, almost equal in age, all deserving of party preferment—three friends: John J. Hardin of Jacksonville, Edward Dickinson Baker of Springfield, and Lincoln. All were rival candidates for nomination to Congress in 1843. Lincoln found hmself out-maneuvered in his own county —Sangamon—and made a delegate to the District Convention,

---

[1] Donald W. Riddle, *Lincoln Runs For Congress* (1948).

with himself and the delegation instructed to vote for Baker. But there was a possibility that a deadlock between Hardin and Baker might develop, in which event Lincoln might be nominated.

Lincoln measured this possibility and cultivated the advantage of it to himself, but he did not deviate from his obligation. When the deadlock occurred Lincoln was farsighted enough to work out a procedure which would fairly serve the purposes of his rivals and himself. He was generous enough to give his friends precedence: he proposed a plan which insured the nomination (election was assumed) of each in turn, with himself last in order.

This was the "Pekin agreement," later to become notorious. As Lincoln understood it, the three agreed that Hardin would be nominated in 1843, that Hardin would not run against Baker in 1844, and that Hardin and Baker would refrain from contesting the nomination of Lincoln in 1846.[2] On this basis Lincoln withdrew Baker's candidacy in 1843. Hardin pledged that he would not be a candidate to succeed himself. Baker was nominated and elected in 1844; after taking his seat he announced that he would not run in 1846.

But when Lincoln's turn came, Hardin was not inclined to abide by the Pekin agreement. He was urged to run for governor but promptly declined this empty honor—the Whigs had never elected their candidate for governer and had no prospect of doing so—and he announced his availability for nomination and election to Congress.

Lincoln's campaign for nomination was, in effect, the task of preventing Hardin from becoming a candidate—the task of holding him to the Pekin agreement. While attending court in the county seats of the Eighth Judicial District, Lincoln quietly "sewed up" prominent Whigs in all the counties, except Morgan County where Hardin lived, securing their pledges to support his candidacy in the District Convention.

He secured their pledges by appealing to the principle of rotation in office, a principle heartily endorsed by Whigs, in terms of the maxim "turn about is fair play." He was so successful that he soon controlled a majority of the prospective delegates.

---

[2] Elections usually were in even-numbered years, but the reapportionment after the 1840 Census was made so late that the election was held in 1843.

He also controlled the Whig press; four newspapers within the district were committed to Lincoln's candidacy, while only one (in Hardin's town) opposed him.

Since Lincoln controlled a majority of the Whigs who were likely to become delegates to the precinct, county, and district conventions (of course with the exception of Morgan County), the only way by which Hardin could forestall Lincoln's nomination was by preventing the holding of the District Convention. Such a move would have met with widespread Whig approval; many Whigs disliked nominating conventions.

Well aware of this, Hardin proposed an interesting substitute. He suggested a preferential Whig primary election in each county, in which the Congressional nomination would be made by ballot and without the candidates electioneering outside their own counties.

Lincoln shrewdly countered Hardin's proposal. He insisted upon the holding of the convention. Meanwhile friendly newspapers and Lincoln's supporters were insisting that "turn about is fair play," and reminding Hardin, as well as the voters, of the Pekin agreement. Hardin had no recourse but to withdraw from the campaign. Lincoln went into the convention unopposed and was unanimously nominated—three years after he began to campaign. Before the election Hardin became a Colonel of Volunteers in the Mexican War, where he was killed in action in the battle of Buena Vista.

In the election canvass Lincoln defeated the redoubtable circuit-rider, Peter Cartwright, the Democratic candidate, and Elihu Walcott, the candidate of the Liberty Party. The campaign was not exciting. The outcome was a foregone conclusion: the Whigs outnumbered the Democrats and at that time the anti-slavery vote was negligible. The vote was light, and Lincoln carried eight of the eleven counties—a better showing than had been made by Hardin or by Baker. He won election by the largest plurality and with the highest percentage attained in the Congressional district up to that time.

Lincoln's patience was called upon in the long wait between the election and the meeting of Congress. He was elected August 3, 1846, and the Thirtieth Congress convened on December 6, 1847. Presently he received his certificate of election and by October the aftermath of the contest had reached the point that he wrote to his friend Joshua Speed, "being elected to Congress, though I am very grateful to our friends, for having done it, has not pleased me as much as I expected."

However this may have been, Lincoln had reached a high point in a political career which had already shown obvious signs of bright promise. He was already an experienced legislator on the state level. He was acknowledged as an aggressive and a sagacious leader in his party's councils. Election to Congress was an essential step toward the future which he envisaged for himself. Although his party was in the minority in his state he had the advantage of the concentration of its strength in the area in which he lived and practiced both law and politics. He knew Illinois well enough to be aware that the steady and now rapid immigration of settlers, especially those who located upon the prairies, would bring many more Whigs to his state. When there were enough to enable his party to control the Legislature Lincoln might reasonably expect to be elected to the Senate. In the Thirtieth Congress he was the lone Whig from Illinois, but he confidently envisioned for himself and for his party a higher attainment than either had yet achieved.

In the fall of 1847 Lincoln rented his Springfield home for a year, at ninety dollars, and set out for Washington with his family.

2

PRAIRIE STATE POLITICIAN IN WASHINGTON

Late in the evening of the second of December, 1847, the travel-weary Lincolns arrived in Washington. They went first to Brown's Hotel, otherwise known, from its sign which bore an effigy of Pocahontas, as the "Indian Queen." Moderate in tariff, it was second to none in hospitality. The registration, "A. Lincoln & Lady 2 children, Illinois," is still a collector's item. The long wait between election and the meeting of Congress was nearing its end. Lincoln, the lone Whig, and six Democratic colleagues were about to represent the Prairie State in the House of Representatives of the Thirtieth Congress.

The route of the Lincolns from Springfield to Washington must be inferred for some of its parts.[1] They traveled first by stage to Alton or to St. Louis, and then went by river steamer down the Mississippi, up the Ohio, and up the Kentucky to Frankfort. They then went by railroad to Lexington, where they visited at the home of Mr. and Mrs. Robert S. Todd, Mrs. Lincoln's father and stepmother, until Thanksgiving Day.

---

[1] Benjamin P. Thomas, *Lincoln 1847-1853* (1952), pp. 44, 48; John William Starr, *Lincoln and the Railroads*, p. 47; *Whig Almanac*, 1851, p. 39. A travel journal of a man who in considerable part paralleled Lincoln's route, and thus provided check points of elapsed time, is worth study. Earle D. Ross, "A Travelogue of 1849," *Mississippi Valley Historical Review*, 37 (1940), 435-41.

Mrs. Lincoln, of course, was much at home in Lexington, and family and social connections between the Todds and Lincoln's Springfield friends were close. Stuart, Lincoln's first law partner and early political mentor, was a member of the Todd family, and Ninian Edwards, Jr., one of Lincoln's intimate friends, had married one of Mary Todd's sisters. Two other of the Todd sisters, Anna Maria and Frances, had married and then lived in Springfield.[2]

One event which occurred in Lexington during this visit was important to Lincoln because of its effect upon him. This was a long speech on the Mexican War, delivered by Henry Clay.[3] Lincoln's father-in-law was vice-chairman of the meeting at which Clay spoke. The great Whig leader developed a view which was reflected in the speech by which Lincoln distinguished himself; Clay emphatically declared that the war was caused by President Polk's order to General Taylor to move his army from Corpus Christi to the Rio Grande. He insisted that war might have been averted if this move had not been made. He referred to Fort Brown as "within the very disputed district," terminology which Lincoln was to use in his own speech. The war, said Clay, was not one of defense, but one of "unnecessary and offensive aggression." Congressman Ashmun may have adopted Clay's "unnecessary" when he formulated the notorious amendment which involved Lincoln in so much bitter criticism. Clay made the point that the purpose of the war had never been made clear—another idea which Lincoln later included in his speech.

This is what Lincoln heard the titular head of his party say of the war. What did Lincoln, the young Congressman-elect, think of it? His Congressional career turned upon the party issue of the war; what he did and what he said about it affected his subsequent career. It is necessary to sketch the situation and Lincoln's reactions to it, in order to understand the position which he took toward it, and in order to appreciate the judgments of his constituents.

Mexicans crossed the Rio Grande and attacked American dragoons on April 26, 1846. At this time Lincoln was a candidate

---

[2] William H. Townsend, *Lincoln and His Wife's Home Town* (1929), pp. 137-61.

[3] *Whig Almanac*, 1848, pp. 7-16.

for nomination to Congress. By the time news of the first hostilities reached Washington the battles of Palo Alto and Resaca
de la Palma had been fought. President Polk presented the situation to Congress on May 11, in a message which asserted that
Mexico had shed American blood on American soil so that "war
exists . . . by act of Mexico." Two days later Congress adopted
a resolution that "by the act of the Republic of Mexico a state
of war exists between that government and the United States."
In the House fourteen and in the Senate two Whigs voted against
the adoption of the resolution.[4]

Back of the war was the annexation of Texas. This was the
inevitable conclusion of the Texan struggle for independence—
indeed, of the settlement of Texas by emigrants from the United
States.[5] What was but the normal process of expansion westward
was soon interpreted as a heinous plot: the minority of militant
abolitionists reiterated that Texas had been annexed for the
purpose of vastly extending the establishment and the political
power of slavery. Despite the fact that most of the settlers in
Texas were not slaveholders, the alleged plot became the Whig
view.

However this may have been, the annexation of Texas was
not merely a vexing aspect of the slavery question. It was an
issue of foreign relations.[6] After a proper interval the Republic
of Texas was granted diplomatic recognition by the United States,
and later by France and by England. There was a widespread
belief that the interests of the European powers might militate
against the security and the interests of the United States.

The Mexican government had declared that the annexation
of Texas by the United States would be regarded as an act of
war and would be followed by hostilities. Ignoring this threat,
annexation was seized upon by President Tyler as a popular
measure. When annexation by treaty failed, it was effected by
joint Congressional resolution during Tyler's administration.
After Polk was inaugurated all that remained was for the Texan

---

[4] Justin Smith, *The War With Mexico* (1919); Alfred Hoyt Bill, *Rehearsal
for Conflict* (1947); Robert Selph Henry, *The Story of the Mexican War*
(1950).

[5] Justin Smith, *The Annexation of Texas* (1941).

[6] St. George L. Sioussat, *James Buchanan, Secretary of State* (1928),
pp. 265-89.

Congress to act and for the formalities of procedure to be carried out. These steps were taken. The Mexican threat was promptly translated into action.

Not much of its plan of victory over Mexico had been accomplished by the United States when Lincoln was elected to Congress. General Taylor, after winning the first two actions, occupied Matamoros, and began his campaign up the Rio Grande and into the Mexican interior. Within two months he had occupied Comargo. In the West the quasi-comic opera liberation of California had been effected by Frémont and others. Just before Lincoln's election the epic march of Kearney and his Missourians (and Mormons) had passed Bent's Fort.

Yet the Mexican war had made its impact upon Lincoln and the Illinois Whigs. When the war began they supported it. One decisive fact stands out: on May 30, 1846, soon after Lincoln had been nominated for Congress, a war rally was held in Springfield. It was well attended. Lincoln joined Governor Ford and three other speakers in an appeal for volunteers, speaking "on the necessity of prompt and united action to support" the war. Lincoln's speech was said to have been "warm, thrilling, and effective." Seventy men were recruited by the rally.[7]

During the long wait between his election and the opening of Congress there appeared no additional evidence of Lincoln's views concerning the war. There is no allusion to it in his campaign speeches nor in his letters. But from his words and deeds in Congress it is evident that Lincoln had shifted from support of the war to the orthodox Whig attitude of opposition. The change in Lincoln cannot be observed and charted, but it can be measured in the columns of his party newspaper, the *Sangamo Journal.*

This excellent Whig newspaper had welcomed the annexation of Texas, and had regarded the Rio Grande as the boundary between Texas and Mexico. It was alarmed at the potential danger to Taylor's army when it was encamped at Corpus Christi, and approved the change of base to the Rio Grande. It welcomed the state of war resolution, although it deplored the words and the alleged partisan purpose of the preamble. But as the war continued the Illinois Whig organ moved to the

---

[7] *Sangamo Journal,* June 4, 1846.

position of the majority of the party. It continued to support . the prosecution of the war, and it gloried in the leadership given by such Whigs as Hardin and Baker. Nevertheless the *Journal* became increasingly critical of President Polk and vigorously opposed the administration's war policy.

Lincoln and his local party newspaper usually held the same political ideas, and it is to be concluded that the change in his ideas about the war coincided with the change reflected in the *Journal*. This had occurred before he heard Clay in Lexington. He greatly admired the party leader, and the Congressman-elect doubtless echoed the voice of his chief. It is probable that this highlight of the Lexington visit was effective in indicating to Lincoln that his proper course as Congressman was to hew to the party line.

When the Lincolns left Lexington they had a choice of routes. The most direct way to Washington was by stage from Lexington to Winchester, Virginia, from which rail travel was available. A longer but much more comfortable route was back to Frankfort by rail and then to Pittsburgh or to Brownsville, Pennsylvania, by river steamer. From either of these two points a shorter journey by stage to the railhead at Cumberland, Maryland, would be required. From Cumberland there was direct rail connection to Relay Station, Maryland, from which a branch line of the Baltimore and Ohio ran to Washington. It is probable that the longer route was taken by the Lincolns; under the best circumstances stage travel with two small children (Robert Lincoln was four and Eddie was less than two years old) would be onerous.[8]

Besides, the mileage was an important consideration—as Horace Greeley was to point out when he became a member of the Thirtieth Congress, and as had appeared from comic aspects of the election in Lincoln's district during his long wait. E. D. Baker, Lincoln's predecessor in Congress, had resigned his seat (after collecting his mileage as a dispatch bearer from the war theatre), and one John Henry, a Whig of no distinction, was elected to fill the vacancy. Henry candidly offered as his reason for becoming a candidate that he was a poor man (adding

---

[8] Thomas (p. 48) believes that the Lincolns went by stage to Winchester. It seems probable that traveling with two small children would determine the more comfortable way of travel. Starr (p. 48) believes that the river steamer was used.

that his opponent was wealthy) and that he wanted to collect the mileage.[9]

The law provided that members of Congress be reimbursed for travel at the rate of forty cents per mile by the usually traveled route. It was 840 miles from Springfield to Washington by the *shortest* route. But since the Congressman chose his route it was likely to be a long one, and, as Greeley said, "exceedingly crooked, even for a politician." Yet the common practice met with little disapproval; payment for mileage was a substitute for adequate salary or *per diem*, and used as such. Lincoln charged $1,300.80 for 1,626 miles, which Greeley calculated was an excess of $878.80 over the usually traveled route.

The Lincolns went first to the "Indian Queen," but did not remain there long. They took residence at the boardinghouse, or "mess," kept by Mrs. Ann Sprigg, on Carroll Row between A and East Capitol Streets. The place stood where the older building of the Congressional Library is now located.[10] Lincoln's three Whig predecessors had lived there.

The Illinois politician had little time for sightseeing before his duties began. Even a brief view would have sufficed for the city as it was then. Washington's population at the end of 1847

---

[9] The full story of John Henry is out of place in the text of this book. However, since political opponents joined Lincoln's war record with Henry's, since Douglas repeated the error in the Lincoln–Douglas Debates, and since the confused charge was made in the Presidential campaign of 1860, it is relevant to state the facts.

Henry took his seat February 5, 1847. What he did met with indignation in the Seventh District. Evidently he submitted to the influence of some antiwar Whig, and voted accordingly. He favored laying on the table a motion to end debate on the so-called $3,000,000 bill for war supplies, voted to attach the Wilmot Proviso to the bill, voted to lay the bill on the table, and voted against the passage of the bill—i.e., he voted against furnishing supplies to the armed forces. When a Senate bill, providing for an additional number of general officers, came before the House, he voted not to concur and against the passage of the bill. When an appropriation bill came up he supported an amendment designed to prevent use of any money for defraying expenses of the war. When the amendment was rejected he voted against the appropriation.

On Henry's nomination and election: *Sangamo Journal*, January 14, 1847, January 28, 1847; *Hennepin Herald*, February 5, 1847; Theodore C. Pease, *Illinois Election Returns* (1923), p. 171.

On Henry's votes in Congress: *Congressional Globe* (hereafter cited as *Globe*), 29th Congress, 2nd Session, pp. 331, 360, 383, 425, 429, 432, 472, 511, 527, 539, 557, 573.

[10] Samuel C. Busey, *Personal Reminiscences* (1895) p. 25.

was about 34,000, including more than 8,000 slaves and about 2,000 free Negroes. Nearby (not then contiguous) Georgetown contained about 8,500 of the people of the District of Columbia. Then, as now, Washington was a city of magnificent distances. Most of its people lived in the area bounded by Pennsylvania Avenue on the south, by an irregular line including 1st, 3rd, 5th, and 9th Streets as far north as L Street; L Street was the northern limit of the settled part, and New York Avenue and 15th Street formed the northwestern corner.[11]

Within this area, aside from the White House and the Capitol, there was little that was impressive. Pennsylvania Avenue had been paved with cobblestones laid over the old surface, and in part of its length this avenue was gaslighted on nights when Congress was in session. The White House had essentially its recent outer structural form, but the Capitol lacked its north and south wings, and a temporary wooden dome covered its rotunda. The foundation of the Smithsonian Institution had been laid and construction of the building was in progress. Government departments were housed in two-story buildings: the State Department where the north front of the Treasury Department was later built and the War and Navy Departments where the State Department now stands.

The Capitol, directly across from Mrs. Sprigg's, was the building most in view. It was small as compared to the completed edifice, and it contained more than it could hold comfortably. The Senate and the House were placed in what are now the connecting rooms between the rotunda and the present chambers; the House sat in the space now occupied by the statues of distinguished legislators, with the Senate opposite. The Supreme Court was relegated to the basement below the Senate, and the Congressional Library occupied the space to the west of the rotunda, south of the Senate chamber.

On his first day in Washington, Lincoln attended to personal and business correspondence.[12] On the evening of December 4 his horizon was broadened to national affairs when he attended

---

[11] Wilhelmus B. Bryan, *A History of the National Capital* (1916), II: 357-61; Rufus R. Wilson, *Washington, the Capital City* (1901), II:66; George Watterson, *New Guide to Washington* (1847).

[12] Roy P. Basler (Editor), *Collected Works of Abraham Lincoln* (1953) (hereafter cited as *CW*), I:416 f.

a Whig caucus to select candidates for the organization of the house.[13] There had been a Democratic majority in both houses of Congress in the first half of President Polk's administration, but the Whigs had carried the mid-term elections, and with a majority in the House, were in a position to organize that larger branch of Congress.

The government, with a Democratic Chief Executive and Senate, and a Whig House, was faced by tasks of great magnitude and difficulty. It must bring the war to a successful conclusion. This did not seem to be hard to do, nor was it, in the military sense. The great battles had been fought and won. General Scott had captured and was holding Mexico City, and fighting was practically ended. But concluding the war involved the solution of a most difficult problem: there must be a government in Mexico capable of maintaining order, collecting revenue, paying its running expenses (the most pressing of which was paying the army, thus keeping it loyal to the current regime), negotiating peace, and carrying out the provisions of the peace treaty. Until this problem was solved it was necessary for the United States to keep armed forces in Mexico.

Also, since it was certain that territory would be annexed, it was an obligation of the Thirtieth Congress to provide territorial government for the land and people now Mexican but soon to become part of the United States. Moreover, since the Twenty-ninth Congress had not done so, territorial government for the Oregon country, whose boundary and status had been determined in the first half of the Polk administration, had to be provided. The war and demobilization must be financed; the transition to peace from war economy must be effected. A dangerous domestic question had been complicated by the war; slavery was rapidly becoming an issue dividing political parties, splitting the nation into sections, and perplexing thoughtful citizens.

Then too, there was the usual spate of domestic questions: the westward movement of settlers was bringing changes in the organization of territories and the internal policies of states, and—a phenomenon not then greatly realized—the tempo of the transition to an industrial economy was accelerated. These were the matters of government which the Thirtieth Congress was

---

[13] *CW* I:417.

called upon to handle; these were the issues which Congressman Lincoln encountered as the scene of his career shifted from state to nation.

What qualities and abilities did Lincoln bring as he moved up the ladder from state legislator to Congressman? He brought experience, sagacity, and success in politics on local, district, and state levels. After defeat in 1832 he had been elected four successive times to the lower house of the Illinois Assembly, in one election receiving the largest vote of all candidates from his county. He had been one of the leading men in the legislature; one of the few who talked most and who dominated the legislative program. He was persuasive and effective in managing measures and men. He was credited with two particularly important legislative acts.[14] One was the notorious Internal Improvements bill of 1837 which had negligible result in its objective but which crippled the economy of the state to the point that it was a major achievement of Governor Ford in 1842 to save the financial credit of Illinois. The other achievement credited to Lincoln's management was the removal of the state capital from Vandalia to Springfield.

Lincoln had grown with his party. He was an orthodox Whig. He accepted his party's principles: high tariff, internal improvements financed by the national government, a national bank, protection of the interests of property and of people of wealth, land policies which served the advantage of speculators rather than of settlers, and general sympathy with the business and professional classes.

As a dominating figure in local politics Lincoln had developed great capacity in managing. He was one of the leaders of the small group which was called by people who disliked it the "Springfield junto," and as such he accepted and promoted organizational devices which were largely responsible for such success as his party enjoyed in Illinois. He advocated the widespread use of the convention system for nominating candidates and for advancing party influence. He was clearly right in this view, but he was unable to induce the Illinois Whigs to adopt it throughout the state. Consequently the Whigs were always a minority in Illinois.

One aspect of Lincoln's Whig party relationship seems today

---

[14] William E. Barringer, *Lincoln and Vandalia* (1949).

to be curious, although when viewed in the perspectives of place and time it is readily understandable: he was in sympathy with and responsive to Southern, rather than to Northern and Eastern Whig policy. He was a "Clay man" in 1832, but in 1836, when the candidates were Webster, Harrison, and White, Lincoln was one with the Springfield Whigs in supporting White of Tennessee, who was well known to be the Southern and pro-slavery candidate. It is not surprising that he did not favor Webster, but it is difficult to understand why, as a Westerner, he did not align himself with Harrison. But of the Eastern, Western, and Southern candidates of the new (then only emerging in the West) Whig party, Lincoln favored the Southern, even though White was the mildest anti-Jackson man of the three. As shall appear, Lincoln's rapport with Southern Whigs was apparent in his associations and policies while in Congress.

Lincoln's sympathy with the Southern wing of his party is simply explained. The "Sangamo region" of Illinois, within which his professional and political career had been achieved, was first settled by Kentuckians. From the beginning the people of that region evinced social and political attitudes which were Kentuckian in origin and quality.[15] How much Lincoln's Kentucky birth and early childhood had to do with his mature views is an open question, but the aspiring Springfield lawyer and politician naturally absorbed and reflected the local ideas and customs.

The point to be emphasized, in depicting Lincoln at the threshold of his Congressional career, is that his experience up to this time had been local. As a state legislator he had come in contact with men of outstanding ability. He had made the acquaintance of Webster and Van Buren. He had recently heard Clay in Lexington. For a long time he had been a reader of newspapers of national circulation. In the long wait between his election to Congress and his journey to Washington he had been a delegate to the River and Harbor Convention in Chicago. There he had seen and heard such eminent Whigs as Senator Corwin of Ohio and the noted jurist, Edward Bates of St. Louis. There Lincoln had made a speech in reply to David Dudley Field of New York, and his effort had been approvingly reported by the

---

[15] John Reynolds, *My Own Times* (1879), pp. 151 f.; William Vipond Pooley, *Settlement of Illinois* (1908), pp. 375-82.

great Whig editor, Horace Greeley. Perhaps he met, or at least saw, Thurlow Weed at the Convention.[16]

But to whatever extent he was acquainted with national leaders, or how well he was informed on questions of national scope, his experience had been local. He knew and had dealt with many politicians on the municipal, county, district, and state levels. There he was himself a leader, of equal or higher ability and standing than those with whom he was associated. Now the Prairie State politician was in Washington. He must measure and be measured by men of national standing, some of them of long experience in that capacity. What he did, what he learned, what he gained, and the standing with which he emerged would largely be determined by his relationships and associations with people of nation-wide experience.

Associations in the more intimate circle of Mrs. Sprigg's boardinghouse would, naturally, grow into closer friendships. Here the most important figure was Joshua R. Giddings of Ohio. Some of the Pennsylvania Whigs who lived there were probably more congenial to Lincoln than the uncompromising abolitionist, Giddings, but none of them appears to have influenced him notably. Two of them, Pollock and McIlvane, supported him for the patronage appointment which he later sought, and Pollock impressed him to the degree that when Lincoln became President he appointed Pollock to the directorship of the mint in Philadelphia. Dickey, another of Mrs. Sprigg's Pennsylvania Whig boarders, worked with Lincoln on bills for the abolition of slavery in the District of Columbia.

The party caucus on that December evening must have been an interesting experience for the newly arrived Lincoln. The dominating figures soon emerged. Lincoln had to make his estimate of the urbane Robert C. Winthrop of Massachusetts, who presently was chosen as the Whig candidate for Speaker of the House.[17] But perhaps even more significant was what he could perceive of the persons who advanced Winthrop, and of the men who opposed him. For these people, who directed and shaped the destinies of candidates and who determined party

---

[16] Robert Fergus (Compiler), *The Chicago-River-and Harbor Convention* (1882), New York *Tribune,* July 17, 1847.

[17] Chicago *Western Whig,* December 25, 1847; Caleb B. Smith to Elisha Embree (Embree MSS), August 26, 1847; Galena *Gazette and Advertiser,* March 14, 1848.

policies, were the important men to cultivate. For a man like Lincoln, who was ambitious for political advancement, it was all important to know them, shrewdly to estimate them, join with them, work with them, and, when necessary, to secure from them the aid of their influence and power.

With one exception there were few Whigs of outstanding ability and achievement in the House of the Thirtieth Congress.[18] The exception was, of course, John Quincy Adams. This sterling man was nearing the end of his noble career, and now was ineffective in party councils. Decidedly below Adams in stature were several worthy party men, some of long experience; men like Vinton of Ohio, Tuck of New Hampshire, Collamer of Vermont, Stewart of Pennsylvania, and Grinnell of Massachusetts. There were stalwart Whigs of considerable ability like Richard W. Thompson [19] of Indiana and James Dixon of Connecticut. There were Southern Whigs of influence and competence, such as Alexander Stephens and Robert Toombs of Georgia and William B. Preston of Virginia. There were Whigs who were adept politicians but unendowed with qualities which would enable them to serve their country as well as they served their party— and their own interests. Outstanding among these were two men named Smith: Truman Smith of Connecticut and Caleb B. Smith of Indiana. These two astute men were, in fact if not by recognition, the managers of the Whig party in the House. Their position was peculiar. When, for example, leadership was needed to write the bill setting up the Department of the Interior it was Vinton of Ohio who ably sponsored the law and managed parliamentary procedure involved in its passage. But Truman Smith was offered the Secretaryship of the new cabinet department, and it was Truman and Caleb Smith who had much to do with the valuable patronage appointments to it—with fateful consequence to Lincoln. There were Whigs of no particular excellence of character, such as Schenck of Ohio, and Whigs who saw no farther than the limits of their districts and states. Among these was Barrow of Tennessee, who later was active in taking his state into secession and the Confederacy.

---

[18] Unless as specifically amplified, authority for statements about persons in the Thirtieth Congress is to be found in the *Biographical Dictionary of the American Congress* and the *Dictionary of American Biography*.

[19] Charles Roll, *Colonel Dick Thompson* (1948).

Lincoln's career in Congress depended in part upon his relationships with his party colleagues. With which ones would he find himself in agreement on party and national issues? With which of the leaders would he associate himself, and to the extent that he led, who of them would go with him? With all Lincoln's ability and experience he was new, inexperienced, and untried on the national level. What he could and would do, what developments would do for and to him, were soon to appear.

3

UNFINISHED BUSINESS

To comprehend Lincoln's Congressional career it is essential to note the political situation in which his Congress, the Thirtieth, was placed. It is of prime significance that Lincoln's term in Congress was the mid-term session of the James K. Polk administration. The Presidential election would occur while this Congress was in office: the incumbent Democratic party naturally sought to remain in power, and the opposition Whig party was determined to displace the Democrats, elect their candidate to the Presidency, and control Congress.

Their task was difficult because in the earlier part of his term the administration policies of Polk had been a brilliant success. When Polk became the first "dark horse" nominee in 1844 the Whigs derisively asked, "Who is James K. Polk?" If this were more than a rhetorical question in 1844 the answer was apparent less than two years later.[1]

One criterion of a successful Presidential administration is the ability of the President to get important measures enacted into legislation. Judged by this standard Polk's achievements were remarkable. Few Presidents have had more important ad-

---

[1] The best biography of Polk is Eugene I. McCormac, *James K. Polk, A Political Biography* (1922). McCormac is the author of the brief biography of Polk in the *Dictionary of American Biography*, XV:34-39.

ministrative measures approved: the settlement of the status of the Oregon country and the fixing of its boundary, the acquisition of California and New Mexico, the replacement of the tariff of 1842 by a tariff with lowered schedules mainly for revenue, and the re-enactment of the Sub-Treasury Act (which had been passed under Van Buren and repealed by the Whigs in the Harrison-Tyler term). All these were realized. Three of them had been accomplished during the period of the Twenty-ninth Congress, and the acquisition of California and New Mexico was completed early in the first session of Lincoln's Congress.

In the achievement of these goals the leadership of Polk was evident. It was he, not the Senate, who took the initiative in the settlement of the Oregon questions. He requested the Senate to give notice to Great Britain that the joint occupation agreement was to be ended, as provided by the treaty. The Senate merely empowered the President to give the notice required by the Convention of 1818. Polk unhesitatingly instructed Buchanan, his Secretary of State, to forward the notice. When Buchanan feared that a determined stand would offend Great Britain, Polk noted in his *Diary* that the way to do business with John Bull was to look him straight in the eye. The outcome demonstrated that Polk was right: instead of the Columbia River, or that plus an enclave north of it, the line of 49° North became the boundary, and the United States took undisputed possession of a vast and rich inland empire.

The annexation of Texas brought on the Mexican War and resulted in the acquisition of California and New Mexico. Here, too, the older historical viewpoint, which was extremely unfavorable to Polk, has been revised. The definitive works of Justin Smith, as well as more popular studies, demonstrate that the Mexican War was not occasioned by a proslavery plot. They show that the moderation and fairness of the United States in the prewar negotiations and the justness of the American claims admit of no question.[2] In any event the policy of expansion was the prevailing view, and Polk, in this instance as in others, gave first-rate leadership.

As to the Walker Tariff of 1846 it is enough to say that the lowered rates, even in war time, produced adequate revenue,

---

[2] Smith, *The Annexation of Texas* and *The War with Mexico;* Bill, *Rehearsal For Conflict;* Henry, *The Story of the Mexican War.*

and that it remained in effect until 1857. The bill has been characterized by Professor Dodd, biographer of its originator, as perhaps the best tariff ever enacted by Congress. It suffices to remark of the reinstitution of the Sub-Treasury that so sound was it and so obviously needed that it has remained in effect since it was adopted as one of Polk's administration measures.

Nor was it only in his four major policies that Polk's leadership warranted for him a standing far above that which he has had in popular estimation. His resuscitation of the Monroe Doctrine from the desuetude into which Presidents after Monroe had allowed it to decline is an indication of farsightedness, more remarkable in that it anticipated the role of the United States as a world power. When the precarious status of Yucatán opened the possibility of a foreign protectorate in Latin America Polk explicity restated the Monroe Doctrine in such terms that his policy came to be called the "Polk Doctrine." "Existing rights of every European nation should be respected," he wrote in his first message to Congress, but "it should be distinctly announced to the world as our settled policy that no future European colony or dominion shall, with our consent, be planted or established on any part of the North American continent." Thus the re-establishment of the Monroe Doctrine as a cornerstone of our foreign policy was another achievement of the Polk administration.[3]

Further, Polk perceived the course of strategic development of the interests of the United States in the Pacific. He believed that England might attempt to acquire the Hawaiian Islands to advance her commercial position in the East. To prevent this

---

[3] Samuel Flagg Bemis, *John Quincy Adams and the Foundations of American Foreign Policy* (1949), p. 535; *A Diplomatic History of the United States* (1950), p. 280.

The recent study by Frederick Merk, *Albert Gallatin and the Oregon Problem* (1950), p. 37, emphasizes the degree to which the Monroe Doctrine had been "washed out" during the administration of John Quincy Adams. Adams then interpreted it to apply only to trading establishments, and Gallatin indicated to Canning in 1826 that "The Committee of the House of Representatives . . . had in their report on the subject of the Columbia River, made during the last session of Congress, disclaimed the principle advanced by Mr. Monroe; that the American government, also, had no intention of acting upon it was evident from the circumstances of their having proposed to Great Britain a certain line of boundary beyond which it was clear that the latter would have the right and power to establish whatever colonies they pleased. It could not be expected . . . that a government should go farther than this in renouncing a doctrine once avowed by them, but we might judge of their intentions by their acts."

Polk formulated as the policy of the United States the maintenance of Hawaiian independence. A recent study points out that the establishment of our Pacific area development was Polk's deliberate plan.[4]

Even more broadly the era of Polk was vibrant with overtones of the prelude to modernity. The President's able Secretary of the Navy established the Naval Academy at Annapolis, where his name is commemorated in Bancroft Hall. His Postmaster General, Cave Johnson, introduced the use of the postage stamp. Not to be credited to Polk, but illustrative of the scientific and mechanical advances which were accelerated by the war, was the rapid growth of the use of the magnetic telegraph, after its first demonstration in 1844. The National Fair, which opened in Washington in the spring of 1846, had on exhibition many items highlighting these improvements.[5] Machinery of iron structure was of a new high quality, due to the process, an anticipation of the Bessemer process, recently discovered by William Kelly. The Fair showed both the Hussey and the McCormick reapers. Soon after, Cyrus McCormick, with an eye to the future, moved his manufacturing establishment to Chicago, thus setting the pattern which enabled the North to win the Civil War.

Of course Mr. Polk was a much misunderstood man. When he declared that if elected he would serve for one term only, nobody believed him, not even when he made this point a factor in his cabinet appointments. He did an unheard of thing when he pledged himself not to run for re-election; to insure that his executive department heads would be that only, he demanded that each, before accepting appointment, sign a statement that he would not be a Presidential candidate in 1848. This put at least one of them, Buchanan, under a severe strain, but Polk thus secured maximum effectiveness in all branches of the executive.

The rehabilitation of Polk is an interesting recent development. Bernard DeVoto pointed out that Polk had a powerful mind and absolute integrity; that he knew what he wanted and got it done, thus having been the one "strong" President between Jackson and Lincoln. Robert S. Henry says that "there is no single Presidential administration in United States history with a more

---

[4] Norman A. Graebner, *Empire on the Pacific* (1955).

[5] Bernard DeVoto, *The Year of Decision 1846* (1943), pp. 211-17.

impressive and complete record of accomplishment—and in all the accomplishments Polk himself played a major part." Professor A. M. Schlesinger, on the basis of his "exceptional record in the White House," rates Polk as among the ablest Presidents, second only to Washington, Lincoln, and (Theodore) Roosevelt. Professor Allan Nevins observes that George L. Rives, Justin Smith, and E. I. McCormac have proved that Polk was "conscientious, unselfish, and truly statesmanlike, with a power of planning for the future matched by few of our Presidents." [6]

It is E. I. McCormac who shows why Polk has not received merited recognition. The reason has to do with the unfinished business of the Thirtieth Congress. In the closing hours of the Twenty-ninth Congress David Wilmot attached his famous "Proviso" to an appropriation bill. Wilmot, a Democrat, was the only member of Congress from Pennsylvania who had voted to pass the Walker Tariff.[7] His vote raised a storm of protest in his district and state. It was perhaps to regain popularity that the disgruntled Pennsylvanian sponsored these words: "*Provided, that . . . neither slavery nor involuntary servitude shall ever exist*" in territories acquired by means of the money appropriated.[8] Polk opposed the proviso, and since the Wilmot Proviso became a symbol of antislavery sentiment and has therefore been popularly esteemed, Polk and all who opposed it have not been esteemed. Since the proviso was not adopted by the Twenty-ninth Congress it was certain to become a point at issue in the Thirtieth.

It was well for Polk that three of his four principal administration measures had been enacted by his first Congress, in which his party commanded a majority in both Houses. For, as has been noted, the 1846 elections had gone against the administration. The Whig opposition had a slender majority of the House in the Thirtieth Congress, and the Democratic majority in the Senate had been reduced. According to the commonly accepted practice, not altogether unknown today, the second Congress of a Presidential quadrennium had as one of its pur-

---

[6] DeVoto, pp. 7 ff.; Henry, p. 49; Arthur M. Schlesinger, *Paths to the Present* (1949), pp. 97 ff.; Allan Nevins, *New York Times*, Book Review Section, March 26, 1950, p. 5.

[7] Charles B. Going, *David Wilmot, Free Soiler* (1924), pp. 94-289.

[8] *Globe*, 29th Congress, 1st Session, pp. 1217 f.

poses the election of a President. The Whig party, encouraged by the voting strength shown in the 1846 elections, was determined that the next President should be a Whig.

In fact, they already had their candidate. General Zachary Taylor, after the battle of Buena Vista, enjoyed something like the status accorded General Douglas MacArthur in the spring of 1951. After he was superseded in the direction of the war by General Scott, Taylor was easily persuaded that a military man of his repute might almost certainly be elected President. This had early been perceived by astute Whig politicians like Alexander Stephens and by such behind-the-scenes managers as Thurlow Weed. Although Taylor had not so much as voted for years, and despite the fact that his training and experience had done nothing to equip him for a civilian administrative position, least of all the Presidency, he was receptive. With utter political naïveté he invited nomination by both parties. When this miracle did not occur he came to the conclusion that he was a Whig, although not an ultra Whig. He placed himself in the hands of friends. When Lincoln took his seat in Congress it was a practical certainty that Taylor would be nominated by the Whigs.

This made the support of the Wilmot Proviso by the Northern Whigs ridiculous, for Taylor owned a plantation in Louisiana with a large number of slaves. Yet the Northern Whigs took up the proviso. Obviously they did so for political reasons, to embarrass President Polk and his party.

Polk had the task of bringing the war to an end with maximum advantage to the United States. It goes without saying that he, too, had political considerations in mind in his handling of the war. He was greatly chagrined that the generals whose reputations were the most enhanced by it were Whigs. While it was in no sense to diminish the standing of Taylor that Polk placed Scott in the superior command, it was easy for the President to see, and it was most unpalatable for him to realize, that one of these two Whig generals would inevitably emerge from the war as an impressive political figure.

Here Polk allowed his political interest to lead him into a conspicuous error of judgment. It occurred to him that he might create an aura of military greatness around an available Democrat. He proposed to do this by having Senator Thomas Hart Benton of Missouri commissioned Lieutenant General and placed in charge of the strategy and conduct of the war. Thus both aspiring Whig generals would be subordinated to a Democrat who was skilled, as they were not, in the political arts and crafts. Benton was, indeed, able. He had sound ideas of strategy for the Mexican War; the plan for the campaign which Scott worked out and so brilliantly executed was conceived by Benton. However, the Missouri senator would have lacked much that was essential to a General-in-Chief, including adequate military knowledge and experience.

President Polk accepted Benton's strategic plan as worked out in detail by Scott, and reluctantly commissioned Scott to execute it. When Scott's campaign was well under way the President sent Nicholas Trist, one of Buchanan's State Department subordinates, to Mexico to negotiate a treaty of peace. When a rift between General Scott and Trist broke into open antagonism Polk supported the General and sent a letter recalling the diplomat. However, by the time the letter arrived Scott and Trist had composed their differences, and Trist wisely disregarded the recall and remained to negotiate the treaty. When Lincoln took his seat in Congress the military phases of the war had been completed, and only a few weeks later the peace treaty was laid before the Senate for its advice and consent. As was expected, the treaty provided, among other things, for the cession of Mexican territory to the United States.

It was obvious, in view of these events, that Lincoln's party was in the difficult position of winning a Presidential election and defeating a party with so substantial a record of important achievements. The position of the Whigs was especially difficult because they had been decisively defeated on all domestic issues. It was hopeless for them to try to revive the issue of a national bank. The Walker Tariff was established and was popular. Nothing was to be gained by inveighing against territorial expansion, for that popular policy had been executed and was in effect.

Nevertheless the Whigs had reason to be hopeful. Although their policy of opposition to the war was unpopular in the South and the West, it appeared to them to have gained for them their victories in the Congressional elections and to have secured for them their majority in the House of the coming Congress. To be sure, the ratification of the peace treaty would end the usefulness of the war as a political issue, but until that event Lincoln and other Whigs continued to exploit it. The war had given them something infinitely more valuable: a Presidential candidate whose popularity, because of his war record, made him unbeatable. The war had also given them, as a by-product, the Wilmot Proviso. Whig leaders were aware that the proviso was potentially dangerous, for it was certain to divide their party as well as the Democrats. But they were confident that with Taylor, a Southern slaveholder, as their party candidate Southern Whigs would accept Taylor in spite of the proviso. They hoped that regardless of the proviso many Southern Democrats would vote for Taylor. Certainly they could use the proviso to embarrass the present administration. Here were two very useful political assets.

The necessity of providing government for the new territories was another issue which could be turned to party account. The most effective tactic would be to delay the organization of territorial government as long as possible, so that if the Whigs were successful in the 1848 election the governors, judges, and lesser patronage officers in the territories would be deserving members of the Whig party. To delay was easy: the threat of the Wilmot Proviso, or other reference to the question of slavery in the territories, would insure long debate. Government for Oregon was a different matter; it could not long be postponed. The annexed Mexican provinces, however, were a useful political issue.

The items were unfinished business for Lincoln's Congress. Naturally his political views were at cross purposes with the President's. He was not in sympathy with any of Polk's policies. He would do everything in his power to bring a Whig in succession to Polk. This was entirely proper. But would he follow his party without discrimination? Would he permit policy to supplant principle, and party to determine policy?

4

"POLITICALLY MOTIVATED QUESTIONS"

The unfinished business before the Thirtieth Congress was resumed in the Whig caucus. The slavery issue, in the form of the Wilmot Proviso, immediately appeared.

With their slender majority in the House, the Whigs needed to unite upon a candidate for Speaker and to present a man who had the backing of the whole party. But the Whigs were divided, and their divisions were increasing. There were cleavages between Eastern and Western, between Northern and Southern branches of the party. In New England there were "Conscience" and "Cotton" Whigs, i.e., some who were abolitionists and some who held the old Federalist attitude toward property. "Cotton" Whigs accepted slavery as the labor system which produced cotton most cheaply, and so helped their New England textile industry.

Thus, as the Chicago *Western Whig* noted, three men held the balance of power in the caucus: Amos Tuck of New Hampshire, Joshua R. Giddings of Ohio, and John G. Palfrey of Massachusetts.[1] These men were unbending abolitionists. When it

---

[1] The antislavery attitude of Giddings and Palfrey was carried to the choice of the Chaplain of the House. The leading candidate was the Rev. Mr. Gurley. He was unacceptable to Giddings and Palfrey because he had once been Secretary of the African Colonization Society!

became apparent that Robert C. Winthrop of Massachusetts would probably be the Whig candidate for Speaker they (Palfrey acting as spokesman) demanded that he make certain pledges: to appoint to committees men who would advocate the Wilmot Proviso, to commit the party to the abolition of slavery (or at least of the slave trade) in the District of Columbia, and to make other abolitionist measures party policies. Of course they knew that if he made these pledges he would not be elected. Winthrop refused to make any pledge. He pointed to his record and said that he would take the chair untrammeled or not take it at all. His forthright answer impressed Southern Whigs and won their support.

But when Congress convened at noon on December 6, 1847, Whig division in the face of the party's small majority made Winthrop's election precarious. However, the Democrats scattered their votes among several candidates while most of the Whigs favored Winthrop. The impasse created by the three abolitionists was broken early: on the third ballot a Southern Democrat and a Southern Whig left the House and one Southern Democrat (Holmes of South Carolina) did not vote. Curiously enough it was the vote of Levin of Pennsylvania, the only member of this Congress elected as a Native American party man, which actually elected Winthrop. The three anti-Winthrop Whigs divided among themselves; Tuck and Giddings favored James Wilson of Pennsylvania, while Palfrey gave Hudson of Massachusetts the only vote he received.[2] Lincoln on all three ballots voted for Winthrop.

After the Speaker took his place the oath was administered

---

[2] This episode is amply reported and documented. Joshua R. Giddings, in his *History of the Rebellion* (1864), pp. 261 ff., offers a version of it which is repeated in further detail in George W. Julian's *Life of Giddings* (1892), pp. 217-21; this account contains a contemporary letter of Giddings to Sumner (December 4, 1847). It also recites the demands made by the three. Palfrey's letter and Winthrop's reply are printed in Robert Winthrop, *Addresses and Speeches* (1852-56), I:612. Winthrop's corrections of misstatements in the Giddings *History* are to be found in the article, "Two Letters of Robert Charles Winthrop," *Mississippi Valley Historical Review*, 38 (1951), 289-96. The Galena *Gazette and Advertiser* had an almost exactly accurate report of the election. "Sigma," the Washington correspondent of the Illinois *State Register* on December 24, 1847 had correct detail. The story is fully told in Charles M. Wiltse, *John C. Calhoun, Sectionalist, 1840–1850* (1951), p. 324 (note, p. 534).

to members of the House. Next day the Clerk was selected and the organization of the House was completed. The Clerk then read the President's Message.

Polk's third annual message was extraordinarily important.[3] Its principal subjects were the prosecution of the war and the current offer of peace. But there was more. This was the message in which the Monroe Doctrine was reaffirmed and extended. Much was said about revenue. Lincoln later characterized the war part of the message as the "half insane mumblings of a fever dream," and referred to the President as a "bewildered, confounded, and miserably perplexed man." This estimate seems hardly fair in view of the forthright statements and the clear-cut logic of the message.

On December eighth the members of the House got their seat assignments. The House in those days met in the present Hall of Statuary. Of that meeting place a contemporary source says "the magnificant apartment is in the form of an ancient Greek theatre, ninety five feet in length and sixty feet in height." The Speaker's chair, elevated on a "richly draped" platform, stood in front of the north entrance.[4] Directly below was the Clerk's desk. Facing the Speaker were the seats of the members, grouped in six semicircular rows, diminishing to three and to two rows toward the front. Behind the Speaker was an entrance for members, with sufficient space that, according to the guide book, it formed a *"loggea,"* which was used as a promenade. The galleries for visitors were reached from the outside by two stairways; they might also be reached from the floor of the House. Of the decorations it is enough to mention that the portrait of Lafayette was then in place and was said to be a good likeness.

Congressmen drew their seat locations by lot. Lincoln's luck was poor; he drew seat 191, a back-row place on the Whig side, to the left of the Speaker, and midway between the two main aisles.

The Speaker appointed Lincoln to two standing committees: Post Offices and Post Roads, and Expenditures in the War De-

[3] *Globe*, 30th Congress, 1st Session, pp. 4-12. James D. Richardson, *Messages and Papers of the Presidents* (1905), IV:532-64.

[4] Watterson, *New Guide to Washington* (1847), pp. 24 ff.

partment.[5] These, as Beveridge says, were good assignments for a new member.

When the session was three weeks old William A. Richardson from Illinois was recognized and presented three resolutions.[6] Richardson had won a thumping victory in a special election to fill the vacancy caused by the resignation of Stephen A. Douglas when Douglas was elected to the Senate. Richardson's resolutions were to the effect that the war with Mexico was just and necessary on our part, that the rejection of peace overtures by Mexico left no alternative but to prosecute the war vigorously, and that the United States was entitled to such indemnity as Mexico's obstinacy and the war's duration made expedient. Nothing was done with these resolutions that day; parliamentary bickering was ended by adjournment. The motion to table them was made the next day.[7] Alexander Stephens offered substitute measures, presenting a moderate Whig view. Pettit, an Indiana Democrat, offered another set and R. W. Thompson, an Indiana Whig, presented still another. Toombs introduced a resolution urging the policy of no annexation of Mexican territory, and the extreme Whig attitude toward the war was expressed in further resolutions offered by Van Dyke of New York.

Presently the experienced parliamentarian, C. J. Ingersoll, mildly inquired whether Richardson had withdrawn his demand for the previous question, adding that he hoped that Richardson would not withdraw it. Richardson still called for the question, and it was ascertained that there was no second. Great confusion ensued. Stephens said that he intended to debate Richardson's resolutions. This raised the question whether they would remain on the calendar. An attempt was made to list them as the order of a later day, but this expedient failed. The Speaker called for resolutions from Illinois, and John Wentworth effectually sidetracked Richardson's resolutions by one which affirmed the constitutionality of internal improvements at federal expense. Nothing more was done with Richardson's resolutions.

On the next day Lincoln secured recognition and offered his momentous Spot Resolutions, which so nearly terminated his political career. They were as follows:

---

[5] *Congressional Directory*, 30th Congress, chart. *Globe*, 30th Congress, 1st Session, p. 19.

[6] *Globe*, p. 59.

[7] *Globe*, pp. 61 f.

Whereas the President of the United States, in his message of May 11th. 1846, has declared that "The Mexican Government not only refused to receive him" (the envoy of the U.S.) "or listen to his propositions, but, after a long continued series of menaces, have at last invaded *our teritory,* and shed the blood of our fellow *citizens* on *our own soil*"

And again, in his message of December 8, 1846 that "We had ample cause of war against Mexico, long before the breaking out of hostilities. But even then we forbore to take redress into our own hands, until Mexico herself became the aggressor by invading *our soil* in hostile array, and shedding the blood of our *citizens*"

And yet again, in his message of December 7– 1847 that "The Mexican Government refused even to hear the terms of adjustment which he" (our minister of peace) "was authorized to propose; and finally, under wholly unjustifiable pretexts, involved the two countries in war, by invading the teritory of the State of Texas, striking the first blow, and shedding the blood of our *citizens* on *our own* soil"

And whereas this House desires to obtain a full knowledge of all the facts which go to establish whether the particular spot of soil on which the blood of our *citizens* was so shed, was, or was not, *our own soil,* at that time; therefore

Resolved by the House of Representatives, that the President of the United States be respectfully requested to inform this House—

First: Whether the spot of soil on which the blood of our *citizens* was shed, as in his messages declared, was, or was not, within the teritories of Spain, at least from the treaty of 1819 until the Mexican revolution

Second: Whether that spot is, or is not, within the teritory which was wrested from Spain, by the Mexican revolution

Third: Whether that spot is, or is not, within a settlement of people, which settlement had existed ever since long before the Texas revolution, until it's inhabitants fled from the approach of the U.S. Army.

Fourth: Whether that settlement is, or is not, isolated from any and all other settlements, by the Gulf of Mexico, and the Rio Grande, on the South and West, and by wide uninhabited regions on the North and East.

Fifth: Whether the *People* of that settlement, or a *majority* of them, or *any* of them, had ever, previous to the bloodshed, mentioned in his messages, submitted themselves to the government or laws of Texas, or of the United States, by *consent,* or by *compulsion,* either by accepting office, or voting at elections, or paying taxes, or serving on juries, or having process served upon them, or in *any other way.*

Sixth: Whether the People of that settlement, did, or did not, flee from the approach of the United States Army, leaving unprotected their homes and their growing crops, *before* the blood was shed, as in his messages stated; and whether the first blood so shed, was, or was not shed, within the *inclosure* of the People, or some of them, who had thus fled from it.

Seventh: Whether our *citizens,* whose blood was shed, as in his messages declared, were, or were not, at that time, *armed* officers and *soldiers,* sent into that settlement, by the military order of the President through the Secretary of War—and

Eighth: Whether the military force of the United States, including those *citizens,* was, or was not, so sent into that settlement, after Genl. Taylor had, more than once, intimated to the War Department that, in his opinion, no such movement was necessary to the defence or protection of Texas.[8]

It may be no more than a coincidence, but the Whig journal, the *National Intelligencer,* had in its December 11, 1847, issue a leading editorial on Polk's message and the Mexican War. In it are almost every one of the ideas which appear in Lincoln's Spot Resolutions, which he offered only eleven days after the appearance of the editorial, and in his Mexican War speech, delivered a month and a day after. Whether or not the quasi-official Whig editorial was a source of Lincoln's resolutions and speech, it is evident from the similarity of content that the new Congressman was orthodox and unoriginal in his double attack on Polk's war policy.

These resolutions were merely read and "laid over under the rule." That is, they were referred for future action if their originator could succeed in getting consideration for them. In this instance no action was taken by the House. The resolutions were neither adopted nor rejected. They were not debated. After hearing them the House went on with routine business. Lincoln made no effort to bring them up again.

What, then, was his purpose in presenting them? As was true of the vast majority of resolutions presented, and of speeches made, the object was not to accomplish anything relevant to the business of the House. Neither Lincoln nor anyone else dreamed that President Polk would furnish the "information" requested. The resolutions and the war speech which followed were presented to embarrass the President by centering attention upon what the Whigs thought was a weak point in his case for the justification of the war.

There was a prompt and emphatic response to the Spot Resolutions in Illinois—not at all the sort which Lincoln presumably expected. The first reference to them was in John

---

[8] *Globe,* p. 64; *CW* I: 120-22.

Wentworth's newspaper, the Chicago *Democrat*, which reported on January 3, 1848, that "original motions being in order Mr. Lincoln offered a series of resolutions on the Mexican War, which were laid over." The leading Whig paper, the Chicago *Journal*, printed the Resolutions in the January 6 issue, remarking that they were "spoken of as being direct and to the point." The favorable estimate of the Washington correspondent of the Baltimore *Patriot* was quoted: "The resolutions of Mr. Lincoln, of Illinois, submitted to the House today, will attract attention from the fact that they stick to the *spot* in Mexico where the first blood was shed, with all the tightness that characterized the shirt of the fabled Nessus! Evidently there is music in that very tall Mr. Lincoln." This paragraph, together with the Resolutions, appeared in the Rockford *Forum's* January 19 issue. Aside from the few newspapers whose editors were friendly to Lincoln these were the only friendly references made.

But the list of hostile reactions was a long one. The Springfield *Illinois State Register* on January 7, published the first of many. Richardson's and Lincoln's Resolutions were published in full. Editorial comment praised Richardson's and condemned Lincoln's:

> Although they are resolutions of inquiry, the tenor of them and especially the preamble, indicate on Mr. *Lincoln's* part such an opposition to the war as was little expected at the hands of his constituents, many of whom have immortalized themselves by their gallantry and heroism in the bloody ravines of Buena Vista and rugged fastnesses of Cerro Gordo. We regret that Mr. *Lincoln* has led the people of this district to apprehend that he is about to follow in the footsteps of his infamous predecessor—*John Henry*—who, on the very day that Col. *Hardin* and his glorious regiment of Illinoisans were pouring out their blood at Buena Vista, voted against a bill providing them with supplies, among which were medicine and surgical apparatus for the sick and wounded.

The Alton *Telegraph* was a Whig paper, but probably because its editor was a returned soldier and a hearty supporter of the war it made only passing allusion to the Spot Resolutions. It remarked merely that a great variety of resolutions about the war were introduced, among them those of Richardson and Lincoln. To notice them intelligently would require more room than the paper could spare.

The Quincy *Whig* published the Spot Resolutions on January 14, and defended them as "based upon facts which cannot be successfully controverted, as to which nation was the aggressor, and upon whose soil the first blood was shed." Of course the *Illinois State Journal* (formerly the *Sangamo Journal*) published them with approval, as did also the paper edited by Lincoln's friend and supporter B. F. James, the *Tazewell Whig*.

Full space in refutation was taken by the *State Register* on January 14, in an editorial: "The War—Mr. Lincoln's Resolutions." This time the argument was dignified and without vituperation, "We venture to say that the grounds which he takes will be repudiated by the great mass of people who voted for him." Beating Lincoln with the John Henry stick again, the *State Register* predicted that if Lincoln followed the course indicated by his resolutions he would, before the close of the session, become as odious as Henry.

The masses in Illinois have committed themselves to the war; 6,000 men enlisted. They cannot accept politically motivated questions of the justness of the war. Mr. Lincoln and the faction to which he has pinned his faith at the outset of his congressional career may throw in the way of the administration as many obstacles to the prosecution of the war as their ingenuity can invent, but they will find that the masses—the honest and patriotic citizens of Illinois—will mark their course and condemn them. . . .

Thank heaven, Illinois has eight representatives who will stand by the honor of the nation. Would that we could find Mr. Lincoln in their ranks doing battle on the side of his country as valiantly as did the Illinois volunteers upon the battle-fields of Buena Vista and Cerro Gordo. He will have a fearful account to settle with them, should he lend his aid in an effort to neutralize their achievements and blast their fame.

The Charleston (Coles County) *Illinois Globe* made the standard Democratic reply to Lincoln; it was clipped and published in the *State Register* on January 14:

Mr. Lincoln

This gentleman has made his debut in Congress by the introduction of a preamble and resolutions on the subject of the precise "spot" where the first blood was shed in the present war. They . . . show conclusively that the littleness of the pettifogging lawyer has not merged into the greatness of the statesman. We regret, as a citizen of Illinois, that a representative from our noble State should thus disgrace her, by offering such trash for the consideration of the grave and dignified legislature of this wide spread republic. Well may the patriotic people of the 7th district lament that they have not a *Hardin* or *Baker* to represent them at this important crisis. Alas poor *Spotty*.

In the same number of the *State Register* a similar statement from the Belleville *Times* was republished. Under a column
head, *Democrat and Whig*, Richardson's resolutions were printed
and Lincoln's were summarized with excerpts quoted. Editorial
comment followed: Lincoln's resolutions, it was said, were designed to put the United States in an odious light. Whig papers
would applaud, but "the entire democracy of Illinois, as well
as the rank and file of his own party will condemn his course
forever. . . . It requires some charity, in one acquainted with
the political history of Mr. Lincoln, not to believe that undying
hatred to his former and successful rival who fell so gloriously
in this very war; has entered into the motives which prompted
these resolutions."

The *State Register*, determined to lose nothing of the opportunity to make Lincoln unpopular, headed its reference to the
war speech (January 28) "Out Damned Spot." On February 25
the *State Register* quoted the Peoria *Press*, which used an allusion to the spotted fever as the occasion to say that

This fever does not prevail to any very alarming extent in Illinois.
The only case we have heard of that is likely to prove fatal, is that
of poor "spotty Lincoln," of this state. This "spotty" gentleman had
a severe attack of the "spotted fever" in Washington City not long
since, and fears were entertained that the disease would "strike in,"
and carry him off. We have not heard of any other person in Washington being on the "spotted list"—and it is probable that the disease
died with the patient.—What an epitaph: "Died of the *Spotted Fever.*"
Poor Lincoln!

Some defense of Lincoln was made in a meeting held in
Canton (Fulton County; not in Lincoln's Congressional district)
which was reported by the *State Register* on February 25. Pro-
Mexican, antiwar speeches were made, the Democratic newspaper claimed. It cited the Canton *Repository* to report that one
speaker reiterated Lincoln's view—that the true boundary between Mexico and Texas was neither the Rio Grande nor the
Nueces but an undefined line between the two rivers. This explanation, said the *State Register* "seems to have been made in
answer to 'Spotty Lincoln's' resolutions of inquiry. We trust
that the information here given of the 'precise spot' will make
'Spotty' quite easy."

A serious rebuke of Lincoln was administered by a nonpartisan mass meeting held in Clark County. As reported in the

Belleville *Advocate* (March 2) it was "*Resolved,* that Abe Lincoln, the author of the 'spotty' resolutions in Congress against his own country, may they be long remembered by his constituents, but may they cease to remember him, except to rebuke him—they have done so much for him, but he has done nothing for them, save the stain he inflicted on their proud name of patriotism and glory, in the part they have taken for their country's cause." The Belleville paper, commenting upon the meeting and its occasion, insisted that Lincoln's course "in denouncing his country, has called forth a stern rebuke from many of his constituents, and will be yet more signally condemned."

A mass meeting of voters of the Apollonia precinct, in Morgan County, held March 13, took strong ground. Feeling ran high there, because this community was situated near Jacksonville, where Col. Hardin had lived. One paragraph of the resolutions adopted read

That as citizens of the seventh congressional district of Illinois we can but express the deep mortification inflicted upon us by our representative in Congress, in his base, dastardly, and treasonable assault upon President Polk, in his disgraceful speech upon the present war, and in the resolutions offered by him against his own government, in flagrant violation to the views of a majority of our congressional electors. That this district has often been afflicted with inefficient *per diem men,* or unfortunate representation, but never until now has it known disgrace so black, so mortifying, so unanswerable. Such insulting opprobrium cast upon our citizens and soldiers, such black odium and infamy heaped upon the living brave and illustrious dead can but invite the indignation of every true Illinoian, the disgust of republicans and condemnation of men. Therefore henceforth will this Benedict Arnold of our district be known here only as the Ranchero Spotty of one term.[9]

This was noted in the *State Register* as "another 'spot' for Lincoln."

Peoria returned to the attack. The *Press* was quoted (May 26) by the *State Register.* Extolling Richardson, Lincoln was disparagingly held to light:

The contrast between his course and that of "spotty Lincoln," exhibits here more than anything else, the wide difference between the sentiments advocated by the democratic party and those which are

[9] As it appeared in the *Illinois State Register,* March 10, 1848.

clung to be the enemies of the country. . . . The miserable man of "spots" will pass unnoticed save in the execration that his treason will bring upon his name. . . . The [views] of [Lincoln] displayed the treason of Arnold, and all the "bloody hands and hospitable graves" disposition of a Corwin. . . . Lincoln will be "dead whilst among the living."

The *State Register* reported a Democratic war meeting in Jo Daviess County which was held on February 24, with similar sentiments voiced. On March 24, it cited the recommendation of the Chicago *Prairie State Argus* that the Seventh District Democrats call a convention to clear up the only "spot" in the proud exhibit of the "banner state." In reporting the meeting of the Seventh District Democratic Convention, which nominated Major Thomas L. Harris of Morgan County, the *State Register* predicted that in Harris' election the people would be "rescued . . . from the foul 'spot' that now rests upon them." Insistently from this time the Spot Resolutions were a factor in the campaign for Congressional election in Lincoln's district.

The *State Register,* on June 9, printed a blast which was headed "Communicated from the Jacksonville *Argus*." After referring to Hardin and Baker it read in part as follows: "The next is the traitor Lincoln . . . who occupies his time in wrangling about 'spots' and franking Webster's speeches, abusing the war and the President, to his constituency. . . . Lincoln is told that his acts are known, and he must not try it again."

Harping upon the same theme on June 13, the *State Register* reiterated that ". . . the brand of Arnold is upon his forehead, and the 'damned spot' will not 'out'." On the twenty-third there was a skirmish with the *State Register's* rival, the *Illinois Journal,* in which it was said that the remarks of General Cooley seemed to have touched the "spot." On July 7, campaigning for Major Harris, the *State Register* quoted the Peoria *Press* again: "This district has heretofore been Whig, and the last man elected in it was Abe Lincoln, whose traitorous course in Congress has brought down upon him the merited curses of his constituents, and they seem determined to wipe out the foul 'spot' by electing the gallant Major Harris."

Two weeks later in its own vein the *State Register* continued: "The seventh congressional district, the only 'spot' in the state where Whigery has an abiding place, is about to be enrolled under the democratic banner. . . . Major Harris is about to take the place of Mr. Lincoln, who . . . never omitted an opportunity to tarnish our national flag."

After the peace treaty had been signed, with Mexico acknowledging the Rio Grande as the border, the *State Register* exulted: "The 'spot' which Lincoln was so anxious to discover has been found—found by the Mexicans, of whom he was the apologist—and found upon American soil. What now becomes of the treasonable arguments, and long-winded tirades of Whig editors and orators on behalf of Mexico? The argument of Lincoln . . . stands refuted by the acknowledgment of the Mexican commissioners." The Congressional elections came soon after, and on August 11, the *State Register* gloated at the Democratic victory by still another reference to the "Spot." Nor was the appellation dropped when the war issue receded into the background. On October 27, 1848, reviewing the Harris–Logan campaign, the *Register* still called Lincoln "Spotty," and as late as October 11, 1849, when Lincoln was spoken of as a possible governor of the Oregon Territory, the Indiana *State Sentinel* made a sarcastic allusion to the Spot Resolutions.

Indeed, they arose to plague Lincoln much later. His old opponent, the *State Register*, reporting the Lincoln–Douglas debates in 1858,[10] again and again rang the changes on the old theme. Douglas used it; he alluded to the Spot Resolutions at Freeport, at Charleston, and at Ottawa.[11] As though they must be eternally revived they were pressed in the Presidential campaign of 1860. During that canvass the Springfield Democrats had a parade. They claimed that Lincoln watched it from the dome of the State House. The Republicans denied the charge, and for weeks, Paul Angle says, a meaningless press controversy argued about the exact "spot" from which Lincoln viewed the procession.[12]

How seriously should these criticisms be taken? It goes without saying that they must be discounted as stock Democratic propaganda. However, some of the meetings at which critical resolutions were adopted were nonpartisan. Even the partisan statements have weight. Lincoln was the representative

---

[10] Issue of September 24, 1858.

[11] Edwin E. Sparks, *The Lincoln–Douglas Debates* (1908), pp. 91, 103, 166 f., 307, 490.

[12] Paul M. Angle, *Lincoln 1854-1861* (1933), p. 343.

not only of the Whigs of the Seventh District, he was representing all of the people of that district. With his colleagues he represented Illinois. Even though the *State Register* was partisan it was undeniably correct in pointing out that the masses in Illinois could not accept politically motivated questions about the war, and in noting that in his resolutions Lincoln had committed himself to a faction of the Whig party.

If Lincoln had opposed the administration's war policy from conscientious motives his opponents ought to have respected an attitude based upon principle. But the Spot Resolutions give no indication of being based upon principle, nor of appealing to principle. They seem to have been a shrewd, clever, and opportunistic means of discrediting the President.

Further, the attitude which evidently prompted Lincoln to formulate and present the Spot Resolutions represented a reversal of his former position. Before election to Congress, and while a candidate for the office, he had supported the war. He had made an effective speech for the purpose of recruiting volunteers.

This is not to suggest that a Congressman ought to reflect only the view of the majority of his constituents. He should act upon the dictates of his best judgment and his conscience. But, as shall appear even more clearly in connection with his Mexican War speech, Lincoln was very much the politician, with reference to the war. He was merely speaking for his party, or for a faction of his party. In effect he was speaking for the East, where the war was unpopular, and disregarding the West, where it was popular.

How seriously Lincoln had offended his constituency is readily discernible. The Spot Resolutions became an issue in the Congressional election of 1848, although Lincoln was not then a candidate. In that election the Seventh District Whigs suffered a stunning defeat. In an unusually heavy vote (2,934 more than in the election which Lincoln won), to the amazement of prognosticators the Democratic candidate carried the district by a plurality of 106. When the ample Whig majorities of Hardin, Baker, and Lincoln (671, 628, and 1,511) were reversed by a clear-cut Democratic majority over the Whigs it is evident that this result indicated a repudiation of Lincoln. A considerable factor in the Whig defeat was public indignation, among Whigs as well as Democrats, over the Spot Resolutions.

5

"MY BEST IMPRESSION OF THE TRUTH"

On January 3, 1848, Lincoln cast a vote which greatly displeased
many of his constituents and embarrassed several of his friends.
The House was engaged in routine business when Houston of
Delaware presented a resolution of thanks to General Taylor.
Had occasion not been turned to partisan purpose some of the
Democrats probably would have voted for it. But Ashmun of
Massachusetts offered an amendment which considerably quali-
fied the tone of the original—his amendment called upon the
House to thank Taylor and his men for their valorous deeds in
"a war unnecessarily and unconstitutionally begun by the Presi-
dent of the United States." Ashmun's amendment was adopted
on a strict party vote (while many of the members of the House
were absent) by the narrow margin of 85–81. Lincoln voted
"Aye." [1]

If there had been any sincerity in Ashmun's amendment,
or in the Congressmen who voted for it, its basis should have
been the prelude to impeachment charges. The President takes
a solemn oath to defend the Constitution. If Polk had violated
it in his order to General Taylor it was the duty of members of
the lower House to impeach him, and the duty of the Senate

---

[1] *Globe,* 30th Congress, 1st Session, p. 95; House *Journal,* 30th Congress,
p. 184.

to try him. When Ashmun's amendment was adopted the 85 persons who voted for it expressed their judgment that President Polk had violated the Constitution. It was their duty to have him impeached.

But having secured the adoption of the amendment the Whigs went blithely on their way. Obviously their purpose was not to vindicate the Constitution, nor even their views of it, but merely to embarrass the President. This was as true of Lincoln who voted for the amendment, as it was of Ashmun, who proposed it.

Then on January 12, 1849, Lincoln made a full statement of his views of the Mexican War. Apparently he had intended to deliver this speech the day before; he secured recognition toward the close of that day's sitting, but a motion to adjourn precluded his opportunity to speak at that time.[2]

Lincoln made his first set speech while the House was sitting as a Committee of the Whole State of the Union to consider the President's annual message. Lincoln had adverted to parts of the message in his Spot Resolutions; now he took the floor to cover all the aspects of it that he chose to discuss.

The speech begins with an allusion to a complaint by the Democrats against the vote on the Ashmun amendment.[3] Lincoln agreed that the affirmative vote ought not to have been given in mere party wantonness. His own vote was given under his best impression of the truth of the case. He would now try to show how he arrived at that judgment.

When the war began, he continued, it had been his opinion that all those who, because of knowing too little, or because of knowing too much, could not conscientiously approve the conduct of the President ought to remain silent, at least until the war were over. Some leading Democrats, including ex-President Van Buren, held this view.

But President Polk had made it impossible for him to maintain his policy of discreet silence. For the President claimed that all votes for war supplies were votes supporting the justice of the government's war policies. Polk regarded every silent vote of supplies as an endorsement of the justice and wisdom of his

---

[2] *Globe,* p. 146; text of speech pp. 154-56.

[3] *CW* I:431-42. The speech should be read in its entirety. I attempt to summarize the content objectively, but Lincoln must speak for himself.

conduct. For example, the President's message stated that Congress, with great unanimity, had declared that war existed "by act of the Republic of Mexico." Lincoln pointed out that when the war declaration stood disconnected from the question of supplies, 67 in the House voted against it; Polk had alluded to the much smaller number of 14 who had voted against the declaration with a broad enabling section. Further, the recently offered resolutions of his colleague, Richardson, forced the issue; Lincoln would be compelled to vote on them some day; he could not then be silent even if he would. Thus he had been forced to examine the annual message. His conclusion was that the President fell short of proof because the truth would not justify him.

The first war message declared that the soil upon which hostilities were begun was ours. That declaration was repeated in almost the same language in each successive annual message. This statement was indeed the central point, the point upon which the President would either be justified or condemned. With particular reference to the message of 1846, Lincoln emphasized the statement about the Texas boundary, and in this, he charged, Polk was guilty of the sheerest deception. "The issue, as he presents it, is in these words, 'But there are those who, conceding all this to be true, assume the ground that the true western boundary of Texas is the Nueces, instead of the Rio Grande; and that, therefore, in marching our army to the east bank of the latter river, we passed the Texan line, and invaded the teritory of Mexico.'" This was paraphrased as meaning "A true issue, made by the President, would be about as follows 'I say, the soil *was ours,* on which the first blood was shed; there are those who say it was not.'"

The speech then went on to analyze Polk's evidence in the form of six propositions: the Rio Grande was the western boundary of Louisiana, the Republic of Texas always claimed the Rio Grande boundary, Texas by various acts had made this claim on paper, Santa Anna in his treaty with Texas recognized the Rio Grande boundary, Texas before annexation and the United States afterward had exercised jurisdiction beyond the Nueces—between the two rivers—and the United States Congress understood that the boundary of Texas extended beyond the Nueces.

Each of these propositions was discussed. Of course it was

true that the Rio Grande was the farthest boundary of Louisiana. But that fact was reduced to an absurdity by illustration: the line between his property and the Chairman's could not still be a boundary after he had sold his property. Then Lincoln denied that Texas had always claimed the Rio Grande boundary line. He admitted that Texas had made the claim, but denied that she had *always* claimed it, and cited the state constitution, which did not contain any reference to boundaries. But, suppose that Texas had always claimed the Rio Grande line; Mexico had also claimed the contrary. (It should be noted that Lincoln did not state the Mexican claim, which was not the line of the Nueces, but the line of the Sabine, i.e., all of Texas.)

Then Lincoln proceeded to the claims. He referred first to the Constitution of the Republic (not the state) of Texas, which explicitly recited the Rio Grande as the western boundary. This, he insisted, was but naked claim, and illustrated: "If I should claim your land, by word of mouth, that certainly would not make it mine; and if I were claim it with a deed which I had made myself, and with which you had nothing to do, the claim would be quite the same in substance."

The treaty between Texas and Santa Anna was next examined. He averred that the agreement was not binding, since it was made while Santa Anna was a prisoner. He questioned whether it deserved the name of treaty, and with intended humor pointed to the supposed source of Polk's reference to it: Niles' *Register*. In its first ten years, he said, the document had never been called a treaty; it had none of the distinguishing features of a treaty; Santa Anna did not assume to bind Mexico, since he signed it only as President Commander in Chief; he did not in it recognize the independence of Texas nor indicate expectation that the war would cease; he said nothing about boundary. Lincoln argued that the document bound the Mexican army to evacuate the territory of Texas, passing to the other side of the Rio Grande.

Lincoln made further reference to the "treaty," without quoting it in whole or in part. From the clause concerning the withdrawal of the Mexican army he drew an astonishing meaning. The "treaty" (as he interpreted it) specified that the Texan army should not approach more closely than five leagues "of *what* is not said—but clearly, from the object stated it is—of the Rio Grande. Now, if this is a treaty, recognizing the Rio

Grande, as the boundary of Texas, it contains the singular feature, of stipulating that Texas shall not go within five leagues of *her own* boundary."

Then came the decisive point: whether Texas before, and the United States after, annexation had exercised jurisdiction beyond the Nueces and between the two rivers.

Before summarizing Lincoln's reference it is necessary to remark that Polk in several messages had emphasized this point, saying that the Texas congress had stipulated the Rio Grande as the boundary and had exercised its jurisdiction beyond the Nueces, that the country between the two rivers had been represented in the convention which wrote the Constitution of the Republic of Texas, and had been represented in the Texas congress; and, as it was included in one of the two Congressional districts of Texas it was now represented in the United States Congress.[4] Polk further pointed out that Congress had recognized the trans–Nueces area as ours by including it within our federal revenue system and by the appointment of a revenue officer resident within the district; this person had been confirmed by the Senate. Polk also mentioned the organization of counties and courts in the area, the establishment of post offices, post roads, and a land office. He went into similar detail of specific acts of Congress since annexation, e.g., the establishment of post offices and post roads.

Lincoln handled this theme as a lawyer. Polk's statement, he agreed, was good as far as it went: jurisdiction extended beyond the Nueces. But Polk did not not say that it went to the Rio Grande. Jurisdiction was exercised between the two rivers, but the President did not say that it was exercised over *all* the territory between them. Then Lincoln used another supposedly simple illustration:

I know a man, not very unlike myself, who exercises jurisdiction over a piece of land between the Wabash and the Mississippi; and yet so far is this from being *all* there is between those rivers, that it is just one hundred and fifty two feet long by fifty wide, and no part of it much within a hundred miles of either. He has a neighbor between him and the Mississippi,—that is, just across the street, in that direction—whom, I am sure, he could neither *persuade* nor *force*

<hr/>

[4] Message of May 11, 1846 (the War Message), Second Annual Message, Third Annual Message; Richardson, *Messages and Papers*, IV:437-43, 471-506, 532-64.

to give up his habitation; but which nevertheless, he could certainly annex, if it were to be done, by merely standing on his own side of the street and *claiming* it, or even, sitting down, and writing a *deed* for it.

Polk's assertion that Congress understood that Texas extended beyond the Nueces was correct. But how far beyond? Congress did not understand that Texas extended to the Rio Grande, because the terms of annexation stipulated that boundary questions should be settled by the United States and Mexico. This must have been the understanding of Texas, for the state constitution was adjusted to this requirement.

Then he proceeded to the question of the spot where the first blood was shed. In response to Richardson's resolutions he had offered his own. To show their relevance he stated his understanding of the rule by which boundary must be ascertained. It was this: wherever Mexico was exercising jurisdiction the land was hers; wherever Texas was exercising jurisdiction the land was hers; whatever separated the actual exercise of jurisdiction was the true boundary. The boundary was the uninhabited country between the Rio Grande and the Nueces.

At this point in the speech the lawyer gave place to the political philosopher, in a passage worthy of Jefferson:

Any people anywhere, being inclined and having the power, have the *right* to rise up, and shake off the existing government, and form a new one that suits them better. This is a most valuable,—a most sacred right—a right, which we hope and believe, is to liberate the world. . . . Any portion of such people that *can, may* revolutionize, and make their *own*, of so much of the teritory as they inhabit. More than this, a *majority* of any portion of such people may revolutionize, putting down a *minority* . . . who may oppose their movement. . . . It is a quality of revolutions not to go by *old* lines, or *old* laws; but to break up both, and make new ones.

Thus Texas was a part of Louisiana, bought from France in 1803 and sold to Spain in 1819. Mexico revolted from Spain, and Texas revolted from Mexico. Now, Lincoln went on, let the President answer my resolutions, candidly and with no evasion. If he can show that the soil where the first blood was shed was ours, "that it is not within an inhabited country, or, if within such, that the inhabitants had submitted themselves to the civil authority of Texas, or of the United States, and that the same is true of the site of Fort Brown, then I am with him for his justification." His reason for desiring this information was that

"I expect to give some votes, in connection with the war, which, without his so doing, will be of doubtful propriety in my own judgment, but which will be free from the doubt if he does so."

But if the President cannot, or will not, answer these questions Lincoln would be convinced of what he already suspected: "that he is deeply conscious of being in the wrong—that he feels the blood of this war, like the blood of Abel, is crying to Heaven against him." Lincoln repeated his belief that Polk purposely involved the two countries in war, expecting to escape blame by the military glory which would accrue from an easily won war. But, mistaken in his assumption of an easy victory, and involved in a long and stubbornly fought war, Polk was in an untenable position. "How like the half-insane mumblings of a fever dream, is the whole war part of his late message!" The President was on the horns of a dilemma: he must get indemnity by territorial annexation or he must levy contributions. At one time he rejected indemnity in the name of national honor and again claimed it with the apparent inclusion of Lower California. He depended upon the maintenance of Mexican national existence, but saw the impossibility of a competent Mexican government being formed. He was inconsistent about prosecuting the war, for his policy of sustained invasion would not win peace.

Finally Polk was criticized because he omitted to predict when the war would end. Lincoln concluded: "As I have before said, he knows not where he is. He is a bewildered, confounded, and miserably perplexed man. God grant he may be able to show, that there is not something about his conscience, more painful than all his mental perplexity!"

Inevitably this war speech, like the Spot Resolutions, stirred the execrations of the *Illinois State Register,* which noted the speech on January 28. Without a copy of it the editor did not know "whether Mr. L. took ground against the war *in toto* or not, but as his name is recorded among the infamous 85, who voted that the war was 'unconstitutional and unnecessary,' we presume that he backed his vote in his speech." With the full text the Democratic paper made a complete refutation in a "SPEECH NOT Delivered in the House of Representatives, in Reply to Mr. Lincoln, of Illinois." This imagined speech occupies almost three columns in the issue of February 18, 1848. The opening part concerns Lincoln's vote for the Ashmun amendment, making the point that anyone who, in principle, opposes

the war and yet votes supplies, shares in the alleged unconsti-
tutional beginning and prosecution of the war. Points of fact are
made against Lincoln, e.g., his denial that for ten years the
Santa Anna "treaty" was not called a treaty; the *State Register*
cited a reference to it, calling it a treaty, by General Filisola.
Ridiculing Lincoln's dialectical conclusion that "within five
leagues" meant within five leagues of the Rio Grande, the
"SPEECH NOT Delivered" cited another document signed by
Santa Anna which expressly stated that the Rio Grande was the
Texas–Mexico boundary. Obviously the purpose of the article
was to correct Lincoln's assertions; to the extent that it was
read it did so.

Senator Douglas delivered what was, in effect, a reply to
Lincoln's speech, although he did not mention Lincoln's effort.
Douglas' speech was fortified with facts and was well docu-
mented. It refuted every point made by Lincoln.[5] The *Illinois
Journal* had printed Lincoln's speech and had dared the *State
Register* to publish it. Now the *State Register* published Douglas'
speech and challenged the *Journal* to print it, offering to publish
Lincoln's speech if the *Journal* would publish Douglas'.

The indignation meeting of the voters of the Appollonia
precinct, already referred to in reaction to the Spot Resolutions,
also fulminated against the Mexican War speech. It was characterized as "base, dastardly, and treasonable," and again as
"disgraceful." [6]

The Chicago *Democrat,* in humorous vein, presented what
was presumably a more effective argument for the Rio Grande
boundary. On February 14, it remarked that

The Whigs don't believe in our title to the Rio Grande when written in prose, but when in poetry they go for it—in 1846 the Whigs
were all singing:

> One morning bright and early
>> The news came safe to hand
> That the Mexicans, ten thousand strong
>> Had crossed ———

What? the Sabine? No. The Nueces? No. The Colorado? No. What
then? The Rio Grande?

---

[5] *Globe,* pp. 221-27.

[6] *Illinois State Register,* February 18, 1848, March 10, 1848.

> O the Rio Grande, O the Rio Grande,
>   We would we were upon your banks
> With rifles in our hand.

And they wished to be on the Rio Grande, did they? And what did they intend to do with those rifles? Nothing more or less than to repel the invasion of 10,000 Mexicans who "had crossed the Rio Grande." This song was sung by the Whigs in 1846, who have since changed their tune.

One of Lincoln's fellow House members made a scathing reference to his Mexican War speech. This was Jamieson, a Missouri Democrat. Vigorously defending Polk, Jamieson turned to Lincoln:

> . . . I desire to injure no gentleman's feelings, yet I must speak out boldly. The gentleman from Illinois, from the Hardin and Baker district, took a strange position before the American Congress for such a representative. Yes, sir; look back and see what your Hardin did. He was a Whig to be sure; he and I met here on this floor, and we disagreed, as far as politics are concerned; yet he went from your district (referring to Mr. *Lincoln*) and fell nobly at Buena Vista. You have a Baker, too, from your district, and that Baker went along under General Scott, and he, too, was in the bloody battle, and at Cerro Gordo commanded when the noble Shields fell with a grape through his lungs. Coming from the district that has been thus represented, both here and in Mexico, it is astonishing to me how the gentleman could make the speech here which he has.[7]

Jamieson's speech was reported by the Washington correspondent of a Louisville, Kentucky, paper. The *Illinois State Register* reprinted his statement:

> I think that Lincoln will find that he had better remain quiet. He will . . . regret that he voted that Illinois officers "fell while leading brave Illinoians to robbery and dishonor . . . in aid of a war of rapine and murder," that he has thrown upon the escutcheon of Illinois the stain of having sent six thousand men to Mexico "to record their infamy and shame in the blood of poor, innocent, inoffending people, whose only crime was weakness." . . . that he has declared by his vote that the "God of Heaven has forgotten to defend the weak and innocent, and permitted the strong hand of murderers and demons from hell to kill men, women, and children, and lay waste and pillage the land of the just."[8]

---

[7] *Globe*, p. 190.

[8] The quotations in this report present a nice literary problem. The reporter obviously quoted from memory, and he may have misquoted

Two other Democrats in the House criticized Lincoln's speech.[9] On February 18 Robinson of Indiana refuted it (and the Spot Resolutions) in a speech defending Polk. His argument was mild enough, but to it he added that Lincoln ". . . had never ventured to tell the people of Springfield district, Illinois, when electioneering for his seat, that the war was unnecessary and unconstitutional; but after he got here he could venture to declare it!" Howell Cobb of Georgia on February 8, argued with "the gentleman from Illinois" to the effect that Corpus Christi was as much the "spot" as was any other place between the Nueces and the Rio Grande. It may be mentioned that if rejoinder was made by only three Democrats not a single Whig in Congress came to Lincoln's defense.

There was vigorous reaction at home. January 21, 1848, the *State Register* excoriated Lincoln for his vote on the Ashmun resolution. The *Illinois Journal* published the war speech on February 10. The next day the *State Register* asserted that the speech had called forth denunciation from many who had voted for Lincoln. It opined that if Lincoln were to run again ("which he will not and dare not do") he would not receive a single vote except from those who put party schemes above national honor. It then published the Clark County nonpartisan denunciation of the Spot Resolutions.

In the weeks that followed the *State Register* reported resolutions of war meetings in a number of counties. Most of these assemblies were Democratic, but some were nonpartisan. In every case the resolutions adopted were in hearty support of the war; whether Lincoln was mentioned or not, the Whig position was attacked. Meetings in Edgar and Perry counties were noted on February 25, in Jefferson on March 17, in Pike and Lawrence counties on March 24, in Morgan and Shelby on April 7, in the Third Congressional District on April 14, and

---

Lincoln. Certainly even the substance of what the reporter indicates Lincoln said suggests the speeches of Giddings and Corwin. It may have been that Lincoln toned down the language of his speech when he put it in written form. See Albert J. Beveridge, *Abraham Lincoln* (1928), I:430 note.

[9] Beveridge (I:428) is in error when he says that with the exception of Jamieson no notice whatever was taken in Washington of Lincoln's war speech. See *Globe*, p. 193, for Robinson's reference to it, and p. 289 for Cobb's.

in Cass, Mercer, and Adams counties on April 21.[10] Lincoln had stirred much opposition to his own and his party's stand.

The St. Louis *Union* was quoted by the *State Register* on March 3, to the effect that Lincoln's "course in denouncing his country has called forth a stern rebuke from many of his constituents, and will yet be more signally condemned." The Morgan County meeting declared that Lincoln had "acted in direct contradiction to the wishes of his constituents of the whole state as well as of this district." In its April 14 issue the *State Register* insisted that Lincoln and his supporters know "that under no circumstances could he have been elected had he avowed the sentiments which he now published, before or during the canvass in which he was elected." With ample allowance for party bias this judgment probably reflected the situation accurately. The paper added that "public opinion requires them to repudiate him, and they do it." This estimate was subsequently borne out in fact.

The Third District (Democratic) Convention denounced Lincoln as unpatriotic and unrepresentative of Illinois. The Sangamon County Democratic Convention congratulated the state for the patriotism of her citizens, but it was "compelled to recognize one unfortunate exception . . . the Hon. Abraham Lincoln, present Whig representative from this Congressional district, who, contrary to the expectations and wishes of his constituents . . . has lent himself to the schemes of such men as Corwin, Giddings, Hale, and others, apologists and defenders of Mexico, and revilers of their own country." Similarly the Menard County Democrats, after the usual denunciations of the Whigs generally, got around to Lincoln, pledging that "we want no man of 'that sort,' and will, determinedly, oppose any candidate who in anywise, gives countenance to such predecessors" as Lincoln and John Henry.

Lincoln might have dismissed these criticisms because they were partisan and politically aimed. But he had friendly criti-

---

[10] The resolutions of the Jefferson County nonpartisan meeting merit quotation as showing the view generally held in Illinois: "We cannot believe that an American Congress would . . . under oath, have declared by almost unanimous vote, that the war existed by act of Mexico if it had not been so.

We cannot believe that a Scott, a Taylor, a Butler, a Hardin . . . would so heartily engage in the prosecution of a war which had been unjustly and unconstitutionally commenced."

cism and warning, too. William H. Herndon was in the field in the Seventh District, and as a close friend of Lincoln's he received numerous personal protests against the Spot Resolutions and the Mexican War speech. "His constituents began to manifest symptoms of grave disapproval of his course on the Mexican War question," Herndon later wrote. "Very soon after [the delivery of the war speech] murmurs of dissatisfaction began to run through the Whig ranks." [11] Herndon at once wrote to Lincoln, reporting the local response to his efforts. But Lincoln was convinced of the correctness of the stand which he had taken, and defended it. A long written discussion between them ensued.[12] Neither convinced the other. It remained Herndon's opinion that the resolutions and the speech sealed Lincoln's doom as Congressman and lost the district to the Democrats.

It is most curious that Lincoln had such slight regard for reports of conditions in his home district. The reason appears to be that, seeing the political scene in national scope, and from the Washington viewpoint, he fell under the influence of Eastern and Southern party leaders and adopted their estimates of what the party stood to gain by opposing the war policies of the administration. He lost contact with the situation in Illinois.

This is clearly indicated in his letter to Herndon, written immediately after he attended a Whig caucus to consider the coming nominating convention. "The whole field of the nation was scanned, and all is high hope and confidence. Illinois is expected to better her condition in this race." [13] This is perhaps the most glaring error in estimating a political situation that Lincoln had ever made. He was assuming the nomination and election of General Taylor, and events proved that this was correct for the nation. But he egregiously exaggerated the possibilities in Illinois. Yet this estimate was more modest than Lincoln's expectation in February, when he thought that with Taylor as candidate Illinois would *certainly* elect one more Whig Congressman besides the supposedly certain one from the Seventh District, and *probably* would give the electoral vote of the state to the Whigs. Apparently the air of Washington was too

---

[11] William H. Herndon and Jesse W. Weik, *Abraham Lincoln* (1889), I:265.

[12] *CW* I:446-48.

[13] *CW* I:490-92.

heady. Lincoln failed to see the signs of the times. He also failed to heed the warnings of his friends.

On the anniversary of the battle of Buena Vista, an occasion which meant much to many people in Illinois, the Reverend J. M. Peck delivered a patriotic oration. He sent Lincoln a copy of his speech, as printed in the Belleville *Advocate*. So far from drawing the conclusion assumed by the sending of the document, Lincoln in his letter of acknowledgment argued his points anew.[14]

Strangest of all was his refusal to heed the warning given him by one of his closest friends and most trusted political advisers. Dr. A. G. Henry (not to be confused with John Henry, the mileage member from Morgan) had favorably impressed Lincoln professionally, and as a resident of Springfield and other towns of the Seventh District the doctor had been an indefatigable worker in the Whig cause. Lincoln had obtained considerable credit for the party organization by state, county, and precinct as set forth in the 1843 Whig circular; the plan was Henry's in design and execution. He was a tower of strength to the Whigs.

While Lincoln was in Congress Dr. Henry was living in Pekin, eking out his physician's earnings by editing the *Tazewell Telegraph*. Dr. Henry wrote Lincoln shortly after the delivery of the war speech. He wrote about a speech which Col. Baker had made and which Henry did not like because Baker took the extreme Whig view against territorial acquisition. This part of the speech Henry had toned down as he edited it for his newspaper. In discussing the matter the doctor made his own estimate of the national and state situation. Lincoln would have trusted it in former days. Dr. Henry then speculated about the stand which Lincoln would take regarding the war. He hoped that Lincoln would not go with Clay against all territorial acquisition. "If you do," Henry wrote, "I am fearful you will be with the minority party for a long time to come. It would be painful in the extreme to part company with you after having fought with you side by side for so long. But if the Whigs as a party join issue with Mr. Polk and take the side of no territory, I shall at the polls (but no where else) *sustain Mr. Polk*." [15]

Lincoln argued his position with Usher F. Linder, a law

---

[14] *CW* I:472 f.

[15] Robert Todd Lincoln Papers, hereafter cited as RTLP.

associate who was then a Whig member of the Illinois legislature. Linder was perturbed at the course which Lincoln had taken. He warned that unfavorable consequences were sure to result from it. He mentioned protests which others had made to him.

In his reply Lincoln attempted to refute all arguments. His critics said that they followed Crittenden's attitude toward the war; Lincoln insisted that he followed him, too. The Democrats, he wrote, forced the Whigs into opposition by interpreting silence as support. He denied that opposing Polk was opposing the war; he and other Whigs consistently voted supplies. He denied that the adoption of the Ashmun amendment stripped Taylor and Scott of their laurels. He denied that the Whigs were tainted with abolitionism for the reason that abolitionists opposed the war. He pointed out that 37 Whigs in the House, all of them slaveholders, had voted for the Ashmun amendment; with one exception they were all Taylor men. Lincoln made it plain that he did not intend to abandon his position.[16] Moreover, he was continuing to disregard the warnings of the Seventh District friends who were his constituents and members of his own party.

It must be repeated that if Lincoln had based his position on principle, and had maintained it as a matter of conscience, he would have been justified in following his course even though it entailed the loss of political friends or resulted in the loss of his Congressional seat to the Democrats. But he had no such motivation. He was still the politician following party policy because he believed that to do so would be of advantage to the party. No doubt he was able to convince himself that the effective policy was the right one. Time showed that, although he retained and realized his ambition for higher political preferment, his course in Congress forced his own retirement for several years, diminished his party's strength in the state, and delivered the one dependable Whig stronghold in Illinois to the enemy.

---

[16] CW I:457 f.

6

LINCOLN AND THE MEXICAN WAR—A CRITIQUE

What attitude toward the Mexican war was normal in Lincoln's day? Certainly not that of Justin Butterfield, a Chicago Whig who was soon to become Lincoln's rival for a patronage job. Butterfield, a blue-light Federalist during the war of 1812, endorsed the principles of the Hartford Convention, and in consequence ruined his political future in New England. He established himself in Illinois. When asked whether he would oppose the Mexican War he is said to have replied, "No, indeed! I opposed one war, and it ruined me. From now on I am for war, pestilence, and famine." [1]

Nor should anyone have been expected to take the chauvinist position of "My country, right or wrong." Col. John J. Hardin was not sufficiently discriminating when he wrote, as the war began, "In our foreign relations I acknowledge no fealty to any party but our country. I believe it is the duty of all true patriots to strengthen the hands of the Govt by every means . . . against all aggression & insult from foreign nations." [2]

The right to criticize administration policies is as proper in wartime as at any other time. The position of John Quincy

---

[1] Usher F. Linder, *Reminiscences of the Early Bench and Bar of Illinois* (1879), p. 87.

[2] Letter dated February 5, 1846, Hardin MSS, Chicago Historical Society.

Adams, for example, was certainly defensible. Nor should a just estimate scorn the position of Joshua R. Giddings; it was mistaken, but it was based upon principle and was consistent.

It is not difficult now to correct mistaken judgments of the Mexican War. It was not brought about by the underhanded machinations of the proslavery interests.[3] This was perceived by Lincoln, who never thought that it was.[4] The United States was not a powerful aggressor, the easy victor over a weak, minor power. A glance at the map might be instructive. Before the settlement of the Oregon questions, Mexico, in territorial extent, was as much a major power as was the United States. Smaller in population and weaker in war potential, she had a much larger standing army, whose cavalry was well trained and efficient.[5] The United States had just grievances against the Mexican government, and had been more than patient in seeking adjustment of them through diplomatic means.[6]

It cannot be conceded that, since Mexico had warned that the annexation of Texas would be regarded as a cause of war, Texas should not have been annexed.[7] Texas, as Lincoln said, had "revolutionized" from Mexico, as Mexico had "revolutionized" from Spain. For ten years Texas had defended herself against repeated attempts by Mexico to reconquer her. Diplomatic recognition had been extended Texas by England, France, and the Netherlands, as well as by the United States. The procedure of the United States in establishing diplomatic relations had been quite correct; there had been no indecent haste.[8]

---

[3] Chauncey S. Boucher, "In *re* that Aggressive Slaveocracy," *Mississippi Valley Historical Review*, 8 (1921), 13-89.

[4] In the recently discovered Wilmington speech: *CW* I:475.

[5] Bill, p. 81. Joel R. Poinsett, who had been a diplomatic representative in Mexico, and who knew Mexico well, wrote to Senator Cass: "The people are warlike, and in Guerrilla warfare are very formidable. Their regular cavalry is by no means despicable, their irregular mounted force the best I have ever seen." (James Fred Rippy, *Joel R. Poinsett* (1935), p. 226).

[6] Smith, *The War With Mexico*, I:58-137.

[7] Smith, p. 82: "The annexation of Texas to the United States was on legal, moral, and political grounds entirely legitimate."

[8] Bill, p. 77, points out that when Mexico threatened war because of the annexation of Texas "Webster snubbed her sharply, pointing out that American citizens were no longer aiding rebels, since Texan independence had been recognized by Britain, France, and the Netherlands as well as by the United States; and even the British minister told Santa Anna that the American attitude was quite correct."

Texas and the United States, as two sovereign nations, had a perfect right to negotiate annexation. No other government had any right to interfere in that matter.

Lincoln had never opposed the annexation of Texas. When that issue was current he took an attitude most unusual for a Westerner: "I never was much interested in the Texas question."[9] Lack of interest in Texas was rare among people on the Western frontier. The "Texas fever" ran high.[10]

The settlement of Texas, with consequent annexation to the United States, was a normal aspect of the westward movement. Emigrants went to Texas much as others had gone to Ohio, to Illinois, to Iowa. Surely Lincoln saw such advertisements as this which appeared in the *Sangamo Journal:*

EMIGRATION
TO THE TRINITY AND RED RIVER COLONY, TEXAS

All emigrants who shall go into this colony and settle before July 1, 1845, will be given 320 acres of land to every family, 160 acres to every single man.[11]

Another advertisement by the Texas Association offered 320 acres of land east of the Brazos River (a more settled area) at eight dollars per acre.[12] These advertisements appeared in issue after issue. Slaves were taken into Texas precisely as they were taken into Alabama: slaveholders (or some of them) moving westward took slaves with them. But as most of the Texas-bound emigrants were without slaves the majority took none. The movement into Illinois was not essentially different; immigrants from slave states brought slaves to Illinois, holding them under the law which permitted long-term indentures.[13]

---

[9] *CW* I:347 f.

[10] Frederick J. Turner, *The United States, 1830–1850* (1935), pp. 352-78; Avery O. Craven, *The Coming of the Civil War* (1942), pp. 180-85.

[11] *Sangamo Journal,* June 26, 1845, and reprinted repeatedly; I have noted 18 appearances of the advertisement until January 22, 1846; there were several issues missing from the file.

[12] *Ibid.,* July 31, 1845; repeated at least 15 times.

[13] Indenture laws for this purpose were passed while Illinois was part of Indiana Territory (1807), retained during the territorial period of Illinois (1809-18), and under the state constitution. There were 133 such quasi-slaves in the whole of Indiana Territory in 1800, 168 in Illinois Territory in 1810, and 917 in the state of Illinois in 1820. See John Moses, *Illinois* (1889), I:324, and Ninian W. Edwards, *The Life and Times of Ninian Edwards* (1870), pp. 179 ff.

This work has asserted that Lincoln, in his Spot Resolutions, his vote for the Ashmun amendment, and his Mexican War speech was not acting upon principle, but was taking partisan advantage of the war issue. The evidence for this judgment appears in his legalistic arguments.

As to the first two of the Spot Resolutions, the answer was plain. The "spot" was within the territory of Spain until 1819. It was within the territory wrested from Spain by the revolutionary government of Mexico. As to the third, the implication that the "spot" was within a Mexican settlement whose inhabitants fled at the approach of the American Army rested upon rumor based upon letters written by soldiers. Presumably the rumor was true. But this had no bearing upon the question of title to the land in which the settlement was located. As to the fourth, Lincoln depended upon inadequate information: he implied that the settlement involved was the only one in the entire "desert" between the Nueces and the Rio Grande. In this he was mistaken.

The crux of the Spot Resolutions was the fifth: whether the people of that settlement had ever submitted themselves to the laws of Texas or of the United States. This point Lincoln developed in the war speech also.

It was on this point that Lincoln rested his case against President Polk. Polk had affirmed, in several messages, that jurisdiction had been exercised by Texas and by the United States, and he had given specifications.[14] Lincoln demanded proof.

It must have been apparent to him when he made the demand that the criteria which he set up were impossible and irrelevant. It was true, and known then, that there were few settlements in the area, and that most of them were on the Gulf and the Nueces. But it was the usual and normal pattern, in the growth of a frontier area, to establish county governments (primarily for providing convenient court facilities) with settlements in the nearer portions of counties which often extended far beyond the settled districts.

For example, when Ohio became a state and Indiana was a territory, one of the frontier counties of Indiana was Knox County. This county covered part of the present state of Indiana

---

[14] Richardson, IV:437-43, 471-506, 532-64.

and more than half of the present state of Illinois.[15] Knox County of Indiana Territory was unquestionably part of the United States in 1790, but there were people in its farther reaches who had never submitted themselves to the laws of the United States or of Indiana Territory, by consent or compulsion, by accepting office, or paying taxes, or serving on juries, or by having process served on them, or in any other way.

As late as 1817, the year before Illinois became a state, one of its twelve counties was Bond, which lay in the form of a long, narrow corridor extending northward to Lake Superior.[16] Save in the area near the county seat, how many people in Bond County then submitted to the jurisdiction of Illinois Territory or of the United States?

Or to take a still later example, John Wentworth related that when Chicago was young (in 1830) a settler who married in Chicago had to go all the way to Peoria, the county seat, for his license.[17]

The settlement of Illinois was perfectly normal, and the pattern of county organization which developed there was quite similar to that which grew up in Texas.

Briefly, the development of Texas in the Nueces–Rio Grande area was as follows: when Texas won independence the old *empresario* land grant system was replaced by the pattern established in the United States.[18] A Land Office was set up through which land grants were obtained.[19] Many grants were made for tracts held under the old title derived through Mexican law; in almost every case, when conflicting claims were adjudicated, the older title was sustained.[20] As early as 1839 the Commissioner of the Texas Land Office estimated that 2,107,000 acres had been legally granted, one-third of which was east of the Rio Grande,

---

[15] James A. Rose, *Counties of Illinois* (1906), pp. 5, 14 f.

[16] *Ibid.*, p. 33; Solon J. Buck, *Illinois in 1818* (1917), pp. 86 f. In 1818 Bond County extended to the state line; even then only the three southern tiers of townships had been surveyed. Fourth-fifths of the 1,384 population lived within the surveyed area, and only forty families north of it.

[17] John Wentworth, *Reminiscences of Early Chicago* (1912), p. 132.

[18] William Kennedy, *Texas: The Rise, Progress, and Prospects of the Republic of Texas* (1841), I:340, 377.

[19] D. W. C. Baker, *A Brief History of Texas from Its Earliest Settlement* (1873), p. 87.

[20] William R. Hogan, *The Texas Republic* (1946), pp. 245 f.

one-sixth west of the Nueces, one-sixth east of the Nueces in the McMullens and the McGloine colonies, and one-third on the San Antonio River.[21]

The area about which Lincoln inquired was represented in the provisional Constitutional Convention,[22] which directed that until the first census was completed there should be two representatives in the Texan Congress from Bexar and one from San Patricio County, and that there should be one senator from Bexar County and one from the senatorial district composed of San Patricio, Refugio, and Goliad Counties.[23] The organic law of Texas provided that counties should be organized, and prescribed the mode, stipulating that a new county might be formed from part of another only upon the petition of 100 free male inhabitants of the area sought to be established as a county.[24] Thus until 1846 there were two counties in the Nueces–Rio Grande area: Bexar and San Patricio. But in 1846 Nueces County was created from San Patricio, and in 1848 Cameron and Starr Counties were created from Nueces, while Webb County was created from Bexar. Kinney and Uvalde Counties were created from Bexar in 1850.[25] Six new counties in the space of four years indicated current settlement, and their organization proved jurisdiction.

Lincoln emphasized jurisdiction. Courts were available. Each county had a chief justice and two associate justices. These officials, in addition to judicial duties, had the task of supervising roads and levying taxes. Each county had a surveyor, who must reside at the county seat and who might appoint deputies. Each county had a board of land commissioners. In 1845 each county was divided into four precincts, from each of which a commissioner was elected. From the days of the Republic each county had a sheriff, clerk, justices of the peace, coroner, and constables; all elected for two-year terms by the qualified voters.[26] Thus, as in Illinois, there were political jobs to be sought.

---

[21] Kennedy, II:380.

[22] *Journals of the Convention,* pp. 3, 4, 10, 17, 21, 70, 71, 367, 373, 374, 377.

[23] Constitution of the State of Texas, Article III.

[24] Wallace C. Murphy, *County Government in Texas* (1933).

[25] Zachary T. Fillmore, *The History and Geography of Texas as Told in County Names* (1915).

[26] Murphy, pp. 9-11; Hogan, pp. 245 ff.

The county courts were required by statute to be held quarterly. The Bexar court met on the second Monday of March, April, October, and November for terms of three weeks. The San Patricio courts met at the same times.[27] Since the county seats were far from the frontier the need for additional courts was what led to the organization of new counties. The *National Intelligencer* on January 27, 1848, carried an item (quoted from the *American Flag,* then published at Matamoros) which was of no help to Lincoln.[28] It exhibited a petition of settlers on the Rio Grande, praying for the establishment of a court in their neighborhood, i.e., praying for a further county division, so that they would not have to make the long journey to the county seat. The petition was granted within the year that it was made.

Lincoln argued that because the area was uninhabited the legal claims of Texas and of the United States were questionable. The same argument might with equal logic have been made about another part of Texas, except that no one questioned the title to the area. The people on the forks of the Trinity petitioned the Texas Constitutional Convention to establish convenient courts for them, since they were "cut off by stretches of uninhabited and, in some districts, uninhabitable country. . . . Neither Nacogdoces nor Robertson have ever established their civil or political jurisdiction over these settlements." [29]

How much of these facts might Lincoln reasonably have been expected to know? He might have been expected to know as much as Douglas knew when he made his speech rebutting what Lincoln had said.[30] Congressman Kaufman of Texas (of whose Congressional district the area was part) spoke several times on these subjects, presenting facts which cut the ground from under Lincoln's assertions and implications. Speaking on June 5, 1848, Kaufman demonstrated not only the legal title of Texas to the Nueces–Rio Grande area, but that legal jurisdiction had been exercised over it. In each statement of fact Kaufman gave his reference to Texas statutes or to other documents which,

---

[27] Kennedy, II:360 f.

[28] The *American Flag* was an unofficial newspaper published by personnel of Taylor's Army.

[29] *Journals of the Convention*, p. 61.

[30] Douglas began by saying, "I shall state no fact for the accuracy of which I have not the most conclusive authority in the books before me."

as he pointed out, were on file in the court and Congressional libraries and were there available to any interested person.[31]

Finally it may be remarked that there was a negative application of Lincoln's argument that jurisdiction established ownership. As Justin Smith observed, there was a time when Connecticut established and exercised jurisdiction over territory which proved to be owned by Pennsylvania.[32]

Interestingly enough, a lawsuit occurred in Nueces County only a few days before Lincoln presented his Spot Resolutions. A Mr. Wayman, who was a merchant, sued an army officer named Porter, alleging that Porter had illegally taken possession of his stock of goods in April, 1847. The defendant argued that the United States Army had taken over the area, and that after this requisition had been made the laws of Texas had no jurisdiction. The Hon. W. P. Morton, district judge, found that the entire territory to the Rio Grande was within the limits of the state of Texas, and that no officer of the United States Army had authority to interfere with the acts of a citizen in his transaction of legitimate business anywhere within the state. He found for the plaintiff and awarded $15,000 damages.[33]

An amusing instance was referred to Lincoln in rebuttal of his point about title to the area. The Philadelphia *Ledger* was the first to report that General Taylor, who had an eye to land values and plantation possibilities, had paid $20,000 for an old Mexican grant of eleven leagues (some 4,000 acres) located between the Nueces and the Rio Grande. No doubt the county court was depended upon to validate the title. The story was bandied widely. The Augusta (Georgia) *Whig* inquired about the ownership of the area before the war; the Boston *Post* humorously replied that some of it now belonged to General Taylor.[34]

The question underlying the Ashmun amendment had a much greater latitude of doubt than any asked in the Spot Resolutions. The growth of constitutional law has settled the question decisively: the war powers of the executive include the authority to order the armed forces where he will at his discre-

---

[31] *Globe,* 659-63, 783-88.

[32] Smith, *War With Mexico,* II:277.

[33] *Illinois State Register,* January 14, 1848.

[34] Clipped in the *Illinois State Register,* September 15, 1848.

tion.[35] But there had been no such decision when Lincoln spoke or when Polk issued such an order. The war powers of the executive grow with every war. They were notably increased during the Mexican War.[36] Ironically, in view of Lincoln's vote on the Ashmun amendment, and his arguments in defense of his vote, the war powers of the executive increased more during Lincoln's Presidency than in any period before or since. Compared to Lincoln's executive orders for the relief of Fort Sumter, increasing the size of the army, payment of military personnel without Congressional appropriation, blockade of the Southern ports, and his putative freeing of slaves by the Emancipation Proclamation, Polk's alleged unconstitutional acts are dwarfed to pygmy proportion.[37]

It is now fully recognized that inasmuch as the annexation of Texas had proceeded to the point reached when he was inaugurated, it was Polk's duty to order the movement of military force as he did.[38] It was his duty to defend the southwestern border of the United States when the Sabine was that border, and to defend the new southwestern border at the Rio Grande when annexation made that river the border.

As regards the movement of Taylor's army from Corpus Christi to Fort Brown, Polk was fully within the right. It is idle as well as incorrect to refer to the area between the Nueces and the Rio Grande as "the disputed territory." There never was a time when Mexico would have recognized the independence of Texas with the Nueces as the border. Mexico never recognized the independence of Texas with any stated border; she insisted that all Texas, to the line of the Sabine, was hers. Texas had not only claimed but successfully defended and maintained the Rio Grande border; she had several times driven Mexican forces from Texas across the Rio Grande. Consequently when Texas was annexed Polk correctly acted upon the fact that the Rio Grande was the border.[39]

---

[35] Smith, *War With Mexico*, II:151.

[36] There is a convenient summary of this question in the pamphlet, "Powers of the President to Send the Armed Forces Outside the United States" (1951). Polk's order is discussed on p. 10.

[37] James G. Randall, *Constitutional Problems Under Lincoln* (1951), pp. 25-47, 48, 73, 118-39, 140-68, 342-404.

[38] Smith, *War With Mexico,* II:38-155.

[39] Hubert H. Bancroft, *History of the North Mexican States and Texas* (1886, 1889), II:279-343; Bill, pp. 50-56.

The clause in the joint resolution of annexation which referred to the adjustment of border disputes applied to the upper reaches of the Rio Grande, and to these regions only. It involved the question whether Texas as annexed actually contained the land on the left bank of the river *to its source,* i.e., in the area which had been in the former province of New Mexico. Texas had made only one attempt to establish a trade route in that region, and that attempt was a disastrous failure—the ill-fated Texas-Santa Fe expedition of 1842.[40] This was the only area where there had been legitimate dispute with Mexico. Dispute was obviated when New Mexico became part of the United States.

The conclusion concerning Polk's executive order is that the war was not unconstitutionally begun by the President. It was futile then, and would be futile now, to argue whether it had been begun unnecessarily. No one can now doubt that Polk was acting in accordance with correct interpretation of the Constitution. However, it was a debatable question when Lincoln was in Congress. Lincoln cannot be convicted of error because the later development, which has made the fact indisputable, had not then occurred.

A critique of the war speech involves several matters. To say the least, Lincoln was anything but candid in his opening statement—that when the war began people who could not approve the President's course should remain silent. The fact was that Lincoln did not oppose the war until he went to Congress. Perhaps prudence caused him to refrain from criticism while a candidate. But the matter went beyond that. While a candidate for Congress Lincoln supported the war; as has been noted, he participated in a war recruitment rally. It follows that either then or while in Congress he was less than sincere.

A conscientious person, presented with the issue that Lincoln drew, need have no difficulty to ascertain his proper course. If Polk interpreted votes for supplies as endorsement of his war policy, and a Congressman regarded that policy as wrong, he could have discharged his duty to his conscience by voting against supplies. This is what some Whigs, such as Giddings, did. But most of them, as Justin Smith so aptly says, "denounced the

---

[40] George W. Kendall, *Narrative of the Texan Santa Fe Expedition* (1844).

war enough to incriminate themselves when they supported it, and they supported it enough to stultify themselves when they condemned it." [41] Lincoln was one of these.

The purely political motive of Lincoln's speech is apparent in his narrowing the issue to the single question of title to the place where the first blood was shed. If this land was indeed American then Lincoln (so he said) would go with the President; if it was in fact Mexican, Polk's course stood condemned. There was no appeal to the rightness or wrongness of the cause of the outbreak of hostilities, much less any question of the rightness or wrongness of war. It was simply the legal question of title.

In his analysis of Polk's case Lincoln used arguments unworthy of a responsible public man. For example, his point that Polk had referred to Texas as part of Louisiana, from which Lincoln drew the analogy that the line which divided your land from mine cannot still be a boundary after I have sold the land to you. Or another analogy: if I should claim your land by word of mouth that would not make it mine, or if I were to claim it by a deed which I had made myself the claim would be worthless. Winning a war of independence is not analogous to asserting a verbal claim, nor was it comparable to writing an invalid deed. Still another fallacious analogy was that of the man who exercises jurisdiction over a piece of land 50 by 152 feet in area between the Wabash and the Mississippi Rivers. The Texan war for independence, and successful defense of claimed territory, were rather different from the illustrative point. It was not Texan claim versus Mexican claim, as Lincoln asserted. It was claim based upon revolution and sustained by repeated and successful defense.

Lincoln's interpretation of the "treaty" signed by Santa Anna simply does not bear examination. This is what the document said:

Article III. The Mexican troops will evacuate the territory of Texas, passing to the other side of the Rio Grande del Norte. . . .

Article VI. The troops of both armies will refrain from coming in contact with each other; and to this end the commander of the army of Texas will be careful not to approach within a shorter distance than five leagues.[42]

---

[41] Smith, II:283.

[42] CW I:435 f; Niles' *Register*, 50:336.

Lincoln tortured these words to mean that Texas should not go within five leagues of her own border.

Did he seriously expect anyone to accept this crafty interpretation? Nothing can be clearer in meaning than the text quoted: the Texan army should not come closer than five leagues distance from the Mexican army in the latter's evacuation of Texan territory. Nothing could be clearer than that once the Mexican army had crossed the Rio Grande and was thus repatriated, Texans—military or civilian—were at liberty to proceed to the river. Lincoln deliberately altered sense: the article refers to the Texan army; Lincoln made out that Texas, not the army of Texas, was not to approach the Rio Grande. He misinterpreted the point that it was the Mexican army, not the Rio Grande, which was to be kept at a distance of five leagues. It is significant that Lincoln did not quote the words of the document when he referred to it. Had he done so the correct meaning would have been obvious, and his own partisan position would have been apparent. The only construction which can be placed upon this part of the speech is that Lincoln deliberately intended to mislead.

The question of jurisdiction has been sufficiently discussed, except to allude to the compromise boundary which Lincoln proposed in his speech. It is difficult to see why he adopted this view. The Nueces would have been a more logical boundary than some yet to be determined imaginary line between it and the Rio Grande. But Lincoln set great store by the idea, taking the trouble to write to Horace Greeley, inviting the editor's acceptance of the midway line as the policy of the New York *Tribune*.[43]

Lincoln laid much stress on the supposed fact that Taylor's army encamped in the confines of an old Mexican settlement, whose inhabitants fled at the approach of the American army. It is, of course, merely a matter of terminology whether these people were called Mexicans or Texans. They were inhabitants of Texas, and subject to the laws of Texas and of the United States.[44] It was unfortunate for them that the army occupied

---

[43] CW I:493 f.

[44] Some of the Texan revolutionary patriots were "Mexicans" in exactly this sense, e.g., Juan Antonia Navarro, who became a member of the Texas Constitutional Convention and was a member of the Texas legislature from the beginning. See Fillmore, pp. 113 f.

their land, but their flight was totally irrelevant to the question of the responsibility for the outbreak of fighting.

In implying that this was the only settlement on the Rio Grande Lincoln was in error and could have been corrected at the time. Laredo by 1840 had a population of 600, most of whom were natives (not American immigrants), and on the road from Laredo to Santa Fe there were several villages. On the Gulf there was the small town of Brazos St. Iago and the port of Point Isabel.[45]

It was ironical that Lincoln so stressed the point that Polk had been unable to bring the war to conclusion. The speech was made January 12, 1848. Polk's plenipotentiary had long been in Mexico. The peace treaty was signed on February 2, only a little more than two weeks after Lincoln spoke. It was transmitted to the Senate on Washington's birthday, and the Senate voted its advice and consent on May 30.[46]

But all this is beside the point. Lincoln was setting up conditions which could not be met. That was his intention. That purpose led to the development of the entire speech: if the President answered Lincoln's questions satisfactorily, Lincoln would reverse his vote on the Ashmun amendment (how he could do that is not explained) and would forthwith associate himself with Polk in the prosecution of the war. "But if he *can* not, or *will* not do this— . . . I shall be fully convinced, of what I more than suspect already, that he is deeply conscious of being in the wrong. . . . He now finds himself, he knows not where." The motive of the speech is revealed: to put the President in the wrong.

As though the political motive of harassing the President were not enough, Lincoln went on to convict Polk the man. Pointing to what he regarded as inconsistencies in the President's messages, Lincoln concluded: "His mind, tasked beyond it's power, is running hither and thither, like some tortured creature, on a burning surface, finding no position, on which it can settle down, and be at ease. . . . As I have before said, he knows not where he is. He is a bewildered, confounded, and miserably

---

[45] There were still more settlements in the area. See Kennedy, II:412, Fillmore, pp. 208, 280. The New York *Herald* reported a new town, Rome, recently laid out 15 miles above Rio Grande City, and referred to new settlements opposite Mier and below Guerrero (October 24, 1848).

[46] Smith, II:233-52.

perplexed man. God grant that he may be able to show, there is not something about his conscience, more painful than all his mental perplexity!" It may be remarked that the imperturbable Polk revealed no awareness of this analysis of his mind and conscience. There is no reference to Lincoln's speech, nor to Lincoln, in the President's voluminous *Diary*.

Since the right to criticize the President is one of the liberties of the American citizen, no one will question Lincoln's right to criticize Polk. One may properly ask what he expected to accomplish by it. The answer is readily forthcoming: advantage to his political party. Strangely enough, in view of the vigorous reactions to it, Lincoln expected that the speech, circulated in his Congressional district, would aid his party in the coming elections. That was the touchstone of the whole issue for the Whigs. Defeated on every domestic question, they were making party use of foreign policy. Within six years the Whig party was dead. The lesson is clear. The Federalist party, defeated on domestic issues by the Jeffersonians, made partisan use of foreign policy from the time of the embargo to the end of the war of 1812. That party died. It may seem strange that the bearing of this fact was lost upon the Whigs in 1846-48. It is clear today.

Lincoln might have made something of his attempt to discredit the administration, had he not phrased his criticism in a form that was sure to be offensive to many of his Whig constituents as well as to many Illinois Democrats. If some New England Whig had made the speech it would have met with little notice. But the war was popular in the West, and for a Western politician to take the position which Lincoln assumed, was to jeopardize not only his own but his party's standing. That is what developed. Without conscientious principle, and actuated only by political motive, Lincoln for the first time in his life was completely mistaken in his estimate of a political situation. Within two weeks he had committeed three costly blunders.

7

THE FIRST SESSION

When Lincoln was in Congress it was a time for greatness. The nation's westward expansion had placed the frontier on the Pacific. There was acute need to provide government for the new territories and problems of great difficulty were involved. The slavery question complicated all of them. Greatness was required to solve them.

But there was no greatness in the Thirtieth Congress. There was politics. Routine business occasioned petty acts and tedious speeches. Senator Benton put it aptly, when he said of a proposal to improve the ventilation of the Senate chamber, "No, sir; no more ventilation! We have quite wind enough, sir! Yes, sir; quite wind enough." [1]

There was more wind than wisdom in Lincoln's Congress. Greatness was evident in the next, in the adoption of the Compromise of 1850. But the same problems appeared in the Thirtieth Congress, and they should have been met then. Nor was greatness shown by Lincoln. The utmost that can be said is that he demonstrated ability, and exhibited industry, attentiveness, and devotion to duty.

Lincoln voted in all roll calls with but seven exceptions, and he was present during five of the roll calls in which his

---

[1] *Globe,* 30th Congress, 1st Session, p. 1085.

vote was not recorded.[2] He merits praise that he never skulked a vote. He assumed his share of routine work. He worked effectively on his two committees, and presented their recommendations to the House.[3] He was prompt in filing petitions sent by his constituents, most of which were requests for land grants for railroad construction.

In fact, he was unusually aggressive. His first act as Congressman, aside from voting on roll calls, was to present a petition from his friend, Dr. A. G. Henry, who had advanced money for supplying Illinois volunteers for the war. Lincoln labored to get Henry reimbursed.[4] He followed the petition with a bill for Henry's relief, and stayed by it tenaciously until it was enacted.[5] Early in the session he gave notice of leave to present a bill to grant land for veterans of the War of 1812 and the Mexican War.[6] The day he presented his Spot Resolutions he presented the first of his railroad land grant petitions.[7] On January 5, 1848, he made his maiden speech.

The subject of Lincoln's first speech in Congress was the government's contract for carrying the Great Southern Mail.[8] The Postmaster General had offered a contract to a Virginia railroad at a lowered rate. The railroad rejected the contract and petitioned for one at a higher rate. In a letter to Herndon, Lincoln referred deprecatingly to his speech: "By way of getting the hang of the House I made a little speech . . . on a post-office question of no general interest. I find speaking here and else-

---

[2] *Journal,* pp. 288, 836, 845, 881, 885, 1181, 1192. All of these few absences occurred in the first session; from the time of taking his seat (three days late) in the second session Lincoln was present and voted in every roll call.

[3] *Globe,* p. 194. Winthrop was criticized by the Giddings coterie for his committee assignments. They asserted that he was under the influence of Southern Whigs. Actually Winthrop withdrew from all familiar associations, took a room at Gadsby's hotel, and there spent three days (while the House was in recess) making up the assignments. That the criticisms were unfounded is shown by the fact that several of the Southern Whigs were dissatisfied with their assignments. See Joseph Borome, "Two Letters of Robert Charles Winthrop," *Mississippi Valley Historical Review,* 38 (1951), 289-96.

[4] *Globe,* p. 56.

[5] *Globe,* pp. 398, 535.

[6] *Globe,* p. 56; *CW* I:460 f.

[7] *Globe,* p. 64; *Journal,* pp. 147, 150 f.

[8] *Globe,* pp. 107-09; *CW* I:423-29.

where about the same thing. I was about as badly scared, and
no worse, as I am when I speak in Court." [9]

The matter was, however, of some importance. Northern
newspapers were seriously inconvenienced by the failure of the
Southern mail to arrive on schedule. Shortly before, the *National
Intelligencer* had noted that the Southern mail had not been received for four days.[10] Botts, a Virginia Whig, had already debated the question, asserting that the Postmaster General had
disrupted the mail service in order to save money. Goggin,
another Virginia Whig (and Chairman of the Committee on
Post Offices and Post Roads), followed Botts, stating the essential
facts and taking the side of the railroad. The fundamental question was one of law: did the Postmaster General have authority
to contract at the higher rate? Goggin absolved the Postmaster
General of intended fault; he concluded that the law had been
misinterpreted.

It is odd that Lincoln, who lost no opportunity to capitalize
party issues, should have defended the Postmaster General. It is
curious, too, that he exhibited ignorance of the House rules to a
degree unusual for a freshman member. In his speech he mentioned what had gone on in committee, and was stopped by the
point of order that committee deliberations could not be made
public. He quaintly remarked that if he had been out of order
he took it back as far as he could; he had no desire to be out
of order, although he could never keep long in order. When he
ended his speech he naïvely asked that his unused time, if any,
might be credited for later use.

It was on January 12 that Lincoln made his Mexican War
speech. A week later he spoke again for the committee.[11] This
time the subject was a petition of two Georgians, Saltmarsh
and Fuller, praying for compensation. They had purchased a
mail contract, and the sale had been approved by the government, but the transfer had not been entered upon the department books. So far as the record showed the original contractors
were entitled to payment, and Saltmarsh and Fuller had received only a small amount of pay. After discontinuing their

---

[9] CW I:430.

[10] *National Intelligencer*, December 20, 29, 1847, January 6, 1848; New
York *Tribune*, June 13, 1848.

[11] *Globe*, p. 197; CW I:442-44.

service they had sued one of the original contractors, but they lost their suit. Then the Post Office Department sued the other original contractor, bringing all the relevant facts to light: the government owed the supposed holders of the contract a sum larger than their indebtedness to the government. Saltmarsh and Fuller were entitled to compensation, and a bill for their relief was entered. Later it was passed.

It was a Congressman's obligation to listen to speeches as well as to make them.[12] There will be occasion to note the repetitiousness of subject matter in routine speeches. Almost all of them followed party tenets. Seldom was anything new or notable said. One speech, however, which Lincoln heard early in the session, impressed him profoundly. It was made by Alexander Stephens, the Georgia Whig. Lincoln wrote to Herndon that "a little slim, pale-faced, consumptive man, with a voice like Logan's has just concluded the very best speech, of an hour's length, I ever heard.

My old, withered, dry eyes, are full of tears yet.

If he writes it out any thing like he delivered it, our people shall see a good many copies of it." [13]

The reader of the printed form of the speech will probably infer that the written form differed markedly from the oral, or will wonder what moved Lincoln to tears. The printed speech is highly argumentative, with little emotional appeal. The nearest approach to purple prose is a passage with "the brightest gem in the chaplet of a nation's glory . . . the last funeral pyre of liberty . . . the land of my home, the place of my nativity, and the graves of my sires." There was a flamboyant reference to the battle of Buena Vista, with eulogistic words about Col. Hardin. Perhaps the reference to the death of Hardin is what deeply moved Lincoln.

Lincoln's remark that the people of the Seventh District would see many copies of the speech prompts the observation that the purpose of most of the speeches in Congress was not to influence Congressmen but to edify constituents. This was forcibly pointed out by the redoubtable Parson Brownlow:

---

[12] Howell Cobb remarked that in the Twenty-ninth Congress there had been more than 75 speeches in the tariff; C. J. Ingersoll added that there had been 92 speeches on Oregon (*Globe*, p. 45).

[13] *CW* I:448.

"A member who addresses either House may be heard through his *printed* speech, but is not heard by members and spectators present. Writing letters, reading newspapers, and smoking cigars, behind the bar, is the order of the day. But this habit of paying no attention to a member while speaking has been contracted in great degree, from the fact of it being impossible to hear a man distinctly, owing to the peculiar construction of the hall." [14] The New York *Herald* remarked to the same effect: "In the House, flippancy, episodical and egotistical diversions, wholly independent of the subject matter, and copious talk to Buncombe are tolerated. A license of manner and of language has become sanctioned by custom and generally prevails. Members talk neither to the subject nor to their colleagues. They are thinking only of their constituents, and intend that their speeches, nicely but cheaply printed, shall be sent home all properly franked and directed." [15]

Lincoln franked many speeches as campaign documents. The *State Register* complained of the flood of speeches by Webster and other antiwar Whigs;[16] Lincoln did not confine his use of the Congressman's free mailing privilege to his own efforts, although he franked his own speeches in large numbers. He sent out 7,080 copies of his speeches, and 5,560 of the speeches of other members. His own cost him $76.80, and he paid for them and for those of others a total of $136.40. It is noteworthy that of the whole sum only four dollars was spent after the first session.[17] The Congressional and Presidential elections occurred that autumn, and little purpose was served by distributing campaign documents after the elections.

Tragedy struck the House on February 21. The day began with the usual routine. A bill to create the office of Surveyor General of Oregon was introduced, petitions were received, and notice of leave to present new bills was made. Another set of resolutions for political effect was offered: Chase, a Tennessee Democrat, proposed the thanks of Congress to several Democratic generals of the war, including Lincoln's old rival, James

---

[14] Rockford *Forum*, May 2, 1848.

[15] New York *Herald*, April 1, 1848, August 12, 1848.

[16] *State Register*, April 14, October 13, 1848. Statements of thanks to Lincoln for sending documents appear frequently in several of the Illinois Whig newspapers.

[17] George Saile Gideon Account Book (MSS), p. 154 f.

Shields. This brought the usual parliamentary maneuvering. Finally there was a roll call on whether the main question should be put (Lincoln voted "Nay"), and Speaker Winthrop rose to put the question.[18]

He was interrupted. "Look to Mr. Adams," cried Hunt of New York. The venerable statesman of Braintree was seen to sink in his seat. He had voted in the roll call, and appeared to be as well as usual. Several members rushed to him. One was Fries of Ohio, a physician. Another doctor, Edwards of Ohio, went to Mr. Adams.[19] The stricken Adams was carried to the rotunda, in the hope that fresher air might revive him, and was then taken, still unconscious, to the Speaker's room. A surgeon was called and Mr. Adams was cupped, with no perceptible effect. Henry Clay came to the room, but Mr. Adams did not recognize him. Tradition has it that during his two days of illness he recovered consciousness long enough to say, "Thank the officers of the House," and then, quite clearly, "This is the last of earth. I am content."

Two funeral committees were appointed, one on arrangements and one to accompany the body to the burial place. The former had thirty members (one from each state and the one territory); on it Lincoln represented Illinois.[20] The committee proved to be too large, and a subcommittee was formed, to which Lincoln was not appointed.[21]

On March 2, Lincoln and those who had the fortitude to remain listened to a harangue by the one representative of the Native American party in the Thirtieth Congress.[22] The occasion was an administration proposal to establish a diplomatic mission in Rome. Levin's speech was what might have been expected of a nativist, and need not be summarized. It was so objectionable that it was not allowed to go without refutation. Purporting to prove the Pope's interference in American affairs, Levin "read" from documentary sources. A few days later Maclay (Democrat) of New York demonstrated that the sources identified by Levin

---

[18] *Globe*, p. 381; William H. Seward, *Life and Public Services of John Quincy Adams* (1849), pp. 333-37.

[19] New York *Tribune*, February 23, 1848.

[20] *CW* I:474 f.

[21] *Globe*, p. 387. John Wentworth represented Illinois on the committee to attend the body of Mr. Adams to Quincy.

[22] *Globe*, pp. 418-21.

contained no such statements. Levin had merely pretended to read.[23] The highly respected C. J. Ingersoll, with the utmost politeness and urbanity, took Levin to task and was insulted by him.[24] Ingersoll remarked that there were only two Roman Catholic Congressmen. "We are a Protestant Congress," he said, "representing a Protestant community. I therefore think it prudent and wise to avoid the excitement which subjects of this kind are apt to create." [25]

A week later Lincoln reported, without a speech, another bill from the Committee on Post Offices.[26]

So far as the record shows there was not much wit or humor displayed in the House debates. Such examples as survive will hardly crack ribs if they are read today. For example, March 18, under the heading "Things in Washington," the New York *Tribune* noted that "the House of Representatives agitated a long discussion . . . concerning the price of mules—De Mulieribus, as a member, no less distinguished for his wit than for his honest eloquence and good sense, was pleased to say." It is perhaps as well that the Congressional *Globe* does not identify the punster; the reader's groan may be directed against Mr. Greeley, whose sense of humor was defective.

On April 3, Lincoln moved to suspend the rules so that the House might consider a joint resolution from the Senate. It concerned contracts for the purchase of hemp for the Navy. Lincoln wanted it referred to the Committee on Naval Affairs. It required a two-thirds majority to suspend the rules and Lincoln's motion failed.[27] He may have had an eye to business for his father-in-law, who was interested in hemp processing.

A party battle occurred on April 19, to settle the contest over the seat of the Sixth Congressional District of New York.[28] Gross fraud had occurred there: in violation of a New York

---

[23] *Globe, Appendix*, pp. 443 f.

[24] *Globe*, p. 439.

[25] Charles Brown, a Pennsylvania Democrat, made an acute observation on Levin's speech: "It is apparent enough that the gentleman is now very desirous of forming an alliance with the Whig party of the South." (*Globe, Appendix*, p. 442.) The coalition was, in effect, made; the Native Americans nominated no candidate for the Presidency in 1848, but "recommended" Taylor.

[26] *Globe*, p. 449; CW I:456 f.

[27] *Globe*, p. 571.

[28] *Globe*, pp. 543-48.

statute 163 paupers had voted at a polling place in the precinct where the almshouse was located. Most of the fraudulent votes had been cast for the Democratic candidate, but some had been cast for the Whig. The House found that neither candidate was entitled to the seat; that the seat was vacant. Lincoln so voted. The upshot of the matter was that in the next regular election Horace Greeley was chosen, with subsequent embarrassment to Whigs and Democrats alike.

Lincoln spoke briefly on May 4.[29] A bill for reimbursing Texan cavalry volunteers for the loss of their horses was the subject. Lincoln's point of interest was that the Texas volunteers ought not be given special consideration; everyone who had similarly lost during service should be repaid. Since the question was one involving the Mexican War, Giddings was against the bill, and Kaufman of Texas felt obliged to make a ringing speech on the service of the men whose loss was thus to be made good.

May 8, Congressional debate began on a serious matter, but reached a development which gave rise to intended humor.[30] A bill similar to that which Lincoln had given notice of leave to introduce, awarding bounty lands to war veterans, was before the House. Inevitably some of the Whigs carried their aversion to the Mexican War to extreme length, whereupon some Democrats ridiculed their attitude by reference to other wars. Lumpkin, a Georgia Democrat, wanted veterans of the Seminole War to be included. Stephens, the Georgia Whig, moved to add "or the Creek Indians in Georgia and Alabama." Hammons, a Maine Democrat, perhaps seriously, proposed to add the survivors of the Aroostook War who had served as much as thirty days. Venable, a North Carolina Democrat, moved similar benefit to "those who served thirty days in the anti-rent war against Big Thunder, and those who served thirty days in the Mormon War, or the Dorr War, or the Whiskey expedition in Pennsylvania, or in the buckshot war." An unidentified member proposed thus to recognize those who had served in the Southampton insurrection in Virginia. Green, a Missouri Democrat, aroused some laughter (so, at least, says the *Globe*) by proposing an amendment to cover all who desired to slay a Mexican, and further

---

[29] *Globe*, p. 727; *CW* I:468 f.
[30] *Globe*, p. 730-36.

laughter was provoked (according to the *Globe*) by the proposal of Edwards, one of the Ohio Whigs, to include particularly "the man who had admitted Santa Anna into Mexico." Beneath this the wit of Congressmen did not descend, at least at this time.

Lincoln spoke briefly, May 11, on a bill enabling Wisconsin to join the Union.[31] His point was that the policy of reserving township sections so as to "enhance" the price of unreserved sections was wrong. He also joined in debate the next day, but this time was not quoted by the *Globe's* reporter.[32] As a member of his principal committee he moved the previous question, thus ending debate, on a post office matter on May 30.[33]

Science occupied the attention of Congress on June 12, when Vinton of Ohio proposed an appropriation for meteorological observations by the Naval Observatory. Immediately Jones of Tennessee moved to amend by striking out "meterological observations" and inserting "Professor Espy, for regulating storms and weather generally." His allusion was to the alleged ability of Professor Espy to make rain.[34] A piece of scientific apparatus was discussed on June 20. Houston of Delaware proposed that the House install an electrical machine to record votes on roll calls. It was noted that an oral roll call consumed from twenty to thirty minutes, and that on some days there were six or seven roll calls. The saving of time would have been considerable.

But House members were interested in things other than machines to expedite the work of Congress. It was on this day that Lincoln made his speech on internal improvements. Wick, an Indiana Democrat, spoke in support of the traditional Democratic idea of the power of Congress to legislate for the territories, Hudson, a Whig from Massachusetts, used his hour for a speech on slavery, and Lincoln's Democratic colleague from Illinois, Orlando Ficklin, spoke for an hour in reply to Lincoln and Hudson. The voting machine resolution was laid on the table.[35]

Lincoln took part in debate again June 28. The theme was a proposed increase in salary for district judges in Virginia. It

---

[31] *Globe,* p. 755; *CW* I:469-71.

[32] *Globe,* p. 762.

[33] *Globe,* p. 797.

[34] *Globe,* p. 826.

[35] *Globe,* pp. 856 f.

seemed to Lincoln that holding eleven courts per year was excessive, but he did not favor the recommended salary increase.[36]

On the Fourth of July Lincoln participated in a ceremony which brought together the maximum number of dignitaries of the government. The cornerstone of the Washington Monument was laid. The President and members of the cabinet headed a parade a mile and a half long. General Quitman, back from distinguished service in Mexico, led the military section. Members of Congress followed. Fraternal organizations were headed by the Masons, who laid the stone. Not the least notable of the personages present were two very old ladies whose lives linked the era of George Washington with 1848 and whose husbands had much to do in establishing Washington's government. They were Mrs. Alexander Hamilton and Dolley Madison. Speaker of the House Winthrop made the address.[37] Mrs. Lincoln must have regretted missing so brilliant an occasion, but she and the two boys had returned to her father's home in Lexington.[38]

Next day the Whig majority pushed partisanship to the front, forcing, over the determined opposition of the Democratic minority, the adoption of resolutions affirming the constitutionality of the principles advocated by the Chicago River and Harbor Convention, to which Lincoln had been a delegate. Of course he voted "Aye." [39]

A week later a development occurred which caused much merriment.[40] For weeks the House had used its time in making speeches designed for the coming elections. Slight attention was paid to pressing measures such as the organization of government for Oregon, California, and New Mexico. Appropriation bills were up, and the time for adjournment approached. But instead of business as usual it was politics as usual. Responsible legislators were worried. The Speaker and other serious men did, on this day, force attention to the civil appropriation bill and to the naval bureaus. But a roll call showed that only 112 members, less than a quorum, were present. The next roll call accounted for only 102.

[36] *Globe*, p. 878; *CW* I:494.
[37] *National Intelligencer*, July 6, 1848; Winthrop, *Addresses*, IV:525 ff.
[38] *CW* I:477 f., 495 f.
[39] *Globe*, pp. 894-96.
[40] *Globe*, p. 926.

The House rules required the presence of members unless excused. Disciplinary action was demanded. The names of the absentees were called, the doors of the House were closed, and the sergeant-at-arms was directed to arrest the absent members and bring them before the bar of the House. He first brought Lahm of Ohio. The Speaker demanded the reason for Lahm's absence. Lahm defended his record for attendance, and stated candidly that in his seven months in Congress he "was compelled to listen to discussions . . . which were exceedingly uninteresting, and very frequently were not pertinent . . . a useless waste of time of the House, and a worse than useless expenditure of the money of the people." He persisted that he had committed no offense and offered no excuse. He was readmitted after paying a fine.

Others were brought, but unlike Lahm they pleaded illness. It was a long drawn out procedure, and at six in the afternoon (in Washington, in mid-July, before the days of air-conditioning) Sawyer of Ohio remarked that the session had lasted nearly seven hours and that it was very hot. He suggested that "now, in order that those who were hungry might go home and get their dinner, and something else needful to cheer the inner man —a little of the critter . . ." [the remaining absentees could be dealt with tomorrow.]

When the affair was resumed it was pointed out that most of the absentees were young and inexperienced. But Sims of South Carolina declared that there were among them some old sinners, including his good friend C. J. Ingersoll [who was indeed an old timer, his first term in the House having been 1812] and his colleague from the Barnwell District, Mr. Rhett, the patriarch of the House [Rhett was 48 years old, Ingersoll was 66]. Botts of Virginia moved the previous question, but the Speaker pointed out that inasmuch as Botts was in the custody of the sergeant-at-arms he was not in order to make a motion. This caused much laughter.[41]

At this point Lincoln, reminding the Speaker that he was still a member, moved the previous question. So it went on and on, with numerous parliamentary objections and with much hilarity. The capstone of Congressional humor was placed by Botts. At his own request he was allowed to explain his absence. He

---

[41] *Globe*, pp. 928 f.

gravely related that although he was a young man he was afflicted with an old man's weakness, lumbago, of which he had recently suffered. He had come to the House yesterday, interested in getting the army bill up for a vote; finding that there was no chance to bring it up he went home and lay down. He had returned today hoping to bring the bill to a vote, but if it could not be done he would go home again. Finishing his excuse, Botts "returned to his seat in a crippled condition, his hand on his hip, and his usually erect figure bent, as with great pain. Instead, however, of meeting with sympathy, the honorable gentleman's misfortune was the source of boisterous mirth to the House, which evidently was not offensive to him, for his good natured face beamed with its invariable cheerfulness." Thus the gaiety of the House of Representatives was enhanced, to the neglect of public business.

Lincoln addressed the House on post office matters on July 19,[42] and five days later, in a session given over to campaign speeches, he obtained the floor when that privilege was sought by many others.[43] He said that he intended to make a full hour speech, but if the House wished to take up the matter before it he would give way. Vinton of Ohio requested him to postpone his speech, and Lincoln acceded. Two days afterward he made his speech on the candidacies of Cass and Taylor.

The Great Southern Mail question came up again on August 2, but this time Lincoln did not speak. On that day a bill highly important to Illinois came up: a Senate bill granting land for the construction of a railroad connecting the upper and lower Mississippi with the Great Lakes at Chicago. Lincoln and his friend Collamer of Vermont (Collamer was Chairman of the House Committee on Public Lands) spoke on the question, but the bill was not acted upon; Caleb Smith moved the consideration of the Oregon Territory bill and his motion carried.[44] The Illinois railroad grant had to await the leadership of Douglas in the Senate and of Harris (who succeeded Lincoln) in the House to be enacted.

Lincoln spoke again on post office matters on August 8. He had been appointed to a committee to which a Senate resolution

---

[42] *Globe*, p. 950.

[43] *Globe*, p. 990.

[44] *Globe*, p. 1027.

(for the relief of persons adversely affected by a change in the post office organization) had been referred. He reported a bill and recommended its passage. It was laid on the table.[45]

In these closing days of the first session a critical question appeared. The civil and diplomatic appropriation bill first came up in July. The Whig majority inserted an item for the removal of obstructions in the Savannah River.[46] Although this internal improvements' item was palpably improper, the Whigs had forced its inclusion in a session when only a bare quorum was present.[47] Democrats attempted to eliminate it, but it was retained. Then in a fully attended session the Democrats showed their resentment: voting on the bill with the improper item in it they forced a reconsideration of the vote by which it had been passed and the whole bill was rejected! [48] The *Globe* reported that there was much confusion and great sensation. Naturally; the government could not have operated without the appropriation—the bill had to be passed to pay the *per diem* and the mileage of members of Congress. After long debate and much party rancor the Savannah River item was eliminated. The Senate had, of course, rejected it.[49]

These party bickerings had not gone unnoticed by that astute partisan in the White House. Polk wrote in his *Diary:*

The body of the Whig party desire to adjourn without adjusting the slavery question by compromise, & to leave the Territories of Oregon, California & New Mexico without Territorial Governments, doubtless in the expectation that in the chapter of accidents growing out of the excitement & agitation which must follow, that they may stand some chance to elect a Whig President. I deplore as a national calamity the want of patriotism which seems to actuate the conduct of the leaders of the Whig Party in Congress. . . .

The House have passed and sent to the Senate the Civil and Diplomatic bill, with an item of appropriation in it for the improvement of the Savannah River in Georgia. The object of it is to force me to give up my constitutional objections and sign the bill, or to compel me to reject the whole bill. My mind is made up. I will veto the bill, if it comes to me on the last night of the session, and if I

---

[45] *Globe*, p. 1049.
[46] *Globe*, pp. 943 f.
[47] *Globe*, p. 948.
[48] *Globe*, p. 954.
[49] *Globe*, p. 1054.

am not over-ruled . . . I will issue my proclamation convening an extra session of Congress for the next day.[50]

Finally the bill without the internal improvements item was passed.[51] Lincoln had voted with his Whig colleagues until he and they had to capitulate. He voted "Aye" on the final bill.[52]

The closing days of the session were hectic. Adjournment had been set for August 14. The Senate held an all-night session for the first time in history;[53] Senators were making a serious attempt to provide the territories with government. The House met earlier and sat later, and finally held evening sessions. On the last day, although the futility of it must have been apparent to him, Lincoln as a member of the Committee on Expenditures in the War Department, asked for suspension of rules to permit consideration of his committee report. The subject was of no importance: the President had transmitted a message and reported Treasury disbursements to Generals Taylor and Cass. The report was intended for use as a campaign document in the coming Presidential election.[54]

So trivial was the point, and so unrealistic was his motion to suspend the rules (which could be done only by unanimous consent), that it must be concluded that in this episode Lincoln, too, was trifling with the nation's interests and adding to the difficulty of transacting business in the closing hours of the session.

The House had concurred with the Senate on a bill setting up territorial government for Oregon,[55] but it did what Polk had predicted; by its delaying tactics it prevented the organization of government for California and New Mexico.

Here also Lincoln voted generally with his party. On the whole he was obstructive with reference to Oregon. During the debate he voted against the extension of the Missouri Compromise line to the Pacific.[56] His purpose was not to open Oregon

---

[50] M. M. Quaife (Ed.), *The Diary of James K. Polk* (1910), IV:34-36.

[51] *Globe*, p. 1070.

[52] *Journal*, pp. 1058, 1059, 1065, 1082, 1083, 1084, 1085, 1091 f., 1092, 1226 f., 1229-31, 1234-36, 1264.

[53] Quaife, *Polk's Diary*, IV:69 f.

[54] *Globe*, p. 1081; *CW* I:517.

[55] *Globe*, p. 1027.

[56] *Globe*, p. 1062.

to slavery, but to maintain the possibility of keeping slavery out of California and New Mexico. Caleb Smith, as chairman of the House Committee on Territories, had worked hard on the Oregon bill, but he had made only dilatory effort to organize the other two territories. Since the administration earnestly desired to have all territories organized, the faithful John Mc-Clernand attempted the hopeless task of inducing the Whig majority to do it. He failed, and the first session of the Thirtieth Congress closed with no action taken by the House for California and New Mexico.

Much verbal effusion was required to drag out the closing session until the Senate could complete its business and present the final bills for the President's signature. When a message from the President (stating his reasons for signing the Oregon Territory bill) was transmitted to the House, a last deliberate insult to the President was made; the House ignored the message. Conger, a New York Whig, went on arguing for the right of his Committee on Printing to sit during the recess. The clock stood at twelve minutes before adjournment at noon. Speaker Winthrop reminded the Congressmen that an important message from the President was in his hands; he would present it if such were the pleasure of the House. Objection was made, but Houston of Alabama asked unanimous consent that the message might be printed. There was objection. Hunt (Whig, New York) begged the gentlemen not to kill the little time remaining. The *Globe* told the story:

> The intense excitement, hurry and confusion attendant upon the closing hours of the session, which had prevailed to some extent during the entire morning, here seemed wrought up to the highest pitch, and at the call by the clerk of each member, the hands of the clock—now rapidly moving forward, and just before the hour of twelve—were intently watched. During the last half hour the Speaker had constantly been engaged in signing bills, and numerous messages had been received from the President . . . and the Senate.[57]

Stanton of Tennessee asked unanimous consent to receive the message. Winthrop put the question. Objection was made. The Speaker warned that the message, if not received, would be locked up until Congress reconvened in December. Objection was maintained. At 11:58 Stanton made another appeal. The

---

[57] *Globe,* p. 1082.

clerk was droning out names in a call of the House when, having reached the name of Richardson of Illinois, the Speaker's gavel fell and the House stood adjourned.[58]

Shortly before its adjournment the Senate had sent a committee to ask the President if he had further communication to make. No House committee made this polite inquiry.[59]

Unimportant matters, such as the business of the government of the United States, were over. Congressmen could now address themselves to what was really important to them: the election of the President of the United States.

---

[58] *Globe*, p. 1082.

[59] The discourtesy was noted by the President; Quaife, *Polk's Diary*, IV:77.

8

ON SAFE GROUND

Lincoln made no more speeches on controversial subjects, after his Mexican War address. Whether this was because of the sharp and widespread reaction to his Spot Resolutions and War speech it is impossible to determine. In any event his next major effort was one which would not excite any antagonism. He expounded, on June 20, 1848, the Whig doctrine of internal improvements.[1] Here he was on safe ground; no Whig would object to an argument for the construction of local improvements at federal expense, and, as things were in 1848, some Democrats might be favorably impressed.

In fact, not a few Democrats, including some leaders and others who were influential, had exhibited signs of abandoning the strict-constructionist attitude toward this question. The Twenty-ninth Congress, with a Democratic majority in both Houses, actually passed a bill making appropriations for the improvement of certain rivers and harbors.[2] Polk vetoed the bill with a stinging message.[3] It could not be passed over his veto. It was in protest of Polk's veto that the River and Harbor Con-

---

[1] *Globe,* 30th Congress, 1st Session, p. 847; *Globe, Appendix,* pp. 709-11; *CW* I:480-90.

[2] Quaife, *Polk's Diary,* II:47.

[3] Richardson, IV:460-66.

vention, which Lincoln attended and addressed, was held in Chicago in July, 1847. John Wentworth, the Democratic representative from the Chicago district, was a leading figure in that convention. He exemplified the dilemma of many Democrats: residents of interior districts, they followed their party in all other respects, but they disagreed with its attitude toward internal improvements to be financed by the central government. There was no difference between Wentworth and the Whigs at this point.

As though smarting under the reproof contained in Polk's veto, internal improvements men presented another such bill in the short session of the Twenty-ninth Congress. The final bill was a curiosity. Originally entitled "An Act to provide for the continuation of certain public works in the Territory of Wisconsin," the bill was so altered by the addition of improvements elsewhere that Wentworth moved to amend the title by adding the words, "and for other purposes." [4] But by whatever title it was designated, it was an internal improvements bill, and it was so recognized by that rigid strict-constructionist, Polk. It was passed too late in the session for him to return it with a veto message. He refused to sign it, but he was not satisfied to permit it to be killed by a mere pocket veto. He submitted to the next Congress the veto message which he would have sent, had there been time, to the Twenty-ninth.[5] Polk gave considerable time and thought to this message. It was not ghostwritten for him by underlings.[6] Inasmuch as Lincoln's speech contains several references to it, Polk's message warrants a brief summary.[7]

It began with reference to the absurd title. The only item in it for work in Wisconsin was one of $6,000 for the harbor at Milwaukee, while the bill appropriated more than $500,000 for the improvement of rivers and harbors in nineteen different states. Next, in view of the demands upon the Treasury because of the war, so much money could not properly be spent even if the use of it were proper. Polk then covered the history of the question. The internal improvements policy had first been advanced about twenty years before, but in a short time appro-

---

[4] *Globe,* 29th Congress, 2nd Session, p. 472.

[5] Quaife, *Polk's Diary,* II:398.

[6] Quaife, *Polk's Diary,* III:116, 166, 169, 179, 244, 247-49.

[7] Richardson, IV:610-26.

priations totaling more than $200,000,000 had been attempted. President Jackson had arrested the development by vetoing the Maysville Road bill. Ending this kind of expenditure had enabled Jackson's administration to pay off the national debt and to operate with a surplus. The vetoed bill made no appropriations for canals or roads, but deepening rivers and improving harbors were internal improvements.

In Polk's view the experience of states demonstrated the inadvisability of the policy. Several states had undertaken public works on so large a scale that they had been perilously involved in debt; in some instances state constitutions had been forced to forbid legislatures to authorize public works without the direct consent of the people. This being true of states where taxes were direct and legislators up for election at short intervals, what would be the national government's condition if internal improvements were constructed at federal expense? There would be no end to the works authorized. There were twenty-nine states then in the Union, with territories on the Pacific: the potential for such improvements was much increased. Since every Congressman would work to secure the maximum appropriation for his district, if the policy were adopted the smallest streams would be deepened and the smallest anchorage enlarged. In application there could not be equal distribution of federal funds to the states; some would surely receive more than others. Even if it were possible for Congress to make such appropriations it would not be expedient.

Nor was it necessary, Polk said. The Constitutional provision enabling states to charge tonnage duties made it possible for states to construct local improvements and pay for them by levying shipping charges. This had been authorized by Congress and done in eight states, the latest of which enabled Maryland to improve the harbor at Baltimore.

Polk gave special attention to the time when the change in policy occurred, especially to the administrations of Monroe and John Quincy Adams. He reviewed the discussions in the Constitutional Convention, referred to the founding fathers, and came to the conclusion that the policy of public improvements at national expense was unconstitutional. The policy could not be based upon the commerce clause. Nor could the general welfare clause apply, for internal improvements at federal expense were not "necessary and proper."

The President concluded by saying that if any great object of improvement were to appear, which could not be paid for by tonnage duties and thus handled by states, only a properly drawn Constitutional amendment, containing adequate safeguards, would enable Congress to authorize and finance it. (If he had a specific instance in mind it was probably the prospect of a transcontinental railroad.) Without change in the basic law there was no recourse but to veto such legislation.

Lincoln evinced surprising naïveté when he took the floor to speak. The House was considering the civil and diplomatic appropriation bill, and Lincoln wanted to discuss internal improvements. So he frankly said that, never wishing to practice fraud upon the House, and desiring to do nothing very disagreeable to any member, he would state in advance that he was about to speak on internal improvements. If he were out of order the Chairman might say so and he would take his seat. The Chairman replied that he would not undertake to anticipate what Lincoln might say, and advised him to proceed; if in the course of his remarks a question of order appeared it would be decided then.

Lincoln began his speech by referring to Polk's veto message, and to the resolutions on internal improvements adopted by the recent Democratic nominating convention, which constituted the party platform. General Cass, the Democratic candidate for the Presidency, had accepted these resolutions and had made them his own.[8]

These two statements had intensified the entire issue. The veto message and the Baltimore platform were essentially the same, the latter being general, the former particular. All who voted for Cass would be forced to accept the stated policy, even though Democrats who voted for him believed in the propriety of internal improvements at federal expense. If elected Cass would not make a constitutional argument, nor any other argument. He would veto all such legislation because that was the policy of his party. The question was verging to a final crisis— friends of the policy must now battle, and battle manfully, or lose all. In this crisis, humble as he was, he wanted to review and contest the positions of the veto message. He would view the general positions, without noting the embarrassed state of the Treasury because of the war.

---

[8] *Globe*, 30th Congress, 1st Session, *Appendix*, p. 709; *CW* I:480.

Lincoln restated Polk's points as follows: internal improvements ought not be made by the general government, first, because they would overwhelm the Treasury, second, because while their burdens would be general their benefits would be local and partial, third, because they are unconstitutional, fourth, because the states could collect enough revenue through tonnage duties to make their own improvements; if they could not collect enough the Constitution should be amended. "Do nothing at all lest you do something wrong," was the sum of it all. Except for such improvements as might be made by state authority, internal improvements must be abandoned altogether, or these doctrines must be resisted and repudiated.

As to the effects of internal improvements on the Treasury, Lincoln admitted that there was a tendency toward undue expansion. This was in the very nature of the policy. A Congressman would rather vote for a project in his own district than for one elsewhere; hence enough projects would be included until every Congressional district was provided for, and the total would be too greatly expanded.

But was this less true of Congress than of a state legislature? As every Congressman must have money for his district, a state legislator must have money for his county. So if this difficulty drove us from Congress it would drive us from the state legislatures also.

Let us see if there is not sufficient power to limit and restrain the expansive tendency, and keep it within reasonable grounds. The President valued evidence from the past; he said that at a certain point in our history more than $200,000,000 had been sought for internal improvements. Why did he not say how much was granted? Less than $2,000,000. This proves that when the power to make improvements "was fully asserted and exercised," Congress had kept within reasonable limits. What had been done could be done again.

There was some truth in Polk's statement that while the burden of improvements would be general their benefits would be local. No such project could be so general as not to be of some local advantage. For example, the Navy was maintained for war and to protect commerce at sea. This function is not different from internal improvements. Driving a pirate from the track of ocean trade is not different in principle from removing a snag from the Mississippi River. Each is done to save life and property, and for nothing else. Yet the benefits of the Navy were in many instances local: the large seaports derived more benefit from it than did the interior towns of Illinois. Lincoln considered the Mississippi; it and its tributaries touch thirteen states. Naturally these thirteen were more interested in the improvement of these rivers than the other seventeen. The burden was general and the benefits partly local.

But the converse was also true. Nothing was purely local and of no general benefit. The Illinois and Michigan canal is an illustration. Apart from its effects it was local; every inch of it was in Illinois. Recently opened to traffic, sugar was carried through it from New Orleans to New York. The New Orleans shipper sold his sugar a little dearer and the New York people sweetened their coffee a little cheaper than before, a benefit (resulting from the canal) not to Illinois, where the canal was, but to Louisiana and New York, where it was not.

Consequently if the nation refused to make improvements because their benefits might be local, a state for the same reason might refuse to make an improvement because its effects might be general. If the argument of inequality were sufficient anywhere it was sufficient everywhere, and would put an end to improvements altogether.

But even if there were some inequality, it did not follow that every good thing should be discarded because it contained some inequality. If so we must discard all government. The national Capitol was built at public expense for public benefit, but was of some advantage to Washington property holders and businessmen. Should it be removed for that reason? If so, where should it be? Should it be located nowhere, and Congress hold its sessions, as the loafer lodged, "in spots about?"

Lincoln said that he made no special allusion to President Polk when he noted that there were few stronger cases of "burden to the many and benefit to the few" and of inequality than the Presidency itself. An honest laborer dug coal at about seventy cents a day, while the President dug abstractions at about seventy dollars a day. The coal was worth more than the abstractions, but what monstrous inequality in the prices!

The true rule, in determining whether to reject or to embrace anything, is not whether it has some evil, but whether it has more evil than good. Why not apply this rule? Why see only evil in improvements?

Lincoln avowed a modest attitude toward the constitutional problem. If he were to attempt an original argument he would not, he should not, be heard patiently, he admitted, for the best and ablest men had covered that ground long ago. As to the constitutional right of Congress to authorize and pay for internal improvements, Lincoln was much more latitudinarian than he had been with regard to the war power of the executive. He was satisfied to quote Chancellor Kent, who inclined to the view that Congress had that power. Lincoln pointed out that while many great and good men had denied it, others as good and great affirmed it. In his opinion the arguments of the latter group were vastly the superior; Chancellor Kent was one of the ablest and most learned lawyers of this age, or any age. Lincoln did not feel that the party opinion of a party President on a law question, such as this, could be at all compared or set up in opposition to such a man as Kent. There could be no better answer than Kent's until actual judicial consideration occurred. No one who is clear on the question of expediency need feel his conscience much pricked by the constitutional question.

Next Lincoln took up Polk's point that the states might make improvements by charging tonnage duties. Tonnage was well enough in its sphere, he granted. It might enable slight improvements in harbors. But it would be inadequate for general improvements. He knew little or nothing in detail about tonnage but as he understood it a harbor would be improved and the work paid for by charges upon the traffic in that harbor. But if any of this money were to be used to make any other improvement inequality would appear. Again, if making improvements depended upon tonnage, how could any new improvement be made? If it were to be paid for by charges upon its own traffic it would be impossible to collect charges because the improvement, e.g., a canal, did not yet exist. It was like the Irishman and his new boots: "I shall niver git 'em on," says Patrick, "till I wear 'em a day or two, and stretch 'em a little."

Then, Lincoln continued, the President evidently does see that there are certain great objects which only the general government can handle, but these would necessitate amending the Constitution. At the same time Polk deems these projects inexpedient—thus contradicting himself. Polk, he said, would remove one impediment only to meet another.

At this point Lincoln was interrupted by a question put by

Meade of Virginia: did Lincoln understand that Polk was opposed, on the ground of expediency, to any and every improvement? [9] Lincoln answered that Polk seemed to give some vague expression in favor of some possible improvements, but in saying even this the President contradicted what he had said elsewhere. Polk felt that the improvements of this broad and goodly land were a mighty interest, but he was unwilling to confess to the people, or to himself, that he had built an argument which, when pressed to its conclusions, entirely annihilated this interest.

As to amending the Constitution, Lincoln was very conservative. As a general rule we would much better leave it alone. No slight occasion should tempt us to touch it. Better not take the first step which might lead to a habit; better to habituate ourselves to think of it as unalterable. The Constitution could scarcely be made better than it is. New provisions would introduce new difficulties, and create appetite for further change. New hands, Lincoln said, "have never touched it. Those who made it have done their work well and have passed away. Who shall improve on what they did?"

Lincoln agreed that the subject of internal improvements was difficult. But no more difficult in Congress than in state legislatures, counties, or the smallest municipalities. One man was offended because a road passed over his land; another because it did not pass over his. One was dissatisfied because a bridge was located inconveniently; another because the county had gone into debt for its roads and bridges. Some struggled to get roads built on their land, then refused to permit them to be opened until the landowner received his indemnity. There was wrangling between wards of cities and streets of wards. There were inequalities, speculation, and crushing of the Treasury. There was but one alternative: they were sufficient or they were not sufficient. They were sufficient out of Congress as well as in Congress, and there was the end. They must be rejected as insufficient, or the people must lie down and do nothing by any authority. Determine that the thing could and should be done and the way would be found.

How to do something, and not do too much, was the desideratum. Let each contribute his mite in the way of sug-

---

[9] *Globe, Appendix,* p. 710; CW I:487 f.

gestion. Lincoln's contribution was this: borrow no money; he was against an overwhelming, crushing system. Congress should ascertain, each year, what money could be spared for improvements that year, and then undertake those which could be made with the money available. Of course it would be difficult to determine what needed to be done; every Congressman would be slow to admit that another's river was more important than his. Lincoln applauded what Vinton had proposed: an agency to collect statistics which would furnish information in facts not subject to whim, caprice, or local interest. The determined sum of money would prevent Congress from doing too much, and the facts would prevent it from doing too little in the wrong places.

Lincoln said that Rhett of South Carolina had deprecated the idea of collecting statistics, objecting to counting all the pigs and chickens in the land. There was not much force in Rhett's objection; Lincoln would omit facts about products which were consumed locally and did not require transportation. But it would be of great value to know of goods produced in one locality and consumed in another, to know a locality's capacity for producing a still larger surplus, the means of transportation and the possibility of their improvement, the hindrances, delays, and losses during transportation, and the causes of loss. Such statistics would show where a given expenditure would do the maximum good. Then the nation might undertake the larger and the states the lesser improvements. Thus "working in a meeting direction, discreetely, but steadily and firmly, what is made unequal in one place may be equalized in another, extravagance avoided, and the whole country put on that career of prosperity, which shall correspond with it's extent of teritory, it's natural resources, and the intelligence and enterprize of it's people."

This speech of Lincoln's, like the Mexican War speech and the Cass–Taylor speech which followed it, was a political document, planned for home consumption and referring to the coming election. There was nothing new in it. This, like Lincoln's other speeches in Congress, was intended to increase the popular irritation against Polk for his two vetoes, and to transfer this antagonism to Cass.

It is worth while to note a few features of the internal improvements speech. For example, Lincoln's apparent generosity in forebearing argument about the embarrassed state of the Treasury cannot be taken seriously. The Treasury was not embarrassed. The Walker Tariff was producing more revenue than its predecessor had brought. The government had had no difficulty financing its operating deficit due to the war; its issue of Treasury notes, handled by Corcoran and Riggs, had been quickly oversubscribed.[10] True, the national debt had been increased. But this could not have been repugnant to Lincoln and the Whigs, who were ardent supporters of the Hamiltonian doctrine that a national debt is a national blessing. And when Lincoln was called upon to vote upon Wilmot's proposed direct tax (designed to add $5,000,000 revenue until the war debt was paid) he voted against it, even though a vote for it would have been an antislavery vote, since the tax would have included slaves with other property.[11]

In this speech, as in others, Lincoln used a kind of dialectic, something of a lawyer's logic, narrowing and shaping an issue to win his point by misrepresenting the position which he was attacking. For example, when he restated Polk's objections to internal improvements, Lincoln put it to his hearers (and readers) that unless Polk's doctrines were resisted there could be no improvement anywhere, by any authority. No such conclusion followed from the veto messages. Polk said that improvements could not constitutionally be made by the general government, and ought not to be made at federal expense if permissible. He nowhere said that they ought not to be made at all, and it was altogether misleading to represent that under the strict constructionist view no internal improvements could be made. Certainly they had been made after Jackson vetoed the Maysville Road bill. An important one, at Baltimore Harbor, was in process at that very time.

Nor did Lincoln correctly represent Polk in the statement about the $200,000,000. Lincoln made Polk out to have said that in the Adams administration application was made for that amount; Lincoln correctly stated that during those four years expenditures totaled $1,879,627.01. But Polk actually said that in the *whole period* during which internal improvements were believed to be constitutional the $200,000,000 were requested. The facts were accurately stated by Polk, inaccurately stated by

---

[10] Smith, *War With Mexico*, II:257 ff.

[11] *Globe*, p. 298; Beveridge, I:437.

Lincoln. Nor did the facts support Lincoln's assumption that inasmuch as expenditures in the Adams administration were reasonable it might be expected that appropriations in other administrations would be small.

The argument concerning inequality was captious. Lincoln's use of analogy is worthy of a study in itself; in his speeches it is used so plausibly that one is likely to be deterred from asking how correctly the analogy is drawn. Lincoln asserted that clearing the ocean of pirates and removing a snag from the Mississippi are the same; both done to save life and property, and for nothing else. Can he have believed that? It is of course true that foiling pirates and removing snags facilitate commerce and save lives. But the nub of the misstatement is in the words *and for nothing else.* Surely he knew that the action of the Navy against pirates was minor and incidental to its whole function. He must have seen that there was an essential difference between the two things done. The Navy existed because only a national agency could do what it did, while clearing snags from rivers was infinitely smaller in scope, involved different jurisdictions, and could be paid for by a different government.

Again, Lincoln's illustration of transport of sugar by the Illinois and Michigan canal was superficial. Did he seriously expect the people to believe that because this improvement cheapened the carriage of sugar the people of the nation ought to pay for the canal? The Erie Canal, a state enterprise, had long since paid for itself and made a profit.

Of course Lincoln was utterly unrealistic in saying that if the general government refused to make local improvements the states might decline to make them, so that they would not be made at all. Equally farfetched was his point that if equality were the criterion the national Capitol must be relocated where it would confer no local benefit.

The comparison of the coal miner to the President invites query. If all the coal mined by all the miners in a day were totaled the value would doubtless be considerable. Yet the results of President Polk's efforts might be accorded greater dignity than to designate them as abstractions and of no greater value than one day's labor of a miner. The addition of Oregon and of the Southwest was not an abstraction, and it was of more than trifling value. But then, such considerations would have been beside the point. A Presidential election was in the offing.

The way by which Lincoln narrowed the constitutional question is an amusing example of his dialectic—of his smooth persuasiveness in developing a proposition until the hearer or reader has adopted his conclusion before it is stated. It was not enough to say that an equal number of able and good men might be assembled on each side. The specific case, and the logic of the particular court decision, must be taken into account. The heart of the constitutional question was that the President must decide it for himself. Polk had not taken his oath to preserve, protect, and defend the Constitution as interpreted by John Marshall or by Roger B. Taney. He had taken his oath to defend the Constitution. He was obliged to protect it as he understood it.

When Lincoln narrowed the issue of Polk's vetoes as being "the party opinion of a party President on a law question as this purely is," so that he could say that "no one who is clear on the question of expediency need feel his conscience pricked" by the matter of constitutionality he was reasoning in a circle. A constitutional question is not merely a "law" question.

In presenting his views of state legislatures authorizing and appropriating for internal improvements Lincoln was in a field in which he had expert knowledge. He ought to have known. It was by his leadership that Illinois in 1837 embarked upon a grandiose system of internal improvements that so nearly bankrupted the state that it was not until 1842 that its credit was assured, the debt funded, and payment begun.[12] In the light of that episode it is amusing that now he said, "I would not borrow money," and, "I am against an overwhelming, crushing system." He did not favor on a national scale what he had favored on the state level eleven years before. Presumably he had learned, or perhaps he had forgotten something.

But he had learned nothing to cause him to alter his Whig views. When he first ran for the state legislature in 1832 he advocated a modest program of public works: since a proposed railroad from the Illinois River to Jacksonville and Springfield would cost $290,000, he proposed instead the deepening of the channel of the Sangamon River, which could be financed. By 1836 he favored the distribution to the states of the proceeds

---

[12] Theodore C. Pease, *The Frontier State, 1818–1848* (1918), pp. 194-235.

from the sale of public lands, so that they could dig canals and build railroads without borrowing money at interest. When the Whig party emerged he embraced its cardinal doctrine of public works at federal expense. Naturally he opposed Polk's views. Naturally he made as persuasive a case in opposition as he could. It was no doubt shrewd for him to hold forth for the resumption of the pre-Jackson policy on a modest scale. It is easy to infer the rest: financing the public works by a high protective tariff and increasing the national debt so that the tariff rates would not be lowered. No doubt this speech was well received by the Seventh District Whigs. In talking about internal improvements Lincoln was on safe ground.

9

PRESIDENT-MAKING

The Thirtieth Congress was a President-making Congress, said
Joshua R. Giddings.[1] The second Congress of a Presidential
quadrennium commonly was.

The political motive behind the stock speeches in Congress
is only faintly suggested by reference to procedure in the House.
There were numerous speeches on the Mexican War in the
Twenty-ninth Congress, most of them airing party views. There
were many more, going over the same ground, in the Thirtieth
Congress. Lincoln spoke early. Following his were no less than
forty-three others which appear as formal speeches in the
Appendix to the *Congressional Globe*, besides "remarks" not
fully reported. When the end of the war made this subject
irrelevant it was replaced by speeches on slavery in the territories. There were thirty-seven of these. There were twelve
speeches on internal improvements, of which Lincoln's was the
sixth. Naturally Lincoln assumed his share of President-making
in a speech which would be printed and widely circulated
thoughout his district and state.

The Democrats, meeting at Baltimore May 22-28, 1848, had
nominated Senator Lewis Cass of Michigan for President, and

---

[1] *Globe,* 30th Congress, 1st Session, *Appendix,* p. 382.

General William O. Butler of Kentucky for Vice President. It is this author's opinion that Cass was worthy of the nomination and would have been worthy of the office had he been elected.[2] Born in New Hampshire in 1782, taken as a child to Ohio, where his grandfather, as a Revolutionary War soldier occupied a land grant, Cass qualified for the bar and practiced with success. As a frontiersman he assumed his obligation, served as a militiaman, and was, when the War of 1812 broke out, Brigadier General of Ohio militia.[3]

Since Lincoln's speech emphasized a detail of Cass's war service, the story of which Lincoln made so much needs to be sketched. Although Cass's duty was administrative rather than tactical, he was ordered to take his troops to Detroit, where they were assigned to the command of General Hull. Cass was fully aware of Hull's incompetence; he violently disagreed with Hull's plan (if plan it might be called) of operations. Hull ordered Cass, with another officer, to take 350 men and march to join another detachment which was supposed to be approaching Detroit. Cass was somewhere near the present Ypsilanti when the news of Hull's surrender reached him. The terms of surrender included Cass and his men. In chagrin Cass broke his sword.[4]

If this were Cass's sole achievement in the War of 1812 Lincoln's good-natured ridicule would not have been questionable. There were deeds much to his credit. Not necessarily praiseworthy is the fact that, leaving his boat in advance of his men, he was the first to set foot on enemy soil. His service under Hull's command was creditable. The only victorious action of the Detroit-Malden "campaign" was an attack led by Cass in which the Americans captured a bridge after sharp fighting in which several British counterattacks were repulsed. After his exchange as a prisoner-of-war Cass became one of General William Henry Harrison's staff officers. His duty involved no combat, but Harrison praised him as an officer of greatest merit. Before the war ended Cass was Major General of militia.

After the war President Monroe appointed Cass military, and then civil, Governor of the Michigan Territory. In this office

---

[2] A similar evaluation is made by Irving Stone, in his *They Also Ran* (1943), pp. 251-66.

[3] Andrew C. McLaughlin, *Lewis Cass* (1899); Frank H. Woodford, *Lewis Cass* (1950).

[4] McLaughlin, pp. 86-129; Woodford, pp. 59, 65-67, 68-71.

he served with distinction. He was not content to handle affairs at the seat of his government; he traveled widely through the territory—an immense area which included not only the present Michigan but what is now Wisconsin and that part of Minnesota which lay within the old Northwest Territory. He administered Indian affairs ably. He had scientific interests; on an expedition which took him through the northern peninsula and to the upper Mississippi he attempted to discover and map the source of the river. He did not succeed in getting as far as Lake Itasca, but he learned of it and made his information known. He furnished the national government, as well as prospective settlers, with a wealth of knowledge of the geography and the resources of the territory.[5]

Cass was always a sound Democrat. He was Jackson's Secretary of War and Minister to France. He was a formidable candidate for the Presidential nomination in 1844. Elected to the Senate in 1845, he was one of Polk's most dependable supporters. His usefulness was the greater during the war, when he manfully labored to secure what was asked in the prosecution of Polk's war policies.

Polk, who had declared in 1844 that if elected he would serve for only one term, maintained a rigidly correct bearing in the matter of the choice of his successor. He was completely silent.[6] But when Cass was nominated the President wrote in his *Diary* that Cass was, to his mind, most deserving of the nomination and said that he would fully support him.[7]

There were practical impediments to Cass's entire availability. He was never proslavery. In this he was indeed a good Jeffersonian. He disliked slavery, and, like Lincoln, he desired to see it on its way to ultimate extinction. As a Democrat he held the view that slavery was the proper concern of the states, and he conceded the right of slave states to maintain the labor system of their choice. Also like Lincoln, he did not want slavery to extend into the new territories. As the slavery question assumed greater primacy, and as the exacerbation of feelings about it developed to an alarming degree in the Thirtieth Congress, Cass was not entirely trusted by thoroughgoing proslavery politicians.

---

[5] McLaughlin, pp. 86 ff.

[6] Quaife, *Polk's Diary*, III:451 f.

[7] Quaife, *Polk's Diary*, IV:134 f.

He reversed himself on the Wilmot Proviso, and voted against it.[8]

The position which he maintained as a candidate was that which Douglas made much better known in 1854 and after, but which was, in fact, contained in the terms of the joint Congressional resolution annexing Texas: the principle of popular sovereignty. It had been, as Douglas pointed out, the uniform practice of Congress to permit the inhabitants of territories to adopt and regulate their own school, banking, tax, and voting systems; it would have been normal for Congress to have left to them the choice of their labor system. Popular sovereignty is commonly regarded as the peculiar concept of Douglas; Cass advocated it long before Douglas brought it to popular attention.[9]

In nominating Butler the Democrats evidently had an eye to countering some of the sentiment which was to carry General Taylor to victory. Butler had won military fame. He fought creditably in the War of 1812; after service in the Northwest he distinguished himself under Jackson at New Orleans. In the Mexican War he had an important command in the hard fought capture of Monterrey, where he was wounded. He was under Scott's command when Mexico City was taken, and he remained in charge of American forces after the surrender. He had also had political experience in the Kentucky legislature (1817-18) and in Congress (1839-43). He had practiced law, but abandoned it for agriculture. Obviously it was his military reputation, together with his Kentucky residence, which made him his party's choice as Cass's running mate. As to slavery, Butler, although a slaveholder, was opposed to the extension of the system.[10]

The Whigs had nominated General Zachary Taylor and Millard Fillmore.[11] In nominating Taylor the party leaders sacrificed every possible criterion save one: availability.[12] Taylor's education, experience, and political background provided him

[8] Woodford, pp. 242-48.

[9] Woodford, pp. 248-71; George Fort Milton, *The Eve of Conflict: Stephen A. Douglas and the Needless War* (1934), pp. 36-38.

[10] *Dictionary of American Biography*, III:271 f.

[11] Holman Hamilton, *Zachary Taylor, Soldier in the White House* (1951), pp. 52-133.

[12] Nowhere is the sacrifice of principle to availability more convincingly illustrated than in the paper which Lincoln wrote suggesting what General Taylor ought to say and do: *CW* I:454.

with not the slightest fitness for the Presidency. He was nominated simply and merely because it was believed—correctly—that his popularity as a war hero would win votes for himself and the party. It was utterly illogical for the Whigs, who had opposed the war, to nominate a war hero. This was perceived and emphatically pointed out by Giddings, and such Whigs as he, who steadfastly refused to support Taylor. When the Taylor boom arose Giddings bluntly said that "those Whigs who have got up this movement in favor of General Taylor, knowing him to be in favor of extending slavery, are men of desperate political fortunes, who have become anxious to share in the spoils of office; they are men who would sell their party, their country and their God for an ephemeral success, or to enable them to bask in the sunshine of executive favor." [13] But the leaders had no qualms. They wanted their party in power, and they were sure that this was the way to do it.

There was also the emotional appeal that Taylor, so they said, had been treated badly by Polk. It was claimed that Polk had dangerously reduced Taylor's force by transferring his troops to Scott, and thus had left perilously exposed the General who had won victories at Palo Alto, Resaca de la Palma, Matamoros, and Monterrey. Nevertheless, these partisans exulted, the gallant leader, with almost none but raw volunteers, had gone on to win at Buena Vista. Then there was nothing for the old soldier to do but return and fade away.

The fact that Taylor was a planter and a slaveholder (he had more than 100 slaves, which put him in the very small group of "large" slaveholders) did not deter the Whig party from nominating him. It did alienate the "Conscience" Whigs of the North and East. What Taylor's nomination actually meant was that the Southern Whigs took control of the party. Many people today suppose that the Whig party, being Lincoln's party, was antislavery. Nothing could be farther from the truth. Three-fourths of the slaves were owned by Whigs, and many Northern Whigs accepted the fact without embarrassment; people as far

[13] From a speech delivered in New Hampshire, clipped in the *Illinois State Register*, August 12, 1847. Henry Wilson of Massachusetts wrote to Giddings, "I think I see a movement for Taylor for President. I hope you anti-slavery Whigs will resist it if it breaks the party to pieces. We must not submit to it. . . . The free state Whigs must dictate the policy of the Party or the Party had better be defeated and broken up." (Giddings MSS, Ohio State Archaeological and Historical Society)

apart as Lincoln and the Massachusetts textile tycoons were Whigs despite the slavery element in their party.[14]

As for Fillmore, it suffices to say that he was a New York politician who had risen to a position of importance in that faction-ridden state in spite of the opposition of Thurlow Weed and Governor Seward.[15] The Native American tinge of the Whig party is to be seen in his career. It is apparent, too, in Lincoln's acceptance of it and the welcome he gave it in 1848; writing to an Illinois friend he exulted that "all the odds and ends are with us—Barnburners, Native Americans, and the Lord knows what." [16]

The decisive factor in 1848 was the momentous meeting at Utica, New York, on June 22, at which the Free Soil party nominated Martin Van Buren and Henry Dodge.[17] This new group absorbed the ineffective Liberty Party, and by the nomination of two Democrats made it logical for antislavery Democrats to add thousands of votes to the antislavery movement. Dodge, however, resigned the nomination. The leaders of the new party shrewdly replaced him with Charles Francis Adams. Adams had been a Democrat until 1836, when he became a "Conscience" Whig. He was unacceptable to "Cotton" Whigs, such as Webster and Speaker Winthrop. The combination of the Democrat, Van Buren, and the Whig, Adams, presaged the siphoning off of a formidable number of votes from the two regular parties.

This was the background of Lincoln's speech. It was observed that when he spoke on July 27 he was not exactly forehanded. The Democrats had taken the field first, with speeches by Clarke of Kentucky, McClelland of Michigan (who was warmly attached to Cass personally as well as politically), and Thompson of Pennsylvania. Then "Tariff Andy" Stewart of Pennsylvania led off for the Whigs, followed by Caleb Smith of Indiana, Toombs of Georgia, and Flournoy of Virginia. Lincoln was the eighth to make a set speech designed for President-making. It is no wonder that he used so much humor, for the "ho-hum" feeling must have been hard to overcome. Nevertheless he overcame it.

---

[14] Arthur Charles Cole, *The Whig Party of the South* (1913).

[15] W. E. Griffis, *Millard Fillmore* (1915).

[16] *CW* I:476 f.

[17] Allan Nevins, *Ordeal of the Union* (1947), I:189-91, 202-08.

His speech is the more illustrative because in it he employed some of the techniques of frontier stump speaking. As Beveridge remarked, if one would imagine him delivering it in a rough and tumble setting, rather than in Congress, one would have a fairly accurate idea of Lincoln as a campaigner in his earlier years.[18] Lincoln's effective humor kept his hearers in an uproar. His manner, a contemporary said, "was so good natured, and his style so peculiar, that he kept the House in a continuous roar of merriment for the last half hour of his speech. He would commence a point in his speech far up one of the aisles, and keep on talking, gesticulating, and walking until he would find himself, at the end of a paragraph, down in the center of the area in front of the clerk's desk. He would then go back and take another *head,* and work down again. And so on, through his capital speech." [19]

Lincoln began by noting that the Democrats objected to Taylor because he lacked principles. But on the matter of the veto power he had one. Clarke of Kentucky had protested Taylor's statement that he would not exercise the veto even though Congress passed a bill of doubtful constitutionality. This, Lincoln said, was what Washington and Jefferson had done.[20]

On such issues as the currency, the tariff, internal improvements, and the Wilmot Proviso, Taylor's stand was at least as well defined as Cass's. For Taylor had said that "the will of the people, as expressed through their representatives in Congress, ought to be respected and carried out by the executive." This was the principle of allowing the people to do what they wanted with their own business. As Caleb Smith had said, "Are you willing to trust the people?"

What the Whigs objected to was binding the President by a party platform. Lincoln argued that a vote for Cass bound the voter to accept every item of his platform. If that voter were for Cass, but in favor of internal improvements, his will was frustrated. Whigs thought this wrong; they had a candidate who would let the people have their way.

Lincoln admitted that he did not know what Taylor would

---

[18] Beveridge, I:456.

[19] Baltimore *American,* clipped in the *Illinois State Journal,* August 16, 1848.

[20] *CW* I:501-16.

do about the Wilmot Proviso. As a Northern man, or, rather, as a Western free-state man, with a constituency and with personal feelings against the extension of slavery, Lincoln hoped that Taylor, if elected, would not veto the proviso. Even if he were to veto it Lincoln would still vote for him, because only his election could beat Cass. The election of Cass would result in slavery going into the new territories and in new wars with new acquisitions of territory into which slavery would go. Cass or Taylor would be elected; which was preferable?

Then Lincoln used the "pot and kettle" argument. There was as much doubt of Cass as of Taylor on the proviso. So on internal improvements: Cass had voted for the bill which Polk vetoed, and then had accepted the veto. Yet a Democrat like John Wentworth claimed that Cass was still for the vetoed policy.

Lincoln went back to his first issue: the Democrats insisted upon a declaration of principles, forcing a platform upon the people. Whigs favored separating the election of the President and the legislative function so that the people might elect whom they pleased and legislate as they desired. This was the true republican principle.

Then Lincoln became humorous. Iverson, the Georgia Democrat, had reproached the Whigs for casting off Henry Clay. Lincoln rejoined: "At the end of his second severe flash, I was struck blind, and found myself feeling with my fingers for an assurance of my continued physical existence. A little of the bone was left, and I gradually revived." It was terribly severe, he said, to be accused of letting Clay out, like an old horse, to root. But he went on (again the pot and kettle), didn't the Democrats turn Van Buren out to root? Using Iverson's words about the Whigs and Clay, Van Buren was "scathed and withered a few for his present position and movements . . . put down . . . down . . . when he was finally to stink and rot." Needless to say Lincoln was not concerned with Van Buren in the battle of extermination between him and his former admirers: "Devil take the hindmost—and the foremost."

As to the Whigs taking shelter under General Taylor's military coattail, what about the Democrats? (Still the pot and kettle.) They had run five candidates under General Jackson's coattail, and now the sixth was under the same cover. They had never ventured, and did not now dare to venture, from under it.

As Polk had been called "Young Hickory," Cass was now "of the true Hickory stripe." "Like a horde of hungry ticks you have stuck to the tail of the Hermitage lion to the end of his life; and you are still sticking to it, and drawing a loathsome sustenance from it, after he is dead. A fellow once advertised that he had made a discovery by which he could make a new man out of an old one, and have enough of the stuff left to make a little yellow dog. . . . If you have any more old horses, trot them out; any more old tails, just cock them, and come at us." This sally had effect. "We give it up," was heard from the Democratic side.

But Lincoln was not ready to give it up. He went on to talk of "the military tail you Democrats are now engaged in dove-tailing onto the great Michigander." Cass's campaign biographers were tying him to a military tail like boys tying a dog to a bladder of beans. They had little material but they were at it might and main. Here Lincoln alluded to Cass's military record in 1812:

He *inv*aded Canada without resistance, and he *out*vaded it without pursuit. As he did both under orders, I suppose there was, to him, neither credit nor discredit in them; but they . . . constitute a large part of the tail. He was not at Hull's surrender, but he was close by; he was a volunteer aid to Gen. Harrison on the day of the battle of the Thames; and as you said in 1840, Harrison was picking huckleberries two miles off while the battle was fought, I suppose it is a just conclusion with you, to say Cass was aiding Harrison to pick huckleberries. This is about all, except the mooted question of the broken sword. Some authors say he broke it, some say he threw it away, and some others, who ought to know, say nothing about it. Perhaps it would be a fair historical compromise to say, if he did not break it, he didn't do anything else with it.

Then in a *reductio ad absurdum* which must have been very funny to his hearers—and to the voters to whom the speech was franked—Lincoln asked, "By the way, Mr. Speaker, did you know that I am a military hero?" He facetiously sketched his Black Hawk War service, and told how he fought, bled of mosquito bites, and came away. He was not at the debacle of Stillman's Run, as Cass was not in Detroit at its surrender, but, also like Cass, Lincoln saw the place soon after the battle. He did not break his sword, because he did not have one, but he accidentally bent his musket. If Cass surpassed him in picking huckleberries, Lincoln did more than Cass in charging wild onions. Lincoln saw no live Indians, but he suffered much from

mosquitos. He concluded: "Mr. Speaker, if I should ever . . . doff
whatever our democratic friends may suppose there is of black
cockade federalism about me, and thereupon, they shall take
me up as their candidate for the Presidency, I protest they shall
not make fun of me, as they have of Gen: Cass, by attempting
to write me into a military hero."

Lincoln became serious for a while, as he discussed the
probable attitudes of the two candidates toward the Wilmot
Proviso. But this theme, too, he deftly turned to a humorous
conclusion. He showed from the record, quite correctly, that
Cass had favored the proviso when it appeared, and had continued to vote for it until recently, when "he began to see
glimpses of the great democratic ox-goad waving in his face,
and to hear, indistinctly, a voice saying 'Back' 'Back sir' 'Back
a little.' He shakes his head, and bats his eyes, and blunders back
to his position of March 1847; but still the gad waves, and the
voice grows more distinct, and sharper still 'Back sir' 'Back I
say' 'Further back'; and back he goes, to the position of Decr.
1847, at which the gad is still, and the voice soothingly says 'so'
'Stand at that.'"

Then Lincoln gibed at Cass as "a general of splendidly
successful *charges* . . . not upon the public enemy, but upon the
public Treasury." He showed that while Cass was governor of
Michigan Territory and superintendent of Indian Affairs he was
paid $96,028, an average of $14.79 per day. During this time, as
Lincoln put it, Cass was doing several things in several places at
the same time, and getting paid for them: as governor, as maintaining an office, as Indian agent, on Indian service outside
Michigan, and as taking commutation of ten rations a day. He
drew pay for superintending Indian agencies at Piqua, Fort
Wayne, and Chicago. He received another commutation of
rations while in Washington, as well as an allowance for traveling. (Lincoln collected these data as a member of the Committee
on Expenditures in the War Department; this is what he vainly
tried to have printed as a committee report.) There was no
reason to suppose that Cass had kept any office other than the
one at his home, but this was less important than his wonderful
physical capacities: he did labor in several places at the same
time, and the labor of several men at the same time.

And his eating capabilities were quite as wonderful! He
"eat" [Lincoln used the old past tense of the verb which is now

a colloquialism] three rations a day in Michigan, and near five dollars a day on the road. He also knew the art of being paid for what he ate, rather than having to pay for it. It must have been very funny when Lincoln closed this subject by saying "Mr. Speaker, we have all heard of the animal standing in doubt between two stacks of hay, and starving to death. The like of that would never happen to Gen: Cass; place the stacks a thousand miles apart, he would stand stock still between them, and eat them both at once, and the green grass along the line would be apt to suffer some too at the same time. By all means, make him President, gentlemen. He will feed you bounteously,— if—if there is any left after he shall have helped himself."

Next Lincoln discussed the point urged against the Whigs that, having opposed the war, their position became untenable when they nominated a war hero. He tried to soften the charge of opposition by distinguishing between the vote for the Ashmun amendment and voting for supplies. He insisted that

if, when the war had begun, and had become the cause of the country, the giving of our money and our blood, in common with yours, was support of the war, then it is not true that we have always opposed the war. With few individual exceptions, you have constantly had our votes here for all the necessary supplies. And, more than this, you have had the services, the blood, and the lives of our political bretheren in every trial, and on every field. . . . Clay and Webster each gave a son. . . . From the state of my own residence, besides other worthy but less known whig names, we sent Marshall, Morrison, Baker, and Hardin; they all fought, and one fell; and in the fall of that one we lost our best whig man. Nor were the whigs few in number, or laggard in the day of danger. In that fearful, bloody, breathless struggle at Buena Vista, where each man's hard task was to beat back five foes or die himself, of the five high officers who perished, four were whigs.

As he had been fair to Cass in saying that there was nothing discreditable in his 1812 war service, Lincoln was now fair to his political opponents:

I mean no odious comparison between the lion-hearted whigs and democrats who fought there. On other occasions, and among the lower officers and privates on *that* occasion, I doubt not the proportion was different. I wish to do justice to all. I think of all those brave men as Americans, in whose proud fame, as an American, I too have a share. Many of them, whigs and democrats, are my constituents and personal friends; and I thank them—more than thank them—one and all, for the high, imperishable honor they have conferred on our common state.

But the Democrats could not make any distinction between the origin of the war and the cause of the country after the war began. They said that the President and the country are one. Yet veterans of the war who are members of Congress had voted that it was unnecessarily and unconstitutionally begun by Polk. As for Taylor, "the noblest Roman of them all," it was enough for him that the nation was at war. He did not ask about its justice.

With only three minutes remaining of his hour, Lincoln closed with a telling allusion to Democratic factions.

Is it all union and harmony in *your* ranks?—no bickerings?—no divisions? If there be doubt as to which of our divisions will get our candidate, is there no doubt as to which of your candidates will get your party? I have heard some things from New-York; and if they are true, one might well say of your party there, as a drunken fellow once said when he heard the reading of an indictment for hog-stealing. The clerk read on till he got to, and through the words "did steal, take, and carry away, ten boars, ten sows, ten shoats, and ten pigs" at which he exclaimed "Well, by golly, that is the most equally divided gang of hogs I ever did hear of." If there is any *other* gang of hogs more equally divided than the democrats of New-York are about this time, I have not heard of it.

Even if there were bias in the evaluation of this as the "crack speech of the day" (as was said by the *Baltimore American*) it undoubtedly was effective. Little need be said in criticism. It has been noted that Lincoln, while mercilessly pillorying Cass's war record, was fair. But it was thinly stretching the point to compare it with Lincoln's own service in the Black Hawk war. Lincoln was less than just, when he referred humorously to Cass's work as governor, in omitting at least passing recognition to Cass's brilliant record. Of course what he said was campaign material; he later referred to Cass as "an able and distinguished member of the [Democratic] party." [21] No onus attaches to Lincoln's sallies in the context of the campaign of 1848.

The most serious criticism of the speech applies to Lincoln's attempt to show that in nominating a candidate with a platform the Democrats were afraid to trust the people, and his claim that Taylor's pledge was trusting the people. This was the merest

---

[21] *CW* II:88.

sophistry. Anyone who works with sources in American political history in this period must note how tenaciously the Whigs appealed to "Whig principles." In their choice of Taylor they were abandoning all principle.

It must be observed, too, that Lincoln's allusions to the Wilmot Proviso and to slavery were more eloquent in the things not said than in things said. It was, as was perfectly understood at the time, a travesty of intelligence to run a slaveowning planter and expect him to be preferred to Cass on the slavery issue. It was known that Cass's attitude toward slavery weakened him in the slave states, where Democrats, in most areas, were in the majority.

Moreover, Lincoln went a great deal too far when he predicted that if Cass were elected slavery would inevitably go into the newly acquired territories, and that there would be more wars to acquire more slave territory. Even though Cass was not elected there is ample reason for believing that the contrary had the greater probability. Douglas adopted popular sovereignty, and based his Kansas–Nebraska Act upon it. Kansas, according to the Census of 1860, had only two slaves. Kansas (before the Civil War, but after the Republican party gained control of Congress) and Nebraska (after the Civil War) were admitted to the Union as states on the basis of the Kansas-Nebraska Act, without the enactment of new or additional antislavery legislation.[22] However, the proper view of this part of Lincoln's speech is to concede that as all is fair in love or war, nothing is unfair in a Presidential campaign.

Most notable of all aspects of this speech of Lincoln's are its references to the Mexican War. It is significant that he did not meet the cogent objections to opponents of the war nominating a war hero. He greatly toned down the Whig opposition to the war. But what is most obvious is the difference between what he said of the war in this speech and in the Spot Resolutions and the formal war speech. In this speech he did all that he could to cancel out the unfavorable reception of the efforts by which he thought to distinguish himself. He labored to regain the esteem which he had lost by taking his earlier position. Here he gave the highest praise to his Whig fellows who had fought

---

[22] James G. Randall, *Lincoln the President* (1945), I:122, 124, 126 f.

in the war. He identified himself with them insofar as he could. He accorded due honor to his dead friend and rival. He was making amends and trying to recapture lost ground.

This was only one of Lincoln's contributions in President-making in 1848. As his best speech in Congress it doubtless had considerable effect. He had reason, because of this speech as well as because of other efforts on behalf of Taylor and his party, to expect some recompense when his single term in Congress ended. At the moment he was not defending Whig principles, but he was manfully doing his share of President-making.

10

THE WHIG STRONGHOLD FALLS

One effect of Lincoln's stand on the Mexican War while he was in Congress was the loss of the Seventh Congressional District by his party. To understand what occurred something must be known of the voting strength of the Illinois Whigs.

The political history of Illinois was shaped by the trends in its settlement.[1] The earliest portion settled was the southern, which was occupied largely by immigrants from Kentucky, Tennessee, and Virginia. The northern part was settled later, and the prairies of the east central region were the last to be occupied. The northern and eastern prairies were settled late because of the lack of transportation. The early immigrants used the river routes and the Cumberland (National) Road. Northern settlement waited for the beginning of steamboating on the Great Lakes, and still more for the development of railroads. Since those moving to the West tended to settle upon the same latitude as their points of departure, southern Illinois was settled mostly by emigrants from south of Mason and Dixon's line, while northern Illinois was settled by emigrants from the Middle States and New England.

---

[1] This subject is briefly sketched in Riddle, pp. 24-34, and fully developed by Arthur C. Boggess, *The Settlement of Illinois, 1778-1830* (1908), (early period) and by William V. Pooley, *The Settlement of Illinois from 1830 to 1850* (1908).

As party divisions developed in the age of Jackson, the majority in Illinois became Democrats, while the Whigs as they emerged were a minority. But as northern Illinois grew in population, the Democratic majority there was reduced, for since most of the settlers in that part were from New England and the Middle States, the party balance in Illinois underwent a profound change.[2]

When Illinois became a state it had only one representative in Congress. The first of them lived in Kaskaskia (southwest Illinois), and the last, during the period when there was only one, lived in Jacksonville—the northward trend is evident. After the census of 1830 there were three Congressional districts; two southern and one northern. When the party divisions emerged the two southern districts elected Democrats, the northern chose a Whig. In this decade the northern district was an immense area, in 1838 containing thirty-four counties. In the next redistricting seven Congressional districts were set up, and, whether by gerrymandering or not, the Whig strength was concentrated in the Seventh. (Until the northern prairies were settled the Whig vote in the north was light; the two districts there elected Democrats.)

In the Seventh District the Whig majority was so large that until Lincoln presented his Spot Resolutions, voted for the Ashmun amendment, and made his Mexican War speech—and especially until these acts occasioned the furor of indignation in the District—there was every reason to expect that whatever Whig were nominated in 1848 would be elected.[3]

Stephen T. Logan had long expected to be that Whig. E. D. Baker, too, was resolved to run. His war record was a valuable asset, and Baker saw to it that he was back in civilian life early enough to attend to his political interests.[4]

The Whig press was silent on the matter, but the Democratic *Illinois State Register*, on September 10, 1847 (while Lincoln was still in Springfield, nearly three months before he arrived in Washington) aired what the Springfield Whigs doubtless would have preferred to remain secret: "The Whig junto here, for a few days past, have been in a 'mess.' While Col. Baker was

---

[2] Riddle, pp. 34-43.

[3] Riddle, pp. 44-59.

[4] *Morgan Journal*, July 24, 1847.

absent, assisting Mr. Polk in his 'butchery of poor Mexicans,' as the Whigs have it, his political friends have stacked the cards against him. Judge Logan claimed his turn in the Congressional wheel, and succeeded,. we learn, in making satisfactory arrangements for a visit to Washington; but the gallant Col. now repudiates the arrangement, and insists that his claims are paramount to those of the Judge."

At all events, Logan made his claim and held it. Baker abandoned his attempt to win nomination in the Seventh District, and removed to another where he had a chance. But Logan's claim was not unchallenged. Pierre Menard (son of the former lieutenant governor of the same name) later wrote to Lincoln of his hope that Lincoln would run in 1850, saying that "I wanted you to be our candidate for I did not like Logan, he is too selfish And I like Baker less—for he is full of imperfection and I was the first one in Tazewell County who began to role the ball against him. I like a man to have some stability." [5]

The Morgan County Whigs, always jealous of the precedence of Sangamon, advanced the name of Col. William B. Warren. Warren had been John Henry's competitor to fill the vacancy caused by Baker's resignation in 1845.[6]

Then came a newspaper editorial which was not only lukewarm toward Logan, but advanced claims for Lincoln. The Lacon *Illinois Gazette* speaking of Logan and Warren, added

> We have a number of men . . . who would make respectable representatives . . .; but none . . . who would be better qualified and more faithfully serve their constituents than the gentlemen named above. Still it is a question . . . whether a change for every Congress is expedient and productive of the greatest good. . . . So far as we are informed, Mr. Lincoln . . . has ably and faithfully discharged his duties; and if he has at no time intimated a willingness or desire to retire at the expiration of the term . . . we are not sure but that the interests of the district would be quite as well promoted by his . . . re-election for another term.[7]

This was loyalty, but it was also inconsistency. Allen Ford, the editor of the *Gazette,* had worked hard for Lincoln's nomination in 1846, and his strongest argument was rotation in office;

---

[5] RTLP.

[6] *Illinois State Journal*, April 13, 1848.

[7] *Illinois Gazette*, April 15, 1848.

he had argued against a second term for Hardin when Hardin used the very same reasons which Ford now adopted for keeping Lincoln in office.[8] Now Mr. Ford was against what he had been for in 1846.

And Lincoln was receptive. Herndon had reported the sentiment in his favor, and Lincoln replied:

It is very pleasant to learn from you that there are some who desire that I should be reelected. I most heartily thank them for their kind partiality; and I can say, as Mr. Clay said of the annexation of Texas, that "personally I would not object" to a reelection. . . . I made the declaration that I would not be a candidate again, more from a wish . . . to keep peace among our friends, and to keep the district from going to the enemy, than for any cause personal to myself. . . . If it should so happen that nobody else wishes to be elected I could not refuse the people the right of sending me again.[9]

But the force of the Pekin agreement was so great that Lincoln did not seek the renomination.

Of course the Seventh District Whigs assumed that their candidate would be elected. Such was the assumption throughout the state. The Beardstown *Gazette,* within the district, predicted Logan's election, and a Whig paper as far away as Galena had the same conviction: "Mr. L., we presume will be elected." [10] A postelection analysis by the Beardstown *Gazette* admitted that the Democratic organization and effort were "not even remotely anticipated by the Whigs." [11]

In his legal practice Logan had accumulated a considerable fortune, which he had augmented by land speculation. He had gone into local politics, being elected to the state legislature in 1842, 1844, and 1846 and a member of the Constitutional Convention in 1847. He was a queer, eccentric man. Careless of dress to an extreme degree, with a great shock of long light hair, he did not make a pleasing appearance. He was extremely stingy. He had a poor speaking voice. But let Herndon, the amateur psychoanalyst, describe him:

His physical build is small—short—thin—and squarely put up and angularly built, running in figure and features to sharp keen

---

[8] Riddle, pp. 84 f.

[9] *CW* I:430-31.

[10] Beardstown *Gazette,* July 26, 1848; Galena *Gazette and Advertiser,* April 21, 1848.

[11] Beardstown *Gazette,* August 16, 1848.

points, lance like. He has light hair—bluish gray eyes—large headed and square headed—stoop shouldered a little now shrunk and shrivelled. He is frailly built—a froth network—nervous—quick—uneasy—restless, full of action and energy. His eye is keen and penetrating: his voice is sharp and shrill—"squeaky and squealy."—His gestures are angular—seesaw sharply up and down—his forefinger long, sharp and bony, striking the palm of his left hand. . . . He used no figures—no metaphors—having no fancy and no imagination.[12]

The Seventh District Democrats made full use of the war issue in selecting their candidate. Thomas L. Harris was born in Connecticut. He was graduated from Washington (Trinity) College in Hartford, where, in his last college year, he studied law. Leaving New England he went first to Virginia, where he taught school, and then to Illinois, where he practiced law in Petersburg, Menard County. He was elected to the legislature in 1846, but when the war broke out he was chosen captain of a company of volunteers and did not take his seat. Assigned to Col. Baker's Fourth Illinois Regiment, Harris had a good record, with special distinction at Vera Cruz and Cerro Gordo. When the regiment was disbanded, Harris (promoted to Major) went to Washington seeking permission to raise his own regiment. When permission was refused Harris returned to his home and, like Baker, looked to the resumption of his political career.[13] He was said to be a strong debater, though not an orator. It was his war record which made him available. He proved to be an able Congressman.

Election campaigns in Illinois were usually rough and tumble and this one was more than that. For the first time the Democrats believed that they had a chance to win, and they put forth every effort.

Logan took the campaign seriously, too. He actually bought a new suit to wear while campaigning. Apparently he made an orthodox and dignified campaign; his typical subjects for speeches were internal improvements, the tariff, and the Mexican War.[14]

The Democrats, pounding upon the war issue, mercilessly and incessantly held Logan to it. Reporting the Democratic Dis-

---

[12] *Abraham Lincoln Quarterly*, 1 (1941), 437 f.

[13] *Illinois State Register*, August 16, 1848, clipping the item from the Norwich, Connecticut, *Aurora*.

[14] Clipped in the *Illinois State Journal*, May 4, 1848.

trict Convention, which nominated Harris, the *State Register* predicted that soon the people would be "rescued from the foul 'spot' which now rests upon them." [15] In the same issue it emphasized the stand which Logan had taken in the legislature with reference to the war, noting his vote on a resolution affirming the justice of the war and pledging the state's resources in prosecuting it. On this Logan and all the other Whigs save five voted "Nay." The *State Register* did not let him—nor its readers —forget this. On May 26 it repeated the reference, and went on to say that "the voters of the District will perceive that Judge Logan by his votes in the state legislature has enrolled himself in the same catalogue with John Henry and Abraham Lincoln. The election of Logan would be an endorsement of the votes and speeches of Messers Henry and Lincoln, the responsibility of which does not now rest with the people. Shall such approval be given to such infamous deeds?"

On June 23 the *State Register*, as the campaign warmed up, published a leading article titled "Five Points in Judge Logan's Political Career." Each "point" began, "BEAR IT IN MIND." Point two was "BEAR IT IN MIND, that Stephen T. Logan, unblushingly endorses the votes cast by *Abraham Lincoln* in Congress." The Peoria *Democratic Press* on June 28 said that "This district had heretofore been Whig, and the last man elected to it was *Abe Lincoln*, whose traitorous course in Congress has brought down upon him the merited curses of his constituents, and they seem determined to wipe out the foul 'spot' by electing the gallant Major Harris. His opponent, Judge Logan, is identified with all the obnoxious measures of the Whig party—denounces the war as 'unjust and unholy,' but goes to his death for Gen. Taylor." The *State Register* reiterated this point on July 21: "It is true that John Henry and Mr. Lincoln rendered themselves obnoxious to the complaints of the people by their votes and speeches on the war. . . . The seventh congressional district, the only 'spot' in this state where whigery has an abiding place, is about to be enrolled under the democratic banner. . . . Harris is about to take the place of Mr. Lincoln who . . . never omitted an opportunity to tarnish our national flag."

Judge Logan was forced to accept the war issue. He spoke on the war at Lacon, and as reported in the Lacon *Illinois*

---

[15] *Illinois State Register*, May 5, 1848.

Gazette a week later, Logan "showed clearly that it was unconstitutionally commenced by the President, in ordering Gen. Taylor to advance to the banks of the Rio Grande, without consulting Congress, the war making power, though then in session." [16] The *Gazette* mentioned that Logan had spoken, evidently making this same speech, at Hennepin, Magnolia, and Henry. Logan was attacked for his war stand in the special campaign paper, *The Ticket,* brought out by the Democrats. *The Ticket* said that Logan had endorsed Lincoln's course in Congress. The Judge unwisely put himself on the defensive by denying the charge. *The Ticket* had said that Lincoln had voted that the war was unjust and unconstitutional, and that Logan had endorsed his vote. Logan retorted that the statement contained two lies: that Lincoln had so voted and that he had endorsed him. The Judge said that

the second lie contained in the charge is that I endorsed the vote as he states it. It would have been a lie if he had said that I endorsed the vote Mr. Lincoln did give. Mr. Lincoln needs no endorsement; his character in this community for talent, integrity, and patriotism needs no endorsement from me or anyone else. What I did say in regard to Mr. Lincoln was, that much as the democrats here abused his speech at the commencement of the war, it was very strange that none of them had undertaken to answer the argument of it.[17]

Logan was overlooking the columns of the *State Register,* for example, its "Speech not Delivered." It should be borne in mind that at the time of this interchange the war was over. What is significant is the insistent linking of Lincoln's stand in Congress with Judge Logan's candidacy.

Logan's demoralization was so great that in this same reply he refuted another charge made by *The Ticket*—a charge which a less irascible man would have wisely left unanswered. *The Ticket* alleged that Judge Logan had been asked to make a contribution to a fund for bringing home the body of a soldier killed in Mexico, and had given fifty cents. The Judge angrily retorted that he had given three dollars.[18] As Judge Logan's wealth was common knowledge his correction must have caused much amusement.

---

[16] The same item was reprinted in the *State Register,* to give it more extensive circulation in the district.

[17] Lacon *Illinois Gazette,* July 15, 1848.

[18] Lacon *Illinois Gazette,* July 22, 1848; *Illinois State Journal,* July 27, 1848.

That wealth was itself a point against the Judge. It led to another assertion, which this time his friends answered. D. P. Fyffe, a resident of Putnam County, reported that the Democrats had charged that Judge Logan favored the Wilmot Proviso because he had six or eight thousand dollars in his pockets as the proceeds from the sale of Negroes who were part of his father's estate.[19]

Such scurrilous statements became common as the campaign waxed hot. The Whigs claimed that Major Harris could not attract people to hear him when he spoke, so that he followed a circus through the district, taking advantage of the crowds who came to see the circus. The Democrats said that "General" Cooley, secretary of the state of Illinois, who was supposed to be supporting Whig candidates, had actually praised Major Harris and had said that he hoped that the Democrat would be elected. The Whigs flatly denied this, and insisted that the meeting addressed by Cooley had ended with three cheers for Judge Logan.

Then the Democrats, on the offensive, alleged that the Whigs solicited Democratic votes, pledging themselves to vote for Democrats for all offices except that of Congressman.[20] There may have been some truth in this statement; it was said that Col. J. L. D. Morrison (of whom more will appear in the present study), who had been elected to the state senate as a Taylor Whig, was pledged to support all Democratic men and measures in the state legislature.[21]

Another ruse of the Democrats was to publish a "German Handbill," a broadside setting forth the anti-foreign attitude which characterized the Whigs generally. The handbill said that Whigs were hostile toward immigrants, cited a travel book written by a German historian which quoted the Whigs as saying that all foreigners should be exterminated by "fire and sword," and charged that Logan as a delegate to the recent State Constitutional Convention had maintained these views. The handbill had three signatures. Two were repudiated. One signer said

---

[19] *Illinois State Journal*, July 27, 1848.

[20] *Illinois State Register*, July 14, 1848; *Illinois State Journal*, August 16, 1848.

[21] Letter of P. B. Fouke to Governor French, August 13, 1848 (French MSS).

that he was out of town when the document was prepared, another said that he had signed it without reading it.[22]

The Whigs circulated the story that one of Major Harris' enlisted men had found a necklace somewhere in Mexico, and, complying with the order forbidding looting, had turned it over to Major Harris. Harris, realizing that the necklace was valuable, had kept it. But the Democrats were not so gullible as to be drawn into dispute. They waited until the election was past, and then invited all Whigs to a banquet at which the central attraction would be a roasted coon (the coon was the pictorial symbol of the Whig party) with the necklace under its chin.

The Whig press did what it could for Judge Logan. The *Illinois Journal* on July 27 (the election was to take place on August 7) in a summing up, copied a laudatory editorial from the Pekin *Mirror*. This praise accorded Judge Logan had been written by Dr. A. G. Henry, ever a wholehearted Whig. The *Illinois Journal* confidently predicted Logan's victory, estimating for him a majority of 500 in Sangamon County, of 300-500 in Tazewell, and of 50-250 in Morgan, Cass, Scott, Logan, and Menard. There was some hardihood in the estimate for Menard, for it was Harris' county. Even so, the leading Whig paper was conceding four counties to Harris.[23]

The *State Register*, fighting aggressively for Harris, hit much harder in its pre-election issue. It still repeated that Logan assumed responsibility for Lincoln's course in Congress. Using as evidence the dispute, long since ended, about the Texas-Mexico boundary, the *State Register* said, "For this every Whig in the House voted, and among them Lincoln, and this vote of Lincoln's is endorsed by Logan." And once more the *Register* got back to the Spot Resolutions.[24]

On August 7 the Whig stronghold fell. Harris won over Logan by a small but decisive majority: Harris 7,201, Logan 7,095. What made this small majority decisive was the difference between Logan's vote and Lincoln's 1,511 majority over Cartwright. Lincoln had carried eight of the district's eleven counties; Logan lost eight and carried only three. The *State Journal's*

---

[22] *Illinois State Register,* July 14, 1848.

[23] *Illinois State Journal,* August 2, 8, 23, 1848; Beardstown *Gazette,* August 16, 1848.

[24] *Illinois State Register,* August 4, 1848.

estimated majority of 500 in Sangamon turned out to be 263, the 300-500 in Tazewell was actually 221, and the 50-250 in Logan was in fact 18.[25]

It is unquestionable that the overturn from a majority of 1,511 to a minority of 106—a change of 1,617 votes—was a repudiation of Lincoln as well as a defeat of the Whigs. There is ample reason to believe that had not Lincoln's war record in Congress outraged the voters of the district Logan would have been elected. This judgment was explicitly affirmed by a Springfield Whig. True, the charge was made by a disappointed office seeker, and is subject to discount for that reason. However that may have been, Caleb Birchall wrote to Secretary of the Interior Ewing that

Mr. Lincoln in a speech delivered by him in Congress, in the Winter of 48, upon the subject of the Mexican War rendered himself very unpopular, and inflicted a deep and mischevious wound upon the Whole Whig party of the State, the consequences of which were clearly manifested in the very next congressional Election that followed—, I refer to the Election of last year The Whig Party selected for their candidate Stephen T. Logan, than Whome there is not a more worthy and talented man in the State both for respectability and talents, (and in a district too that gave Genl Taylor a Majority of 1483 votes, and Which has never been known to elect a Locofoco before,) The Whigs were defeated by over 100 votes.[26]

Many Whig voters must have drawn the same conclusion, for many Whigs voted for Harris.

It was believed by Beveridge that the soldier vote decided the election.[27] When Lincoln won in 1846 the total vote was light (1,279 less than in 1844). Probably the decrease was caused principally by the absence at the front of qualified voters. The total vote in 1848 was 3,042 more than the whole vote when Lincoln was elected. By August, 1848, all Illinois volunteer regiments had been demobilized, and the veterans had returned to their homes. The proportion of soldier voters could not have been less in the Seventh District than elsewhere in the state, and it was certainly higher than in the northern counties. Unquestion-

---

[25] *Illinois State Journal,* August 8, 1848; *Illinois State Register,* August 11, 1848.

[26] Caleb Birchall to Thomas Ewing, June 6, 1849, Archives of the Department of the Interior.

[27] Beveridge, I:461 note.

ably many Whig soldiers, as well as civilians, voted for Harris.

Another index of the loss of Whig votes is found by comparing, by percentages, the vote which Logan received with that of his predecessors. In 1846 Lincoln had won 56 per cent of the total. If Logan had made the same showing he would have received 8,098 votes instead of 7,095. As compared with Baker's 52 per cent in 1844 he would have received 7,520. As compared with Hardin's 53 per cent in 1843 he would have received 7,765. It appears that Beveridge was right: the soldier vote was the deciding element. The Democrats, making the most of their best chance, brought every available Democrat to the polls.[28] But there were not enough Democrats in the Seventh District to have accounted for the size of the overturn. A large number of Whigs voted for the Democratic candidate. This was the ultimate repudiation of Lincoln's stand on the Mexican War —not by Democrats only, as might have been expected, but by Whigs.

The contemporary analyses of the result are interesting. The *Illinois Journal* on August 8, without many definite returns (the election had been held the preceding day and distant precincts had not reported), conceded Logan's defeat. "This has been effected by the 'military spirit,'" it said, and taking such comfort as it could from the fact added that this "shows how old Zack will walk over the course in November." But after the official returns were in the *Journal* had a different explanation: the Whigs had been "cheated and lied out" of the election.[29]

Other Whig papers agreed that the war spirit was the reason for the Whig defeat. On August 15 the Quincy *Whig* said

The feeling of the people seems to run strong for military men. We notice in every election that comes to our knowledge, they have been elected . . . breaking over party lines and carrying counties hitherto firm in attachment to the opposite party. . . . In the Sangamo District . . . even so small a pattern of military man as Maj. Harris succeeds over Judge Logan, for Congress when there is in the District a well known Whig majority of 1200-1500. But Harris is a Major, we believe, among the sucker chivalry, at the Battle of Cerro Gordo, and that fact with the unscrupulous exertions of unscrupulous partisans was too much for Judge Logan & he has fallen a victim to the military fever.

---

[28] Beardstown *Gazette,* August 16, 1848.

[29] *Illinois State Journal,* August 16, 1848.

The Lacon *Illinois Gazette* agreed that the result must be mainly ascribed to the "war spirit which animates the people of the State." [30] The Quincy *Whig* noted that the Belleville *Times* (a Democratic paper) believed that Logan was defeated because of the unpopularity of General Taylor in the District.[31] The Beardstown *Gazette* concluded that the "well directed and simultaneous effort in every part of the district" [32] by the Democrats had won the election.

The *State Register* had its own explanation, which it stated emphatically in the postelection issue of August 11:

The Whigs about Springfield are attributing their defeat to Judge Logan, solely, alleging that the Judge's unpopularity brought about the result. This will not do, gentlemen; you must put the saddle on the right horse. It was the crushing load Logan had to carry in the shape of Whig principles, and the course of the Whig party for the past two years. Besides his own dead weight, Logan had to carry the votes of the Whig party, including Lincoln, that the war was unconstitutional and unnecessary. If this whig reasoning will apply to Logan, why not to Stuart and Edwards who were defeated running for the state legislature? The former received but 22 and the latter 16 more votes than the Judge in Sangamon. "Acknowledge the corn," whigery is getting in bad odor.

In the same issue the point was restated:

The "Spot" Wiped Out

When Henry was elected to Congress from this district no one heard his views in relation to the war, for he was elected to fill a vacancy, and the interregnum between the issuing of the writ and the election was too brief to admit of a canvass. When Lincoln was elected he made no declaration of principles in regard to the war before the people, as he himself tells us in his first speech in Congress. Therefore the people of the seventh Congressional district were not responsible for the anti-war speeches and anti-war votes of these gentlemen. But it was otherwise in relation to Logan. He had committed himself in the legislature against the war, and his sentiments were well known to the people,—and they promptly rejected him. This proves that . . . they are patriotic, true lovers of their country.

Lincoln was himself at least disingenuous in reference to the loss of the district. In a letter on the general political situation he said of the Seventh District that

---

[30] Lacon *Illinois Gazette*, August 12, 1848.

[31] Quincy *Whig*, August 22, 1848.

[32] Beardstown *Gazette*, August 16, 1848.

I would rather not be put upon explaining how Logan was defeated in my district. In the first place I have no particulars from there, my friends, supposing I am on the road home, not having written me. Whether there was a full turn out of the voters I have not yet learned. The most I can now say is that a good many whigs, without good cause, as I think, were unwilling to go for Logan, and some of them so wrote me before the election. On the other hand Harris was a Major of the war, and fought at Cerro Gordo, where several whigs in the district fought with him. These two facts and their effects, I presume tell the whole story. That there is any political change against us in the district I cannot believe. . . . I dislike to predict, but it seems to me the district must and will be found right side up again in November.[33]

He was correct in his forecast, but clearly wrong in his diagnosis. It is regrettable that there is no information of his conclusions when he became fully informed of the details.

The estimates of two Democrats are interesting enough to warrant citation. Col. Charles Oakley, a Chicago attorney, wrote to Governor French that "I regard the victory in our 'dead' district equal to that of Buena Vista; it has mortified and humbled the Whigs more than any occurrence which has taken place in the State for many years." James Shields, once a minor Illinois politician, now an ex-Brigadier General of distinction, and soon to be appointed governor of Oregon and elected to the United States Senate, also commented on the election in a letter to Governor French: "You have elected my noble friend Harris and redeemed the lost district. . . . No man in the State can appreciate the victory more than I can—for I have experienced the tender mercies of the Whigs of Springfield." [34]

Incidentally, the Seventh District election was newsworthy outside Illinois. The New York *Herald* reported Harris' victory in its August 23 issue.

There was some compensation to the Whigs in the 1848 Congressional election, despite the loss of the Seventh District. Col. E. D. Baker kept intact the slender hold of the Illinois Whigs in Congress by winning election in the Sixth (Galena) District.

When it became apparent that Baker could not be nominated in the Seventh District, he cast about for another place. He was

---

[33] *CW* I:518 f.

[34] French MSS.

touted for the office of governor,[35] but he was too sagacious to accept the sacrificial role of Whig candidate for that office. Removal was necessary. He lost no time in establishing residence in Galena.

Baker's decision indicates that he sensed the political effect of the population trend. There was considerable Whig strength in the Galena lead-mining region, but the interior counties, until 1848, had been Democratic. Yet a significant shift had appeared in the past three Congressional elections. In 1843 the Democratic vote was 51 per cent of the total, in 1844 it was 52 per cent, but in 1846 it dropped to 46 per cent, although in that election a Democrat won.[36] The cause of the change was the rise of the Liberty Party vote: 2 per cent in 1843, 3 per cent in 1844, and 5 per cent in 1846. This shows the influence of the New England and Middle States antislavery migration to northern Illinois. Baker no doubt saw that accelerated immigration there would be advantageous to the Whigs, as it proved to be. Except for 1850-52 so long as the party existed it had Congressmen from northern Illinois.

Baker announced his plan to move on April 11, and he arrived in Galena on April 18.[37] The Whig Convention had been called for the twelfth (later changed to the fourteenth) of June, so that he was able to address some of the county conventions.[38] His principal rival was Elihu Washburne (who succeeded him in 1852), but Baker was easily nominated.[39] His opponent was ex-Lieutenant Governor Joseph B. Wells. The campaign was hard fought, and only to a lesser degree than that in the Seventh District a rough one. Democrats said that Baker had left Springfield because his reputation there had become odious, and that he was spending money freely for election purposes and buying votes. It was alleged that he had mulcted the government by

[35] Charleston *Courier* and *Illinois Globe,* clipped in *Illinois State Register,* April 21, 1848; New York *Herald,* April 27, 1848.

[36] Pease, *Illinois Election Returns,* pp. lv, 140, 147, 158.

[37] *Illinois State Journal,* April 7, 1848; Galena *Gazette and Advertiser,* April 11, 18, 1848; New York *Tribune,* May 12, 1848.

[38] Galena *Gazette and Advertiser,* April 25, 28, 1848; New York *Tribune,* May 9, 1848.

[39] Galena *Gazette and Advertiser,* June 16, 21, 1848; Oquawka *Spectator* (with statistics of the balloting), June 21, 1848; Lacon *Illinois Gazette,* July 1, 1848; Rockford *Forum,* July 5, 1848.

receiving money as a bearer of war dispatches.[40] The Galena *Jeffersonian* collected these purely propaganda items and published them in pamphlet form. But Baker won. For Lincoln this meant pleasure in his friend's success, but trouble in his remaining period in Congress. For after Taylor's election the patronage became important, and Baker demanded equal voice with Lincoln in dispensing it. The effects of this demand, some of them fateful to Lincoln, will appear.

---

[40] So charged the Galena *Jeffersonian*, September 14, 1848.

11

CAMPAIGNING FOR OLD ZACH

In one of the debates with Douglas, Lincoln referred to Henry Clay as "my beau ideal of a statesman, the man for whom I fought all my humble life." [1] He was conveniently forgetting the Presidential campaign of ten years before, when he labored manfully for the nomination and election of one who was not his beau ideal of a statesman.

Alexander Stephens, whose forensic effort had made Lincoln weep, was one of the first to sense the potential advantage to the Whigs of the political promotion of General Taylor. [2] As early as December, 1846, Stephens had foreseen the Taylor boom and had organized the "Young Indians," a group of Whig Congressmen who were of his views. Lincoln joined this group and was extremely active in its work, especially in disseminating campaign material. [3]

If the Illinois *State Register* can be believed, Lincoln had espoused the cause of Taylor for President as early as August,

---

[1] *CW* III:29.

[2] Myrta Lockett Avary, *Recollections of Alexander Stephens* (1910), pp. 21 f: "It was I . . . who made him President. Soon after the first battles of the war . . . I urged on the anti-war party that Taylor was our man; I got his nomination in a Whig convention in Georgia in 1847."

[3] Beveridge, p. 441.

1847, before he left for Washington. November 5 of that year
the Democratic paper recalled a "caucus of Whigs in this city in
August" at which speeches were made by Baker, Logan, and
Lincoln, "and the meeting finally resolved to go for Taylor 'without a why or wherefore'." Lincoln's attitude from early December
can be traced. Only six days after his arrival in Washington he
wrote to Richard Yates that he had heard from Duff Green that
Calhoun and the forces he could control were preparing to support Taylor. Lincoln added that there were a great many Whigs
in Washington who were opposed to Taylor. He revealed his own
attitude in the words "whom I fear cannot be brought to do it":
but he was for Taylor.[4] The same view was expressed January 1,
1848.[5]

There is a letter which was published in the *Illinois Journal,*
January 6, under the heading "Politics at Washington." Internal
evidence indicates that Lincoln was the writer:

> Being so entire a stranger, I have not got much into the way of
> things here yet. . . . I talked a considerable while with Crittenden, or
> rather he talked *to* me, about the next Presidency, from which I am
> satisfied he is strongly in favor of General Taylor, although he did not
> say so directly. Duff Green is strong for Taylor, and assures us that
> Mr. Calhoun, with what influence he can bring to bear, will take the
> same course. . . . He says that the Whigs ought to be satisfied with
> knowing that Gen. Taylor is a Whig and a friend of Mr. Clay, while
> he, as a Calhoun man, is willing to take him without knowing any
> more than is publicly known. . . . There are still a great many wishing
> to run Mr. Clay.

Lincoln's preference for Taylor had fully matured by February 9, when, declining an invitation to a Taylor rally in Philadelphia, he wrote that he was "decidedly in favor of General
Taylor as the Whig candidate for the next presidency." His
letter was read with others from "distinguished Whigs" who were
unable to attend.[6] On February 20 Lincoln made suggestions to
U. F. Linder of Illinois concerning the strategy of the campaign.[7]
To Elihu Washburne, rival of Baker for nomination to Congress,
Lincoln wrote that the hope of Taylor's being named was a little

---

[4] *CW* I:419.

[5] *CW* I:422 f.

[6] *CW* I:449. Lincoln was fully committed to Taylor on February 17, 1847
(*CW* I:452).

[7] *CW* I:453, 457 f.

higher than it was when Washburne left the capital, that Clay's recent letter had not helped his interests, and that some anti-Taylor men favored Scott or McLean. He urged Washburne to insure that his Illinois district send a Taylor delegation to the Convention.[8]

To Archibald Williams, a Whig of some influence in the Quincy District, Lincoln wrote that "Mr. Clay's chance for an election, is just no chance at all. He might get New York; and that would have elected him in 1844, but it will not now; because he must now at the least, lose Tennessee, which he had then, and, in addition, the fifteen *new* votes of Florida, Texas, Iowa, and Wisconsin. . . . In my judgment, we can elect nobody but Gen: Taylor."[9] This was indeed sacrificing principle for availability. Mr. Lincoln was certainly not fighting for Henry Clay, his beau ideal of the statesman, when he wrote that letter.

Lincoln was not a delegate to the Whig National Convention, but he was so anxious about the outcome that he attended it.[10] Naturally he talked with the Illinois delegates, with whose procedure he was highly displeased. His appeal to Washburne had been futile, for three of the northern delegates were for Clay and one was for Scott. What particularly irritated Lincoln was that the Clay and Scott men persisted in their choice on the second and third ballots, not shifting to Taylor until the fourth and last.[11]

After the convention Lincoln expressed his satisfaction at the outcome. His reasons are hardly creditable: "By many, and often, it had been said that they would not abide the nomination of Taylor; but since the deed has been done, they are fast falling in, and in my opinion we shall have a most overwhelming, glorious, triumph. One unmistakable sign is, that all the odds and ends are with us—Barnburners, Native Americans, Tyler men, disappointed office seeking locofocos, and the Lord knows what."[12] The Barnburners were not with them long; when the Free Soil party was formed and Van Buren its candidate they

[8] *CW* I:467.

[9] *CW* I:467 f.

[10] *CW* I:476, 478.

[11] *National Intelligencer,* June 10, 1848; New York *Tribune,* June 10, 1848.

[12] *CW* I:476 f.

went with that group. It was doubtless true that votes were to be gained from the other odds and ends, but that ephemeral advantage hardly compensated for the obvious liabilities of, for instance, the Native Americans.

Lincoln was grossly overconfident of his party's November prospects. In the June 12 letter he said that "some of the sanguine men here, set down all the states as certain for Taylor, but Illinois, and it as doubtful." [13] This would have been a landslide exceeding anything before or since.

He was politician enough to question so wild an estimate, and to go to work on Illinois. He did so in the same letter, and no doubt he wrote many like that to Richard S. Thomas on June 19: "Do you know any democrats who will vote for Taylor? And if so, what are their names? Do you know any whigs who will not vote for him? and if so, what are their names? and for whom will they vote?" [14] The information garnered from replies was, of course, used in franking out campaign literature.

For other estimates Lincoln wrote to William Schouler of Massachusetts (evidently they had met at the convention) and to Thad Stevens of Pennsylvania.[15] Stevens wrote a detailed reply. The correspondence with Schouler led to Lincoln's being invited to speak in Massachusetts. On June 25 he heard from a faithful worker, John Morrison, explaining why Morrison had not attended the convention, and giving a favorable report of the outlook in Edwards County, a Whig island in southern Illinois.[16]

Some of the news from Illinois was not encouraging. Herndon wrote Lincoln a much less optimistic report than Lincoln had given him. Lincoln had received one of Herndon's letters after attending a caucus in which the whole field of the nation was scanned, with nothing but high hope and confidence; even Illinois was expected to better herself. Then he read Herndon's report of the defection of several Whigs who were named and of others not named. Lincoln tried to stir his partner. He directed him to organize a "Rough and Ready Club" of all the shrewd wild boys about town (he named some likely prospects), each of whom must do what he could: some speak, some sing, and all

---

13 *CW* I:477.

14 *CW* I:479.

15 *CW* I:516, II:1.

16 RTLP.

"holler." [17] On July 10 he wrote Herndon again, with some satisfaction for his response to the suggestions made. On the same
day he wrote to S. A. Hurlbut, a minor politician of northern
Illinois, and sent him a copy of the new Whig campaign paper,
The Battery.[18]

Lincoln had received Schouler's reply to his letter about
August 25, and on August 28 he wrote to Schouler thanking
him for its encouraging news. He was still over optimistic. He
told of Caleb Smith's reception in Cincinnati, and said that even
in the Connecticut Reserve the news was good.[19] This is, to put
it mildly, surprising. The Western Reserve was Giddings' field.
It was more Yankee than New England. It was simply incredible
that that hotbed of abolitionism, which elected the uncompromising Giddings for term after term, was swinging to Taylor. But
Lincoln thought it was. Despite the defeat of Logan, he was still
refusing to believe that there was any change against his party
in the Seventh District.

After Congress adjourned on August 14, Lincoln remained
in Washington, working with others at franking out documents.
He expected to be so engaged for two weeks when he wrote to
Schouler, but the time stretched out longer; he was in or near
Washington until early September. He was busy; the group sent
out 15,000 to 20,000 documents a day.[20]

The Illinois Whigs got around, on August 23, to the appointment of some Assistant Electors, i.e., men who were expected
to make stump speeches throughout the state.[21] Lincoln was one
of them, but he did not assume the task immediately. Instead
he spoke several times in and near Washington, and then went
for the same purpose to Massachusetts.

He had made one speech locally as early as June 10, and
since it has only recently come to light it is relevant to report it.
It was made at Wilmington, Delaware. The *State Journal* of that
city noted on June 13 that after the nominating convention
"several distinguished Whigs" attended the "ratification meeting"

---

[17] *CW* I:490 f. *The Illinois State Journal*, July 13, 1848, reported the
first meeting of the Springfield Rough and Ready Club.

[18] *CW* I:498 f.

[19] *CW* I:518 f.

[20] Beveridge, I:449.

[21] *Illinois State Journal*, August 23, 1848; Lacon *Illinois Gazette*, September 9, 1848.

in Wilmington: Congressmen Haskill of Tennessee, Cabell of Florida, Houston of Delaware, and Lincoln.

The first speaker introduced, to the assembled multitude was the "Lone Star of Illinois," Hon. Mr. Lincoln. He was received with three hearty cheers, and delivered an eloquent and patriotic speech on some of the principles of the Whig party and the standard-bearers they had selected to carry out their measures. He referred to the history of James K. Polk's administration—the abuse of power which characterized it—the high handed and despotic exercise of the veto power, and the utter disregard of the will of the people, in refusing to give assent to measures which their representatives passed for the good and prosperity of the country. The manner in which the present Executive had carried on the Mexican war should condemn it and the Loco-foco party before the whole people. He did not believe with many of his fellow citizens that this war was originated for the purpose of extending slave territory, but it was his opinion, frequently expressed, that it was a war of conquest brought into existence to catch votes. Admitting, however, that the disputes between Mexico and this country could not have been settled in an amicable manner—admitting that we went into the battle field as a last resort, with all the principles of right and justice on our side, why is it that this government desires a large sum of money to gain more territory than will secure "indemnity for the past and security for the future?" During the whole war this was the stereotyped motto of the administration; but when the treaty was sent to the Senate, the Executive not only included enough of territory for this purpose but actually extended the boundaries and made an agreement to pay the Mexican government $15,000,000 for the additional territory. This subject demanded attention, and although he had means of information, it had never been satisfactorily explained to him. Mr. Lincoln referred to other topics in an eloquent manner, and concluded with a few patriotic remarks on the character and long services of the Whig candidates.[22]

After Congress adjourned Lincoln spoke at a bipartisan meeting in Seneca, Maryland; Major George Peters, a free-trade Democrat and owner of a large number of slaves, and Lincoln supported Taylor, while two others replied.[23] (Lincoln was characterized as a high protective tariff, free soil, Wilmot Proviso, abolition Whig.) This was August 24; two days later he addressed a meeting of the Rough and Ready Club at Rockville, Maryland. His speech was interesting, the *National Intelligencer* said.[24] Lincoln and Brady of Pennsylvania spoke at another

---

[22] *CW* I:475 f.

[23] Frederick, Maryland, *Republican Citizen*, September 1, 1848.

[24] *National Intelligencer*, August 29, 1848.

Rough and Ready meeting on August 31, apparently in Washington.[25] It was presumably in Washington where he spoke on September 5 at a meeting to celebrate Taylor's first military achievement, the defense of Fort Harrison in the War of 1812.[26]

Then, on or about September 9, Lincoln left Washington for his speaking tour in Massachusetts. He probably went to New York by rail and by steamer to Norwich, Connecticut. He completed his journey to Worcester, Massachusetts, by rail.[27]

It is inferred that Lincoln's junket to Massachusetts was at the invitation of William Schouler, editor of the Boston *Atlas,* with whom he had been in correspondence.[28] At all events he spoke in Worcester September 12. That invitation came by default. The chairman of the Whig city committee had called the meeting and announced it, but all speakers who were invited to address it declined. On the day of the affair no one was engaged. Hearing that Lincoln was at a local hotel, the chairman, as late as sundown, hurried to call upon him and invited him to be the speaker. Lincoln was agreeable, and accepted. He was introduced as a representative of free soil. Newspaper reports mentioned his tall, thin figure, his "intellectual face, showing a searching mind, and a cool judgment." Lincoln spoke for an hour and a half, interrupted with warm and frequent applause. He expressed himself modestly, speaking "this side of the mountains, where, as supposed in Illinois, every one was supposed to be instructed and wise." [29]

The summary of his address shows that it used the material of his entertaining speech in Congress.[30] He affirmed that the party and its candidate had principles and that Taylor's Allison letter set them forth. Lincoln lauded Taylor's pledge not to use the veto.

---

[25] Baltimore *Clipper,* September 2, 1848.

[26] *National Intelligencer,* September 5, 1848.

[27] Starr, pp. 49-51.

[28] Reinhard Luthin, in his article, "Abraham Lincoln and the Massachusetts Whigs," *New England Quarterly,* 14 (1941), 619-34, says that there is some inconclusive evidence that the invitation was at the behest of the Massachusetts Whig Congressman, Charles Hudson, who had become impressed by Lincoln's speaking ability. Cf. Beveridge, I:468 note.

[29] Luthin, p, 625; Arthur P. Rugg, "Abraham Lincoln in Worcester," *Worcester Society of Antiquity Proceedings,* 25 (1910), 228; Boston *Daily Advertiser,* September 14, 1848.

[30] *CW* II:1-5.

Then Lincoln proceeded to the primary theme in that locality: slavery. In a considerable overstatement he averred that the people of Illinois agreed entirely with the people of Massachusetts on slavery, except perhaps that they did not so constantly keep thinking about it. He said that there should be no lawful interference with slavery in the slave states, but that slavery must not be permitted to expand. He declared that the Whigs were in advance of the Free Soilers in this principle, because free soil was the *only* principle of the new party; that votes for the Free Soil candidates would tend to increase the probability of slavery expansion, since they would subtract principally from the Whig vote and thus make for the election of Cass. The Whigs, he said, deserved credit for opposing the Mexican War; the Free Soilers supported it. He praised Taylor's war service, discussed the origin of the war, and closed with expressions of confidence in the outcome of the election. At the close of his speech there were three rousing cheers for Illinois, and three for Lincoln.

A later reminiscence of the speech remarked that Lincoln's style and manner of speaking were novel, but that his stories were admirable in humor and interspersed with passages of true eloquence. His sarcasm on Cass, Van Buren, and the Democratic party was inimitable, and he was often urged to "go on; go on!" [31]

Next day the Massachusetts State Whig Convention was to meet at Worcester. Lincoln was making a speech at the railway station when a special train bringing such prominent Whigs as Rufus Choate, Speaker Winthrop, and Nathan Appleton arrived and cut short the address. Lincoln heard Choate and Winthrop before leaving for his next stop. [32]

This was at New Bedford, where he spoke on September 14. [33] No report of this speech is extant. The next day he made the first of two speeches in Boston. This one was at Whig headquarters. The Boston *Atlas*, the voice of Lincoln's friend Schouler, made a thumbnail summary which shows it was the same as that given in Worcester. It was a glorious meeting, said the *Atlas*. [34]

At Lowell on September 16 Lincoln shared the platform at

---

[31] Luthin, p. 626.
[32] Luthin, p. 627.
[33] Luthin, p. 627.
[34] CW II:5, *Boston Atlas*, September 16, 1848.

a Whig rally held in the City Hall. The Lowell *Courier* rated his speech as most able, masterly, and convincing, and said that he was frequently interrupted by applause.[35] From Lowell, Lincoln went to Dorchester, accepting an invitation extended by one of his listeners at Worcester. The Dorchester meeting was full and enthusiastic, according to the Boston *Courier* of September 20. On the nineteenth Lincoln spoke at Chelsea, and the Boston *Atlas* said that his speech there was hard to beat for aptness of illustration, solidity of argument, and genuine eloquence.[36] At Dedham he spoke by arrangement made by a local newspaperman, George H. Monroe, who invited Lincoln at the suggestion of Schouler. He had to shorten that speech because of the departure of his train for Cambridge.[37]

The Cambridge meeting was a ratification of the Worcester convention nominations. Two ward clubs arranged it. Lincoln's speech was an explanation of the principles of the Whig candidates and an argument for their support by everyone who honestly desired to restrain slavery and to insure constitutional and republican government.[38] At Taunton on the twenty-first he made the same speech as that given at Worcester.[39]

The highlight of Lincoln's Massachusetts experience came on September 12, when he attended, and spoke at, a great rally held in Boston's Tremont Temple. Ex-Governor Seward of New York was the principal speaker. Naturally the newspapers gave full space to the main speech, but Lincoln's was noted and summarized by five papers.[40]

It is said that Lincoln was extraordinarily impressed by Seward. The governor's son, subsequently writing of his father's career, relates their conversation at their hotel after the meeting.

---

[35] Lowell *Courier,* clipped in the Boston *Daily Advertiser,* September 20, 1848.

[36] Boston *Atlas,* September 20, 1848.

[37] "Lincoln's Visit to Dedham, Massachusetts," Dedham Historical Society MSS, September 30, 1947; Massachusetts Historical Society *Proceedings,* October, 1916, pp. 30-36.

[38] Boston *Journal,* September 21, 1848.

[39] Taunton *Daily Gazette,* September 23, 1848.

[40] Boston *Atlas,* September 22, 1848; Boston *Evening Traveler,* Septemtember 23, 1848; Boston *Daily Advertiser,* same date; Boston *Courier,* same date; Boston *Herald,* same date. The Boston *Chronotype,* a Free Soil newspaper, noted the speech unfavorably; this was reported in the *Illinois State Register,* October 13, 1848.

Lincoln said, "Governor Seward, I have been thinking about what you said in your speech. I reckon you are right. We have got to deal with this slavery question, and got to give much more attention to it hereafter than we have been doing." [41]

It is unlikely that Lincoln had much success on this tour. The Cotton Whigs were predisposed to Taylor; they did not have to be won. Nor were Lincoln's speeches shaped to influence them. By stressing the slavery issue he labored to prevent Conscience Whigs from deserting their party to vote for Van Buren and Adams. The Massachusetts election returns show a majority for the Whigs in the eastern counties, where the Cotton Whigs were strong. But the Free Soilers won in the Worcester area, where Lincoln had striven to prevent defection. The antislavery movement was rapidly rising to political power in the Bay State; Sumner's star was ascending.[42] Lincoln could not counter so powerful a movement—nor could anyone else. He could claim credit for manful effort in Massachusetts, but that he won many votes for Taylor is doubtful.

How many did he win in Illinois? For now he must discharge his obligation to work as "Assistant Elector" in his own state. There was not much time remaining. He went to Albany, where Mrs. Lincoln joined him, and where he is said to have met with Thurlow Weed and Millard Fillmore.[43] From Albany he and Mrs. Lincoln went to Buffalo by rail. There they took the steamer *Globe*.[44]

The lake steamer trip gave Lincoln the opportunity to take a much needed rest. There were other benefits. A view of Niagara Falls became the subject of a lecture delivered subsequently. Watching the maneuvering of a boat over a shallow gave him the idea of a device which he patented during the short

---

[41] Frederick W. Seward, *William H. Seward*, II:80.

[42] Joshua R. Giddings campaigned extensively in Massachusetts in 1848. He and Sumner represented the attitude of the majority of the Massachusetts Conscience Whigs, who went into the Free Soil movement in large numbers. It is unlikely that Lincoln was able to stem the tide stirred by Giddings and Sumner.

[43] Joseph F. Newton, *Lincoln and Herndon* (1910), p. 36.

[44] Starr and Thomas believe that Lincoln traveled by lake steamer to Detroit, and overland to Chicago. This seems improbable. See the Lacon *Illinois Gazette*, October 14, 1848. A fellow passenger on the steamer *Globe* later wrote to Lincon recalling the lake journey. Harry E. Pratt, *Concerning Mr. Lincoln* (1944).

session.[45] Inasmuch as the *Globe* docked in Chicago on October 5 and Lincoln spoke there on the sixth it is indicated that the Lincolns remained on the steamer for the full distance, rather than debarking at Detroit and going by stage and railroad to Chicago.

Lincoln knew that many Illinois Whigs had only reluctantly accepted Taylor.[46] This was evident in the stubbornness of the Clay and Scott delegates to the convention. It had been demonstrated by other evidence. The difference in view between the Whigs of the northern and the southern parts of the state was basic. Even in the Seventh District it was only late and unwillingly that Clay had been abandoned. The *State Register* remarked that the Tazewell party paper (no doubt Dr. Henry was responsible) was the hottest Taylor paper in the state, but "was for Clay if it had been possible to nominate him." The Quincy *Whig* reported sentiment for Corwin, of all people, and proposed a compromise ticket of Taylor and Corwin. "What a team it would be! Think of it!" exclaimed the *Register*.[47] The *Lake County Visiter,* published at Little Fort (soon to be renamed Waukegan), even after the convention, refused to support Taylor, saying caustic things about Whigs running a slaveholder.[48] Taylor was almost as hard for the Rockford *Forum* to take, but it fell in with the advantage of availability, even before the Convention.[49] The *State Journal* was hardly more than lukewarm, but belatedly it accepted Taylor and ran orthodox campaign material.

After spending a night at the Sherman House, Lincoln was the principal speaker at a Whig rally which was scheduled to meet in the Court House, but because of the size of the crowd was held in the public square. According to the Chicago *Journal* Lincoln "enchained" his listeners for two hours in a speech which

---

[45] On Lincoln's patent, see Ida M. Tarbell, *The Life of Abraham Lincoln* (1900), II:20-22 (illustration); Louis A. Warren, *Lincoln Lore*, No. 889, April 22, 1946. The issue of the patent involved the writing of a letter to Lincoln by Daniel Webster. The model of the patented device was fashioned by Walter Davis in his Springfield shop. See CW II:32-36.

[46] Letter of Justin Butterfield, Jr., to Joseph Gillespie, Gillespie MSS, Chicago Historical Society, Vol. 14.

[47] *Illinois State Register,* June 18, 1847, January 21, 1848.

[48] *Lake County Visiter,* Little Fort, June 1, 1848.

[49] Rockford *Forum,* April 14, 1847.

was said to have been one of the best ever heard or read during the campaign. He was followed by Stephen A. Hurlbut. Next evening Baker "enchained" his audience for *three* hours, the *Journal* said.[50]

Lincoln's next effort for Taylor was at Peoria on October 9, with J. Young Scammon as the second speaker. The hostile *Democratic Press* of Peoria reminded its readers of the Spot Resolutions. "As soon as the *spot* where he should stand was designated" he made his speech.[51]

Sarcasm greeted him on his arrival in Springfield on October 10. The *State Register* noted his arrival and added: "We are pleased to observe that his arduous duties since the adjournment of Congress in franking and loading down the mails with Whig electioneering documents have not impaired his health. He looks remarkably well." [52]

It is more than odd that with only four weeks remaining before election Lincoln made no speeches between the date of his arrival and October 19. It is regrettable that no explanation of this fact has been found. It is still more odd that insofar as can be ascertained he made only two speeches in his home neighborhood. In these he was roughly handled. He spoke at Beardstown on October 19.[53] Two days later he spoke in Jacksonville. There his platform opponent, Murray McConnel, attacked Lincoln for his war attitude, asserting that Lincoln had misrepresented his constituents. Lincoln was sufficiently stung to reply. He refused to believe that a majority of his constituents had favored the war. This was an extremely vulnerable defense, and McConnel pounced upon it: how, then, did Lincoln explain his party's defeat in the recent Congressional election? The *State Register* was informed by its Jacksonville correspondent that Lincoln was "used up" by McConnel. "Lincoln has made nothing by coming to this part of the country to make speeches," the Morgan County writer concluded.[54]

Lincoln spoke in Petersburg, the county seat of Menard County while attending court there on October 23. This time

---

[50] Chicago *Journal*, October 6, 7, 13, 1848.

[51] Peoria *Democratic Press*, October 11, 1848.

[52] *Illinois State Register*, October 13, 1848.

[53] Beardstown *Gazette*, October 19, 1848.

[54] *Illinois State Register*, October 27, 1848.

the *State Register* claimed he was "used up" by William Ferguson.[55] It appears that Lincoln concluded that no good purpose was served by his continuing to speak in this part of the district. If he were not "used up" at least he beat a strategic retreat. What is most curious of all he made no speech in Springfield. The conclusion is inescapable. Lincoln was so unpopular in Springfield and its environs that although he was an official party spokesman it was inadvisable for him to speak there.

Instead he made an intensive canvass of the northern part of the Seventh District (with one speech outside the district at Bloomington on October 28).[56] This was a rational move. For in all his speeches Lincoln was aiming at potential Free Soilers, claiming that a vote for Van Buren was an indirect vote for Cass and thus for slavery. And by far the most of the potential Free Soil votes in the Seventh District were in the northern counties of Putnam, Woodford, and Marshall.

On this tour Lincoln was joined by Dr. A. G. Henry. Did he need a guarantor to save him from such embarrassment as he had experienced at Jacksonville and Petersburg? At all events for six consecutive days Lincoln traveled through this area and Tazewell County. He and Henry spoke on October 30 at an afternoon meeting in Metamora, and next afternoon at Magnolia. Lincoln spoke alone that evening at Hennepin, and on November 1 he and Henry spoke at Lacon.

Here Lincoln was on friendly ground, and was sure of a favorable press; Allen Ford, editor of the Lacon *Illinois Gazette*, had been Lincoln's warm supporter since his campaign for nomination to Congress. Consequently the two speeches received full report in Ford's paper. On the following day Lincoln and Henry spoke at a meeting in Washington, which as a village of "Old Tazewell" was as safe a Whig precinct as could be found. The speaking tour was concluded in the two larger Tazewell towns, Tremont on the third and Pekin on the fourth. Here, too, Lincoln was in the area friendliest to him in all the Seventh District. Pekin was now Dr. Henry's home where he edited the local Whig paper. Lincoln's reception was pleasant; the press records no hostility.

---

[55] *Illinois State Register*, November 3, 1848.

[56] Beardstown *Gazette*, October 25, 1848; *Illinois State Journal*, October 27, 1848; Lacon *Illinois Gazette*, November 4, 1848, Peoria *Democratic Press*, November 8, 1848.

Lincoln, Baker, Henry, *et al.*, were not the only vote getters for Taylor. The General's horse, "Old Whitey," was cited as a factor during the campaign, and there was a reference to General Taylor's dogs. One of the amusing items of the campaign was the discovery, too late to be effective, that Old Whitey was a native of Illinois. The usually rational *Illinois State Journal* ran the following: "This famous horse claims Green County in this State for his birth place. The statement is well founded. Had the fact been known, Old Zach would have got a sweeping majority in Green." [57] The *Journal* failed to make it clear whether Greene County horses or men would have produced that result, but it would have required the horse vote to have captured that Democratic county, which had voted Cass 1,128, Taylor 853, Van Buren 36. The Galena *Gazette* during the campaign noted the arrival of Old Whitey in Washington.[58] No less important a politician than Crittenden was advised of that safe arrival, Orlando Brown writing to him that "Old Whitey has arrived safely with a few hairs left in his tail. I hope that I will be fortunate enough to find a few drops left in my barrel. I don't see why one can't come as safe as the other." [59]

Lincoln voted for Old Zach in Springfield. No doubt he took consolation in Taylor's election and in his victory in the Seventh District. But it must have been bitterly disappointing that Illinois had gone for Cass. Even though Van Buren and Free Soil had carried eight northeastern counties (including Putnam in the Seventh District) the very considerable loss of Democratic votes to the former Democrat, now Free Soiler, had not sufficed to enable Taylor to carry the state.

The loss of Illinois by the Whigs was important to Lincoln. It was no encomium of his success as an Assistant Elector. The vote in Putnam County was despite his major argument—that slavery restriction would be furthered by electing Taylor. In view of what had occurred in Jacksonville and Petersburg Lincoln could not easily have concluded that he had won many votes for his candidate.

But the national victory of the Whigs was more important

---

[57] Clipped in the *Illinois State Journal*, November 17, 1848.

[58] Galena *Gazette and Advertiser*, August 9, 1849.

[59] Orlando Brown to Crittenden, July 16, 1848, Crittenden Papers, Library of Congress; Galena *Jeffersonian*, April 13, 1848.

to Congressman Lincoln. For at some point during his term he changed his mind about returning to the law. He did not contemplate immediate candidacy for elective office, but after the close of the short session of Congress he became a determined aspirant for a patronage appointment, and a weighty reason for his claim was the value of his labors in behalf of the national ticket and for Taylor.

He was entitled to take satisfaction. He had early sensed political indications, and had been one of the first to promote the candidacy of Taylor. He had worked loyally for his nomination. He had spent a hot summer in Washington, working with the Young Indians sending out campaign literature. He had traveled widely and had worked diligently for the party and for the party's candidate. The incoming administration owed him more than a little for his efforts.

12

THE SHORT SESSION

When President Truman compared the Fiftieth Congress with the "do nothing" Eightieth, he might have considered the Thirtieth as another Congress which had been dilatory in its legislative duty. The second (short) session of Lincoln's Congress carried over from the first a backlog of problems of major magnitude. Territorial government had been provided for Oregon, but the need for it in the newly annexed territories was pressing. The discovery of gold in California, the commerce of the California ports, the Santa Fe trade, the settlement of the Mormons in Utah—all these intensified the need. But the Thirtieth Congress failed to meet it.

When the House reassembled on December 4, 1847, its personnel was almost the same as earlier with two significant differences. The contest over the disputed New York seat had been settled by the election of Horace Greeley, editor of the influential Whig paper, the New York *Tribune,* and the vacancy caused by the death of John Quincy Adams had been filled by the election of Horace Mann, whose great work in education was yet to come.[1]

Lincoln was not present when the House resumed meeting. He appeared on the seventh. This time he was not accompanied

---

[1] *Globe,* 30th Congress, 2nd Session, p. 1.

by Mrs. Lincoln. He took quarters with his fellows at Mrs. Sprigg's. He was given the same committee assignments that he had in the first session.[2]

Interesting matters quickly came in the short session. One of them seems, a century later, decidedly modern. Lawrence, a New York Democrat, offered a resolution proposing a constitutional amendment providing for the direct election of the President and the Vice President; each candidate to be credited with that proportion of a state's electoral vote which he had polled in the popular vote.[3] Andrew Johnson offered a homestead law.[4] Homestead legislation was offered during the short session also by Horace Greeley and Embree of Indiana.[5]

The short session was again the occasion for repeated but always unsuccessful attempts to induce Congress to make land grants for the construction of the Illinois Central and other railroads in Illinois. A few days after the House convened Ficklin, Smith, McClernand, and Wentworth gave notices of leave to introduce bills for that purpose; Lincoln did the same later.[6] Representatives from Illinois presented numerous petitions praying for the necessary legislation.[7] Nothing was done by this Congress.[8]

The vexing question of territorial government for the new territories appeared less than two weeks after the opening of the session. Root, an Ohio Whig, offered a resolution that the appropriate committee be instructed to report bills organizing the territories and excluding slavery from them.[9] At once the lines

---

[2] *Globe,* p. 22; Beveridge, I:479. Lincoln's colleagues, Embree and Tompkins, who had lived at Mrs. Sprigg's during the first session, had quarters elsewhere during the short session.

[3] *Globe,* p. 25.

[4] On this day Lincoln, following the Whig majority, voted to instruct the Committee on Ways and Means to report a new tariff bill restoring the principles of the bill of 1842. The Whig majority forced the adoption of the resolution. Nothing came of it.

[5] *Globe,* pp. 38, 454.

[6] *Globe,* pp. 25, 26, 38, 39, 559.

[7] Petitions on this subject, endorsed by Lincoln, are in the National Archives (RG 233 HR 30 A. F. 18). All were referred to the Committee on Public Lands.

[8] Douglas sponsored an Illinois railroad bill which passed the Senate of the Thirtieth Congress, but failed in the House. The story of the legislation which passed in the next Congress is told by Milton, pp. 9-11.

[9] *Globe,* p. 39.

formed: antislavery men favored and proslavery men opposed the resolution. After much parliamentary maneuvering it was adopted (Lincoln voting "Aye"). But this was only the first skirmish of a prolonged struggle. Various tactics were attempted. Caleb Smith brought out a bill for the organization of California.[10] But then, and with each new effort, little more was accomplished than the making of speeches about slavery.

Toward the end of December a long drawn out debate started. It was precipitated by Horace Greeley's exhibit, in his *Tribune*, of the mileage fees paid to Congressmen.

Greeley had directed one of the *Tribune* reporters to collect data. The reporter was rebuffed by the Committee on Mileage, but was cordially received and given full cooperation by the Secretary of the Treasury. The information secured was published in the December 22 issue of the *Tribune*. Greeley made it clear that he accused no individual. He criticized the law. The nub of the question was not the forty cents per mile charge, but the interpretation of "usually traveled route."

The figures were interesting, and their publication excited no little repercussion and some sense of guilt. Of course some of the members who had collected what Greeley declared were excessive amounts were sensitive. Debate was opened by Sawyer, an Ohio Democrat who had been listed with an excess of $281.60, although Schenck, who lived 70 miles nearer Washington had been paid only $2.40 in excess.[11] Schenck indicated the seriousness with which he regarded the matter by offering to swap with Sawyer.

But Thomas J. Turner, an Illinois Democrat, was not appeased by jocularity. He defended himself and attacked Greeley.[12] The shortest post route for Turner was 832 miles, but he had been paid $1,664 for 2,080 miles. He had based his claim upon the route via the Great Lakes, the Erie Canal, and New York City. Richardson from Quincy, Illinois, received $1,334.40 ($329.60 less than Turner was paid) although the shortest route for him was six miles farther than Turner's.[13]

---

[10] *Globe*, p. 71.

[11] *Globe*, p. 108.

[12] *Globe*, p. 108.

[13] New York *Tribune*, December 22, 1848. The article and statistical table were reprinted in the *Whig Almanac*, 1850, p. 30.

The mileage question came up again and again.[14] In the time-consuming debate Greeley was badgered into explanations and forced to admit minor errors. Yet, although he weakened his case by parliamentary ineptness, he performed a useful service by forcing attention to what had, for years, been a palpable abuse. The fact was that Congressmen were underpaid, but public opinion supported the low *per diem* remuneration. As a result perquisites such as mileage and charges for stationery took the place of an adequate salary account.[15] A bill providing fair pay had been passed by the Fourteenth Congress, under the sponsorship of Calhoun in the House. Public opinion was so outraged that the bill was repealed by the next Congress, and the old system reinstated.[16]

Greeley's effort resulted in the passage of a new mileage bill. This law required that the distance between Washington and a member's home be the shortest post-route, prohibited the payment of "constructive mileage" (i.e., payment for travel between sessions although the member remained in Washington), fixed *per diem* at only four dollars when a member was absent without excuse, prohibited the distribution of free books to members, and circumscribed payments from the contingent fund. Lincoln voted for the passage of the bill.[17]

On the same day that the mileage debate began Lincoln was appointed to a special house committee on erecting a marble column at York, Virginia, to commemorate the surrender of Cornwallis.[18] It was a large committee. No report was made of its meetings. The assignment perhaps brought Lincoln into somewhat closer relation with Wilmot, who represented Pennsylvania.

The second session of the Thirtieth Congress was a "lame duck" affair. The Democrats had lost control of the Presidency and this made the Whig majority in the House even more contemptuous of the administration. Its conduct in the short session

---

[14] *Globe,* pp. 200, 224-31, 271-74, 338, 371, 406, 568, 574.

[15] One of the many instances of the abuse of the system was that of Morse of Louisiana. He paid about $100 in travel expense, and charged about $2,000.

[16] *Annals of Congress,* 14th session, pp. 1122-34, 1158, 1183 f. See Charles M. Wiltse, *John C. Calhoun, Nationalist 1782–1828* (1947), pp. 112 f., 124 f., 128-30.

[17] *Globe,* p. 574.

[18] *Globe,* p. 112.

displayed more than one instance of disregard that was little short of insulting. For example, a month after the session's opening Stanton, a Tennessee Democrat, pointed out that messages from the Chief Executive had been on the Speaker's table for several days. Some had been received during the first session, months ago. Speaker Winthrop cited the House rule that the House was the judge of its procedure, and made the point that the Speaker was the servant of the House, not of the President. The messages were not read.[19]

Flippant contempt reached a greater depth soon after. Houston, a Democrat from Alabama, proposed an appropriation of $10,000 for the painting of the portraits of all Presidents since Washington (whose portrait was already in the White House). Andrew Johnson, always on guard against unnecessary expenditures, proposed to reduce the amount to $5,000; the honest yeomanry, he said, would not submit to large appropriations for such purpose. Curbed by the Chairman (C. B. Smith) on the ground that his remarks were out of order, Johnson withdrew his original amendment and offered another, striking out $9,999 of the appropriation. Schenck then moved to amend Johnson's amendment by specifying that the remaining dollar be used to procure a portrait of President Polk.[20]

One of the forward-looking proposals presented to Lincoln's Congress was a resolution offered by Amos Tuck. A preamble recited the evils of war and asserted that the people were disposed to cooperate in preventing the outbreak of new wars. The resolution would have instructed the Committee on Foreign Affairs to invite the Secretary of State to confer with other nations and to draft treaties which would submit future disputes to arbitration. Tuck's intent was to establish a congress of nations to determine international law and settle international disputes. He tried again to get the resolution before the House, but both times he failed.[21]

The slavery question had blocked attempts to provide territorial government for California and New Mexico. But presumably it would not arise in considering organization of territorial government for Minnesota. A bill for this purpose was intro-

[19] *Globe*, p. 144.
[20] *Globe*, 335 f.
[21] *Globe*, p. 267.

duced; it was the Senate bill, framed under the leadership of Douglas.[22] C. B. Smith brought it before the House for his committee, recommending that it be passed promptly. But the cumbersome House rules were a hurdle: the bill contained an appropriation, and all appropriations must go before the Committee of the Whole. This made delay inevitable.

When the Minnesota bill came up again it was necessary to suspend the rules to bring it before the House, and this took time.[23] Then Rockwell, a Whig from Massachusetts, raised the point of order whether the bill might be amended. It became clear that he intended to amend it by including the antislavery restriction of the Northwest Ordinance. Immediately parliamentary obstructions multiplied. But presently the main question was taken: the consideration of amendments offered by the Committee on Territories. The first item was trifling as such, but indicative of the bitter partisanship in the House: to specify the effective date of the bill as the tenth day of March, 1849. The obvious motive was to make it impossible for the present Democratic administration to appoint the territorial officials. The point was so petty that the amendment was rejected. Then a motion to lay the whole bill on the table (insuring indefinite postponement) was defeated. Lincoln voted "Aye" on the rejected amendment and "Nay" on the motion to table. Seven amendments were adopted without debate, some clauses eliminated, and then the question of effective date reappeared. Kaufman of Texas noted that the purpose was to take appointments out of Polk's hands. But the studied discourtesy was deliberate. The most intransigent Whig knew that no Democrat who might be offered appointment would be foolish enough to accept an office with assured tenure of less than two weeks. But the amendment was adopted; Lincoln so voted.[24]

Even so, the Minnesota bill was not passed by the House until February 28, dangerously close to the end of the session.[25] Fortunately the Senate was less obstructive, but even with its more efficient organization the delay caused by the House gave

[22] *Globe,* p. 448.

[23] *Globe,* p. 485.

[24] *Globe,* pp. 581-83.

[25] *Globe,* p. 617.

scant time for it to consider amendments. The bill was passed by the Senate on the last day, March third.[26]

A highly constructive piece of legislation stands to the credit of the Thirtieth Congress: the establishment of the Department of the Interior. But this bill met with opposition in the House. Vinton of Ohio sponsored the act finally adopted, and since he was a Whig he could not be charged with administration bias.[27] But White of New York tried to displace Vinton's bill with one of his own. Cobb of Georgia moved to refer the bill to the Committee of the Whole, which, as Vinton protested, would have buried it as deep as the bottom of the ocean. He made a strong plea to persuade the House to reject Cobb's motion. When it seemed that Vinton's view would prevail, other obstructive tactics were used. Finally the bill was ordered to be engrossed. Vinton invited debate and possible amendments.

But Cobb remained a determined opponent of Vinton's bill. When it was brought up Cobb raised the question of a message from the Senate, treating a routine matter as one of high importance. Vinton, for the moment outmaneuvered, had to acquiesce. Then when he moved to reconsider the earlier vote, making it clear that he did so only to present opportunity for further examination of the bill, Alexander Stephens came to Cobb's aid by moving to lay the motion on the table. It was done. Late in the day, however, the calendar was cleared, Vinton's bill came up, it was read a third time, and it was passed.[28] Lincoln voted for its passage. The establishment of this department became an important factor in his later attempt to get a patronage appointment for himself.

On February 14, 1848, the provision of the Constitution which required the counting of the electoral vote was carried out, although by no means solemnly. Preparation was begun earlier, when Barrow (a Whig of Tennessee) and McClelland (a Democrat of Michigan) were appointed the House's tellers.[29]

---

[26] Actually it was Sunday, March 4. For the passage of the Minnesota Territory Bill by the Senate, see *Globe*, p. 681.

[27] *Globe*, pp. 513, 542 f. The establishment of the Department of the Interior was on the recommendation of Walker, the Secretary of the Treasury, under whose jurisdiction the functions of the new department had been until its establishment.

[28] *Globe*, pp. 542 ff.

[29] *Globe*, p. 491.

On the fourteenth Barrow presented his resolution notifying the Senate that the House was ready to proceed, and inviting the Senate to the House chamber for the official count.

Evidently the Senate was unconscionably tardy, for the House ran out of business. At length Sawyer, an Ohio Democrat, suggested that inasmuch as there appeared to be no business some way be found to dispense with the resolution which had been sent. This occasioned laughter, which led Sawyer to say, "we on this [the Democratic] side of the House give up this matter. We do not want to contest it further (renewed laughter), We believe we are beaten (roars of laughter), and I move a reconsideration." Several members demanded, "A reconsideration of the election?" To occupy time, apparently, someone moved that a new hall for the House, better adapted to its work, be provided. Cocke of Tennessee suggested that the ladies in the gallery be admitted to the floor of the House. Atkinson of Virginia objected on the ground that the House was no place for ladies; they would be in bad company there.

Fortunately, as though to prevent the quality of Congressional wit from descending further, the Senate appeared, led by Vice President Dallas, and took seats in the semicircle in front of the Speaker. Jefferson Davis was the Senate's teller. The Vice President, at the Speaker's right, presided. He briefly stated the procedure which would comply with the constitutional requirements, and the canvass of the vote was made accordingly. Dallas presented to Senator Davis the certificate sent by the Maine electors, which was read by Davis. The figures were written in duplicate by the tellers. Davis presented the results from ten states, and the two House tellers reported the remainder in turn.

The irrepressible little Alexander Stephens, after the Vice President had formally certified the vote of Maine, rose and suggested that the reading of the remaining results be omitted. Dallas ruled that no motion was in order; no other procedure could be followed.

When the scrutiny of the returns from the states was completed, the Vice President found, to no one's surprise, that Zachary Taylor had received a majority of the electoral votes for President, and that Millard Fillmore had received a majority of the electoral votes for Vice President. Therefore, he officially pronounced, they had been elected. The joint meeting then dissolved, the Senate returned to its chamber, and on motion of

Barrow the remaining duty of the House was discharged by the appointment of two members to notify the President and the Vice President-elect of their election. And then (to quote the *Congressional Globe*), the House adjourned.[30]

The volume of House business yet to be transacted was apparent by this time, and next day Truman Smith, the influential Whig of Connecticut, undertook to do something about it. He attempted to have House rule 34 suspended from February 25 until the end of the session.[31] This was conservative enough. This rule was a time-consuming device. By it any member might offer an amendment to any motion before the House, and speak on it for five minutes. In practice this *pro-forma* amendment was used by members to make five minute speeches upon whatever subject was on their minds. The custom was for a loquacious Congressman to offer an amendment, make his speech, and withdraw his amendment.

Conservative as Smith's proposal was (it would apply on eight days only) it failed. Schenck of Ohio, always an obstructionist, objected, and it was laid on the table.

Another attempt to expedite business failed the next day. Caleb Smith of Indiana proposed that rule 26 be altered so that the previous question could not be moved on the same day that it was ordered.[32] This expedient would have prevented the purely parliamentary tactic by which action could be indefinitely postponed. It was a favorite means of last resort to block or delay passage of bills when it seemed probable that a favorable vote was likely to follow.

Long John Wentworth of Chicago made a forthright speech on Caleb Smith's proposal.[33] He was eager to expedite business, but he deemed this means as ill adapted to that purpose. What he wanted was for members to have the courage to face issues and vote upon them. Under the present rule members who were afraid to vote upon a delicate question could prevent the vote being taken by voting against the motion to put the previous question; if Smith's plan were in effect they would not have to do even that. Under the rule important legislation was often

---

[30] *Globe*, pp. 434 f.

[31] *Globe*, p. 542.

[32] *Globe*, p. 543.

[33] *Globe*, pp. 548 f.

effectually blocked. For example, Wentworth said, although a majority professed to favor a bill for the suppression of the slave trade in the District of Columbia, it slept the sleep of death on the Speaker's table. So also slept the territorial bill, which would not be touched unless an indignant and betrayed people awoke Congress to its duty. The Wilmot Proviso, homestead legislation, the direct election of the President, and other weighty measures stood no chance. "With some politicians," he said bitterly, "the people lose all importance after election." Caleb Smith's proposal was also laid on the table.

Undoubtedly strong measures were needed, but the cumbersome House rules effectually impeded action. Frequently there was so much disorder that business was interrupted. This led Turner of Illinois to propose that an experienced police officer be posted in the galleries.[34] This was not done, but the House voted to meet at 11 o'clock instead of noon.

Tempers were frayed, and partisanship reached a new low when a detail of the peace treaty was brought up.[35] The House had before it a bill to carry out the provisions of Article 12, involving the payment of $15,000,000 to Mexico in consideration of her cession of territory. Grinnell of Massachusetts offered an amendment disavowing the protocol of the treaty. Of course this was purely obstructionist. Vinton, motivated only by an impartial desire to have the provisions of the treaty carried out, was making an objective statement of the case when the disorder became so great that he was compelled to stop speaking.

No sooner had Vinton's reasonableness disposed of the Grinnell amendment than Schenck offered one still more palpably partisan, to the effect that no payment to any surveyor of the new boundary should be made until such surveyors were authorized by law. Polk already had surveyors on the field to run the boundary, acting under the terms of the ratified treaty. Obviously Schenck wanted those patronage jobs to be at the disposal of the incoming administration. His proposal was ruled out of order. Ashmun offered another similar to Schenck's. It, too, was ruled to be out of order, but the Speaker's ruling was reversed by vote of the House.

Then Schenck made a speech which seems now to be in-

---

[34] *Globe,* p. 554.
[35] *Globe,* pp. 554-59.

credible, and must have seemed so when he made it. He reviewed his attitude toward the war, and deplored the acquisition of Mexican territory. Fully to appreciate his next point a reminder of the situation which then existed is useful. Schenck spoke on February 19, 1849. Gold had been discovered in California more than a year before. While Schenck spoke a small chest of fine California gold lay on a table in the War Department. Since 1848 the Eastern newspapers had carried stories of the discovery at Sutter's Mill. President Polk had referred to it, in a masterpiece of understatement in his annual message of 1848: "recent discoveries," he said, "render it probable that these mines are more extensive and valuable than was anticipated." His reference was, of course, part of his recommendation that territorial government for California and New Mexico be provided. By the time that Schenck spoke the forty-niners were on their mad way. With that background let the *Congressional Globe* report his speech:

The acquisition of these distant territories had brought with them . . . nothing but trouble. Without them we should have been saved from questions of difficulty, the end of which no man can see, the agitation and adjustment of which are even now threatening to destroy the harmony, or even the very existence of our Union. It is true that as a part of this acquisition there has come a region rich in mineral wealth, which seems to have almost stolen away the senses of our people. But was the country any more a blessing to us on that account? He feared not. . . . If it were not irreverent so to speak, he would say that, in the Providence of God, it seemed as if this abundance of gold in California had been permitted to be discovered so that it might work retributive justice on us for having stolen the country from Mexico. . . . This "gold fever" . . . threatened to convert us all into a nation of gamblers.

This from the future author of a book on draw poker!

Schenck had been speaking on a *pro forma* amendment, the suspension of which had failed of adoption. His amendment authorized and directed the President "to enter forthwith into negotiations with the Government of Mexico for the surrender to the said Republic of all the territories known as New Mexico and California."

Incredible as it seems, Schenck's amendment was defended by Root of Ohio, and much time was wasted debating it. The mysteriousness of the ways of Congress appeared in the adoption of Schenck's amendment! But when the amended bill came up the vote adopting Schenck's amendment was reconsidered, and the amendment was rejected. It was a motley group who last voted in its favor, including the die-hard abolitionists Ashmun, Giddings, Horace Mann, and Palfrey, and the two proslavery Georgians, Stephens and Toombs. Then the bill was passed. Lincoln voted against Schenck's amendment and for the bill.[36]

The California question was mauled again on February 22. Earlier John Wentworth had candidly pointed out that it was commonly understood that no territorial bill would be passed by this Congress: "It was an old farce which they were playing . . . in order to humbug the anti-slavery people of the North. . . . There was a disposition . . . to create an impossibility to act. . . . There was a balance of power among the northern men on this floor, who were playing one game here, and another at home. To take up the bills would be to expose their own course." [37] As though in confirmation of Wentworth's charge, Gregory, a New Jersey Whig on the Committee of Commerce, offered a bill to extend the revenue laws of the United States over California and to establish a collection district there. Desirable as this minimum was, it was opposed by every parliamentary tactic possible under the House rules. Turner of Illinois pointed out the dereliction of duty in failing to provide the protection of territorial government where these laws would operate. Giddings brought into the open the latent implication of the slavery question by asking whether extending the revenue laws would not also extend the coastwise slave trade. The bill was passed, although it had to be done over again later.[38]

Next day Turner made a speech which tacitly accepted the assumption that territorial government would not be provided by this Congress, and proposed that the two territories be permitted to come into the Union as states.[39] This was done a year later in the case of California.

The candor of Wentworth and Turner (and others) apparently had effect. On February 27 a bill for California territorial government was debated. The parliamentary wrangling exceeded anything which had preceded. During debate the antislavery clause of the Northwest Ordinance was written into the bill.

---

[36] *Globe*, p. 559.

[37] *Globe*, p. 553 f.

[38] *Globe*, pp. 583 f.

[39] *Globe*, pp. 587-90.

McClernand of Illinois made a highly rational speech. He stressed the urgent need for territorial government, citing the instance of the murder of an emigrant family from Illinois (a Mr. Reed, his wife and five children). McClernand wished that a bill could be passed which would definitely and forever settle the slavery question. But the debate soon lost all pacific temper. As though the Northwest Ordinance clause were not enough, a substitute bill containing the Wilmot Proviso was offered instead. The substitute bill included New Mexico, and to the great umbrage of Kaufman of Texas, Greeley (who was responsible for the inclusion of New Mexico) proposed that New Mexico contain much of the territory claimed by Texas.[40] The impossible substitute bill was rejected, and the original bill passed, Lincoln voting for it.[41] But alas! it conflicted with the Senate bill, which was not acceptable to the House. As Wentworth predicted, no bill was passed by the Thirtieth Congress.

In spite of wrangling to obstruct essential legislation, another necessary act of high quality was passed by the House on March 1. This was the act providing for the seventh Decennial Census.[42] It was sponsored in the House by Palfrey, who had shown little ability in mastering House procedure, and, except for admirable consistency in his antislavery views, little interest in legislation. In the census bill he demonstrated the value of having a scholar in politics. His bill was a substitute for one previously written. As is well known, the data of the Seventh Census (of 1850) are much more inclusive and of greater value than those of earlier census reports.

Inasmuch as March 4 fell on Sunday in 1849, the inauguration of the new administration had to be held on March 5. This was of small consequence. What was important was that Congress must complete its work on the third. The volume of business at the end of any session was enormous, but only the reading of the record demonstrates the folly of the members of the Thirtieth Congress in their earlier procrastination and their stubborn refusal to accept measures to expedite work.[43] To illustrate,

---

[40] *Globe,* pp. 605-08.

[41] *Globe,* pp. 608-12.

[42] *Globe,* pp. 638 f.

[43] In view of the failure of the Thirtieth Congress to enact vital legislation, it is ironical that during the last days of the session a joint Congressional committee on the inaugural ball (of which Lincoln was a mem-

Congress was supposed to adjourn no later than midnight on the last day, but even with the expedient of night sessions so essential a measure as an appropriation bill was not ready for the President's signature until Sunday morning.

The triviality of the routine business on the three days of March has to be illustrated to be believed. With appropriation bills yet to be passed, not to mention final action on the territorial bills, Dixon (Whig, Connecticut) brought up a report on the then hotly debated question whether Dr. Jackson or Dr. Morton was to be credited with the first use of anesthesia in surgery.[44]

But Congressman Schenck could be depended upon to resort to something more farfetched than any colleague could think up. Still later that same evening he moved to suspend the rules to take up a bill for the relief of the captors of the frigate *Philadelphia*.[45] This would have gone back to the War of 1812; no doubt Schenck would have made an impassioned plea for the widows and children of that gallant band. But the *Globe* was unusually terse. It has only one word: Rejected.

There can be no doubt that there was a concerted agreement, based upon quite unidealistic motives, to determine what legislation should and should not be considered and passed by the House in the closing days of the session. On the next to the last day the first person to be recognized was one of the inner group of Whigs, Truman Smith. He pointed out that on the calendar of the Committee of the Whole there was a bill to establish a board of commissioners on Mexican claims. As Chairman of the Committee on Foreign Affairs he urged that the bill ought to pass, and moved a suspension of the rules to bring it up. Strange to say, two-thirds so voted. Then as the bill was being read Truman Smith interposed and said that inasmuch as

---

ber) was busy planning that social affair. The Chicago *Journal* reported the committee's achievements on March 1, 1849. No blame attaches to the committee members for giving time to this adjunct to the inauguration of the President. But they, including Lincoln, are censurable for failing to enact needed legislation, and for voting down proposals to expedite Congressional business.

[44] *Globe*, p. 642. Instead of following the suggestion of Dr. Oliver W. Holmes (that the busts of the two doctors be placed on a common base, with the word "Ether" inscribed beneath them), Dixon defended the claim of a third doctor, a man named Wells.

[45] *Globe*, p. 644.

he had a substitute bill it would save time if further reading were omitted. McClernand, doubtless suspecting what was planned, but powerless to prevent it, demanded that the bill be read. Smith then said that he was instructed to offer three amendments, and went on to say that instead of doing so he would offer a substitute bill (which turned out to be the Senate bill on the same subject) to which he would attach the three amendments. He sent his amendments to the Speaker, and the substitute bill with the amendments was read.[46]

Whether or not the House members perceived it, this bill set up valuable patronage jobs. Probably that is why it was lifted out of its order on the calendar and kept on its way to passage in the crowded last hours of the session. More than likely the Whigs who were personally interested in the bill's patronage possibilities saw nothing ironical in their zeal to pass it.

The Whig cohort worked together. Presently, while the claims bill was being debated, the Army appropriation bill came to the House from the Senate. The advocate of the claims bill yielded for the purpose of getting the money bill referred to the proper committee, and committees were permitted to meet while debate proceeded. Then by what at a later date would have been called steam-roller tactics, hostile amendments to Truman Smith's bill were voted down, the bill was read for the second and third time, engrossed, and passed.[47] One wonders whether anyone remembered what had happened to the bill to implement Section 12 of the peace treaty, when every dilatory tactic in the book was used to prevent the passage of a bill which, like this one, was designed to carry out provisions of the treaty. The only fact essential to complete the story is that Caleb Smith of Indiana, who worked closely with his namesake from Connecticut, became a member of the board set up by this bill.

John Wentworth demonstrated that he was in earnest in his caustic remarks about the fear of some members to vote when the slavery issue emerged. The Senate had sent a bill extending the Constitution and the laws of the United States over the new territories—conceding defeat in the attempt to organize territorial government. Wentworth favored the Senate bill. He had the courage to propose an amendment, attaching the Wilmot

---

[46] *Globe*, pp. 656-61.
[47] *Globe*, p. 662.

Proviso to the Senate bill. His amendment was rejected without a roll call.[48]

This came up late in the afternoon. Early in the evening Wentworth returned to his attempt, this time offering the slavery restriction clause of the Northwest Ordinance. Amid great excitement this amendment was ruled out of order. Appeal was made, and by the narrowest of margins (85-84) the Chairman's decision was sustained.[49]

Antislavery men flocked to Wentworth's aid. Several other antislavery amendments were offered and rejected. One which disturbed the usually imperturbable Polk proposed that the laws of Mexico remain in force until repealed by Congress. This was a typical Whig dodge. To continue Mexican law would be an indirect way to prohibit slavery. But Mexican law validated the institution of peonage, with the peons attached to the land— thus giving the landowner all the advantages of slavery while relieving him of all obligation to care for his dependent laborers. When Polk went to the Capitol to sign bills he carried with him a written veto to use in the event that the bill passed. But it did not.[50]

Indeed, it appeared that Congress would adjourn without even extending the revenue laws to the new territories, for when the last Senate amendment came up for debate it was defeated. Lincoln voted against it, thus aligning himself with those who declined to give minimum protection to the people of those extensive territories.[51]

The House sat until 11 o'clock on Friday night, and later than that on Saturday (and Sunday). On Saturday, when it was obvious that the volume of business would be very great, Ashmun took the floor to ask the House to appropriate $400 to reimburse a sculptor who had made a bust of John Quincy Adams. It was more than doubtful that the House could be induced to use the time to do what Ashmun asked. However, Grinnell, another Massachusetts Whig, settled it. He said that he did not wish to

---

[48] *Globe,* p. 663.

[49] *Globe,* p. 663.

[50] *Globe,* pp. 663 f; Quaife, *Polk's Diary,* IV:365.

[51] *Globe,* pp. 664 f. This is perhaps the most discreditable vote that Lincoln cast as Congressman. His ill-advised act was prompted, apparently, by his following the majority of his party.

hear the name of John Quincy Adams connected with money in this Hall; he offered to make the payment himself if the House would adopt the remainder of Ashmun's resolution (accepting the bust and placing it in the Speaker's room). It was done.[52]

Regard for the revered Adams justified Ashmun's using time as he did, but nothing could excuse the utter silliness of a resolution of Horace Greeley, which was read a second time before it had to give way to the naval appropriations bill. Greeley, with entire seriousness, proposed to change the name of "The United States of America" to "Columbia," "in grateful acknowledgment of our obligations to, and in tardy atonement for the injustice hitherto suffered by, the great discoverer of this continent." [53]

Characteristic behavior of Andrew Johnson enlivened the weary members toward the close of the session. A conventional resolution of appreciation of Speaker Winthrop "for the able, impartial, and dignified manner in which he has discharged his duties" was offered by McDowell of Virginia while Howell Cobb was temporarily in the Chair. The resolution, which no doubt others expected would be adopted without demur, was violently objected to by the Tennessee Democrat whose stubbornness was already proverbial. He moved to strike out the word "impartial", harangued against Winthrop, particularly criticizing his committee assignments and his giving recognition to speak.[54]

The long day wore on, with little of interest and in the late hours little of importance. The House must remain in session until appropriation bills had been finally disposed of, and various members used the available time to attempt the passage of bills. John Wentworth, for example, made a last valiant attempt to resuscitate the Senate bill making a land grant for Illinois railroads. He failed.[55]

Lincoln's friend, Richard W. Thompson of Indiana, did however, achieve something of a triumph in one of the last things done by the Thirtieth Congress. "Dick" Thompson was a moderate on the slavery question. He exhibited the practical usefulness of accepting a basic minimum, rather than lose all, by sponsoring

[52] *Globe*, p. 692.

[53] *Globe*, p. 594.

[54] *Globe*, p. 695.

[55] *Globe*, p. 698.

in the House a substitute for the Senate bill (which had been rejected by the House) extending the Constitution and laws of the United States over the new territories. He made a brief but impressive speech, warning of the consequences of failure. Again every conceivable obstruction was used to block Thompson's proposal. Time wore on, and when the hands of the clock reached 11:15 (before midnight) they ceased to move—the clock was stopped to preserve the legal fiction of adjournment before midnight. To make a long story short, Thompson's effort was crowned with success. Four time-consuming roll calls were required, Lincoln always voting for the passage.[56] Finally the House agreed to the Senate bill as amended (i.e., extending the revenue laws over California).[57]

These closing hours had their incidents of boisterousness and disorder. Representative Meade of Virginia pushed his fist into Gidding's face and seized him by the collar. Later Johnson of Arkansas got into fisticuffs with Ficklin of Illinois, and Inge of Alabama joined the brawl. Ficklin got the worst of it with some loss of blood.[58]

Early Sunday morning (by the sun; it was still Saturday night by the House clock) it became apparent that there was no point in waiting longer for communications from the Senate. The House then performed a duty conspicuously omitted at the end of the long session; it sent a committee to the President, notifying him that the House was ready to adjourn, and asking whether he had any further communications to make to the House.[59] Just before Rockwell of Connecticut reported for the committee, the President's secretary brought a message that the President had signed the Civil and Diplomatic Appropriations Bill and the bill extending the revenue laws over California. Rockwell reported that the President had no further communication to make to the House.[60] At 7 o'clock Sunday morning Kauf-

---

[56] Globe, pp. 696 f.

[57] Globe, p. 697. Petit, an Indiana Democrat, attempted to filibuster the bill. He forced a delay of roll call until nearly midnight, and then embarked upon an hour-long speech. But the clock was stopped, and at the end of his hour business was resumed.

[58] Julian, Life of Giddings, p. 220; Giddings, History of the Rebellion, p. 209; Giddings, Diary (final entry).

[59] Globe, p. 698.

[60] Globe, p. 698; Quaife, Polk's Diary, IV:369.

man of Texas moved adjournment. The Speaker made a graceful speech of appreciation and farewell, and the House of the Thirtieth Congress adjourned *sine die*. Lincoln had had his last experience as a member of a legislative body.[61]

---

[61] *Globe*, p. 698. Lincoln was elected to the State Legislature in 1854, but he resigned before taking his seat.

13

SLAVERY

"The agitation of the slavery question is mischievous and wicked, and proceeds from no patriotic motive by its authors. It is a mere political question on which demagogues & ambitious politicians hope to promote their own prospects for political promotion. And this they seem willing to do even at the hazard of disturbing the harmony if not dissolving the Union itself. Such agitation with such objects deserves the reprobation of all the lovers of the Union & of their country." Thus wrote the President, alluding to activities of certain members of the Thirtieth Congress.[1] The record bears him out.

In the first (the long) session of Lincoln's Congress the slavery issue came before the House many times. A certain trend can be observed in Lincoln's votes: he voted consistently to receive and refer antislavery petitions. December 21, 1847 a petition was presented by citizens of the District of Columbia, praying for the repeal of all laws establishing the slave trade in the District. On a motion to table Lincoln voted "Nay."[2] A week later Caleb Smith presented such a petition from citizens of Indiana; Lincoln voted against tabling it.[3] Two days later Amos

---

[1] Quaife, *Polk's Diary,* IV:251.

[2] *Globe,* 30th Congress, 2nd Session, p. 60.

[3] *Globe,* p. 73.

Tuck offered a petition of residents of Philadelphia that money from the sale of public lands be applied to the extinction of slavery throughout the nation. Again Lincoln voted against tabling.[4] He voted similarly on other occasions.[5] This much is clear. Lincoln was consistently with the principle so nobly vindicated by John Quincy Adams: the right of citizens to petition their representatives, and the duty of legislators to receive and consider petitions.

But it does not follow that an antislavery attitude is discernible in these votes. Amos Tuck, on May 29, 1848, asked unanimous consent to introduce a resolution. It directed the committees to which the antislavery petitions had been referred to report a bill. He moved to suspend the rules in order to get the resolution before the House. On the motion there was a clear-cut division between the proslavery and the antislavery men. All abolitionists and antislavery men voted to suspend the rules. Southern members, Whigs and Democrats alike, and a few Northern Whigs voted against suspension, thus blocking consideration of the resolution. Lincoln was one of the majority voting against consent to introduce the resolution.[6]

Lincoln presented only one antislavery petition. On February 28, 1849 he offered the "petition of J. M. Sturtevant and others, citizens of Morgan County, Illinois, praying for the abolition of the slave trade in the District of Columbia."[7] This solitary instance contrasts strongly with the activity of the militant antislavery men. Palfrey, Tuck, and Giddings (and Horace Mann in the short session) presented numerous such petitions, with many signatures. Tuck and Giddings referred antislavery petitions of citizens of Illinois; Tuck offered that of William Brown and 21 others of Winnebago County, and Giddings handed in one of 813 citizens of the same county. Again Giddings brought three: one of E. R. H. Parker and 52 other ladies of DuPage County, another of Alice Coleman and 367 ladies, and still another of Rhoda L. Barbour and 81 other ladies of Illinois. Giddings was easily the champion antislavery petition presenter; on one oc-

---

[4] *Globe*, p. 82.

[5] *Globe*, pp. 180, 391; *Journal*, p. 325.

[6] *Journal*, p. 840.

[7] *Ibid.*, p. 568; DNA RG 233, HR 30A F5 (3).

casion he had a petition which carried no less than 8,773 signatures.[8]

The fact that Lincoln presented only one antislavery petition is not to be stressed. The probable reason that he offered only one is that his constituency was not opposed to slavery. Naturally militant opponents of slavery routed their petitions through abolitionist Congressmen.

Another instance of Lincoln's moderateness toward the slavery question during the first session was his reaction to the great excitement which developed when about eighty slaves were rescued from a Washington slave jail, placed on a steamer to transport them to freedom, and were retaken and returned to the jail. The affair stirred bitter debate in Congress. When the acrimony reached a dangerous point, Brown, a Mississippi Democrat, moved to lay the whole subject on the table, on the ground that the excitement ought to be allowed to pass, and moved also that report of the debate ought not to be made public. Lincoln, who had taken no part in the debate, voted with the majority to table.[9] What Giddings did shall appear.

Nor had Lincoln uttered a word of protest when a Negro waiter in a Washington boardinghouse was seized by three slave traders. That outrage was another occasion for Giddings to exert himself. He used it to introduce resolutions to investigate the advisability of abolishing the slave trade in the District, or to relocate the national capital in a free state.[10] Lincoln was silent.

Another conspicuous instance developed during the first session. A private bill, providing compensation for a slave who had been abducted by the British in 1814, came up. The abolitionists voted solidly against it, with Giddings taking the lead. To him it was a highly important question, and by their votes on it he divided the sheep from the goats. He praised Root, Palfrey, and Tuck. He held Truman Smith in contempt. He did not mention Lincoln, but his classification would have been automatic: Lincoln voted for the bill.[11]

---

[8] *Globe,* 30th Congress, 1st Session, pp. 319, 360, 402, 481 (this is the petition with 8,773 signatures), 533, 544, 761, 827; *Globe,* 30th Congress, 2nd Session, pp. 323, 394, 431, 480.

[9] For the whole incident, *Globe,* 30th Congress, 2nd Session, pp. 641, 649-673; for Brown's resolution and Lincoln's vote, *Globe,* 672 f.

[10] *Globe,* 179 f.

[11] *Globe,* pp. 784 f.

The most important vote involving slavery which Lincoln gave in the first session was on the bills setting up territorial government in Oregon. Polk foresaw the problems which inevitably arose, and attempted to settle them by having the Missouri Compromise extended to the Pacific. He did not assume, however, that this would necessarily open all territory south of the line to slavery. On the contrary, he assumed that since it was not suited to slave labor it would probably not be slave territory. He also correctly saw that the best way to handle the question was to consider California first and alone, and to permit her to become a state without going through the territorial period; understanding perfectly that if this were done California would be a free state. Polk's hope, in recommending the extension of the compromise line, was that each question would be met by itself, and the dangerous agitation of the slavery question would be avoided.[12] Nevertheless when the matter was first proposed in the House (August 11, 1848) the extension was voted down by the decisive vote of 82-121. Lincoln voted against the extension.[13]

Earlier Lincoln had voted to table the Senate bill for territorial governments in Oregon, California, and New Mexico; the bill occasioned a most violent discussion of slavery.[14] The House action stirred the President to write in his *Diary* under that date that he regarded the vote as most unfortunate, adding his belief that if no Presidential election were pending the bill would have passed.[15]

The House framed its own bill for Oregon alone. It included the antislavery clause of the Northwest Ordinance. Proslavery men stubbornly tried to eliminate this provision, but they were outvoted; Lincoln voted to retain it.[16] The bill was passed by the Senate August 12, the next to the last day of the session, in an all-night meeting.

The implication was obvious. Territorial organization for Oregon could be secured: because it lay so far north it certainly would not become a slave state. But because California and New

---

[12] Polk, *Diary*, IV:12 f, 20 f, 65, 66 f, 207.

[13] *Globe*, p. 1062.

[14] *Globe*, p. 1007; *Journal*, pp. 1124, 1126.

[15] Quaife, *Polk's Diary*, IV:34.

[16] *Globe*, p. 1027, *Journal*, pp. 1154 f.

Mexico lay correspondingly south, latitude alone insured argument over slavery. Latitude was sufficient; it did not matter that factors of soil, climate, and probable economic development were all unfavorable to slavery there. Thus the stage was set for acrimonious discussion of slavery in the short session—and for the crisis of 1850.

Early in the second session the question arose. Within a week from the beginning the abolitionist Palfrey asked leave to introduce a bill repealing all acts of Congress establishing slavery and the slave trade in the District of Columbia. Lincoln voted "Nay."[17] But on the same day, when Root offered a resolution instructing the Committee on Territories to offer a bill for territorial government for New Mexico and California, excluding slavery therefrom, Lincoln twice voted in favor of the resolution, which was adopted.[18]

A similar "yes and no" attitude was evinced by Lincoln presently. There was a motion to reconsider the vote on the Root resolution, and then a motion to table the motion to reconsider. On the motion to table Lincoln voted "Yea" with the majority.[19] But when Giddings introduced a bill "to authorize the people of the District of Columbia to express their desire as to the existence of slavery therein," Lincoln voted to table it.[20] It is odd that although he consistently voted to receive antislavery petitions he opposed the passage of a bill which would have enabled an expression of opinion.

Shortly after this Lincoln showed himself clearly on the proslavery side. Gott, a New York Whig, presented a resolution looking toward the abolition of the slave trade in the District. Lincoln voted to lay it on the table, deserting Giddings, Mann, Collamer, Palfrey, and Tuck, who voted against tabling. Lincoln was consistently negative, voting against the main question (to adopt), and when the main question was put, voting against adoption. His vote did no good; the Gott resolution was adopted.[21] It was, however, to be the occasion of further bitter debate.

---

[17] *Globe*, p. 38; Lincoln voted against granting Palfrey leave to introduce his bill.

[18] *Globe*, p. 39.

[19] *Globe*, p. 55.

[20] *Globe*, pp. 55 f.

[21] *Globe*, pp. 83-85.

A long and angry debate began on December 23. A bill was brought up, by parliamentary legerdemain, which had been reported earlier by Burt (Democrat) of South Carolina. The bill was for the relief of the heirs of one Antonio Pacheco, proposing to pay them $1,000 to compensate for a slave transported to the West in 1837.[22]

This was the story: Pacheco had a slave, Lewis, who was hired by the army in the Seminole wars as interpreter and guide. Lewis was captured by enemy Indians, and held by one of their chiefs, Jumper. Claimed by Pacheco when the war ended, the slave Lewis was regarded as having acted with the enemy, and on General Jessup's order he was transported with the Indians and was thus lost to his owner.

The facts were agreed to in majority and minority committee reports, but the minority recommended that Pacheco was not entitled to relief. Translated into nonpolitical terms, the incident was the means for another explosive airing of the slavery issue: the majority of the committee was proslavery and wanted to make a test case of the slave Lewis, the minority was antislavery, opposing payment not in dispute of the facts, but on the ground that there was no such thing as property in a slave. It became a test case, a *cause célèbre*, with Giddings the protagonist.

Giddings was well suited to that role.[23] He represented a hotbed antislavery district (part of the Connecticut Reserve in Ohio). He was absolutely consistent in his views. He had opposed the annexation of Texas. He had regarded the Mexican War as a proslavery move and opposed it at every point. His position in regard to the slave Lewis was predictable, as was his attitude toward government in the newly acquired territories. Whatever could be construed as the antislavery side of a question was his side.

He was as fearless as he was consistent. When the eighty slaves taken from the slave jail were recaptured the incident threatened to result in riot. An antislavery journal, the *National Era*, did much to fan the excitement, and a mob threatened to destroy its press. Mobs surrounded the jail, promising dire injury

---

[22] *Globe*, p. 95.

[23] *Dictionary of American Biography*, VII:260 f; Julian. References in present work are based upon Gidding's own writings (letters, speeches, and *Diary*), the *Congressional Globe*, and the *Journal of Congress*.

to anyone abetting the attempt to free the slaves. Giddings coolly walked to the jail, presented himself as a member of Congress, demanded to be taken to the men who had been captured while helping the slaves to escape, and offered to defend them in court. (Hannibal Hamlin, then a Senator, later Vice President in Lincoln's first term, joined Giddings at the jail and made the same offer.) Giddings received threats while going and returning, but he fearlessly faced the mob.

Much of his abolitionist speaking in Congress was with the purpose of inciting opposition. In a letter to his daughter Molly he wrote that "in about another week God willing I shall raise another riot. But the fellows are getting cool and I don't think that I shall be able to strike the *raw* so as to make them kick." [24] He struck the raw and made them kick in the short session, most effectively in the case of the slave Lewis.

It was the purpose of Giddings and his associates to have full debate on the bill for the relief of the heirs of Antonio Pacheco. By dint of parliamentary battling they had their way. To Giddings the case was of the first importance. "This subject," he wrote in his diary, "rests with so much weight on my mind that I cannot sleep at night and is visibly affecting my health." [25] He planned the attack with great care, marshalling his co-workers so that one of them, Dickey of Pennsylvania, presented the parliamentary motion; Giddings knew that if he openly took the lead the motion would be blocked. He prepared his own speech with great care. When he made it he wrote to his wife that "I was full of the *Spirit,* and you may judge of my effort when I say that I had not spoken ten minutes before the sweat rolled down my face, and my underclothes [were] as wet as though I had been in a river. . . . Doughfaces actually turned pale. Those who were never known to vote for freedom before came over and voted with us." [26]

Giddings was pleased by the help he received. Mann and Palfrey counseled with him in the preparation of his speech. Dickey aided him manfully. "Even Grinnell of Massachusetts . . . voted against laying the bill on the table. . . . Gott is now one of the most inveterate free soil men we have. So is Greeley. . . ." [27]

---

[24] Giddings Papers, Library of Congress.

[25] Giddings, *Diary*, Ohio Archaeological and Historical Society.

[26] Giddings letters, Ohio Archaeological and Historical Society.

[27] Giddings, *Diary*.

But Giddings got no help from Lincoln. Lincoln voted to terminate debate, and to lay the bill on the table.[28] However, when the bill came up on January 6 he voted that the payment should not be made. The vote was close, and Lincoln took the floor to ascertain that his "Nay" was so listed.[29]

The final outcome was that on January 19 the vote by which the bill had been rejected on the twelfth was reconsidered. This placed the bill again before the House. When it was again voted upon it was passed 105-95. Lincoln voted against reconsideration, and against the bill when it was reconsidered.[30] He thus indicated his agreement at this time, although his vote on a similar bill in the first session was in contradiction, that the Constitution did not recognize property in a slave.

Now the Gott resolution again became a thorny issue. By its terms the appropriate committee was instructed to report a bill abolishing the slave trade in the District. There was a long debate on December 27 on a motion to reconsider the vote by which the Gott resolution had been adopted. When it was moved to lay on the table the motion to reconsider, the abolitionists and antislavery people unitedly voted "Aye," but Lincoln voted "Nay" with the majority.[31] When the debate was resumed the motion to reconsider was, after bitter wrangling, forced before the House. Lincoln voted with the majority to reconsider.[32] It is noteworthy that in his votes on Gott's resolution Lincoln aligned himself against Giddings and the abolitionists. Yet when Goggin moved to lay the whole subject on the table, Lincoln with the majority (which included the abolitionists) voted "Nay." [33]

It is difficult now, more than one hundred years after the event, to picture the excitement which this heated debate caused. When Gott's resolution carried it was a stunning surprise to the proslavery men. They immediately attempted to have its adoption canceled. When their attempt was decided by the Speaker to be against the rules, something of their feeling is suggested by the

[28] *Globe,* pp. 123, 129.

[29] *Globe,* p. 177.

[30] *Globe,* p. 303.

[31] *Globe,* p. 107.

[32] *Globe,* p. 216.

[33] *Globe,* p. 216.

proposal of Holmes of South Carolina: that every Southern member leave the House and refuse to take further part in the debate.[34]

The conference of Southern Senators and Representatives, led by Calhoun, was in part in reaction to the adoption of the Gott resolution. President Polk viewed the conference with sincere alarm and did all that the proprieties of his office permitted to weaken its effect.[35] But Calhoun was in deadly earnest.[36] The "Address of Southern Delegates in Congress, to their Constituents," which was in effect Calhoun's pronouncement, began with a reference to the current situation, and noticed bills presented in the present session, including the Gott resolution and others such as that of "a member from Illinois." Thus was Lincoln's proposed substitute for the Gott resolution marked by the great Calhoun.[37]

On January 10 Wentworth brought the Gott resolution up again. This time the last resort of obstruction was used: so many members were absent that a call of the House was required. Again there was a sudden epidemic of "sickness." But no one was deceived, and Wentworth held the floor. His purpose was to force a vote on the resolution, and he caustically pointed out that there were many who would be glad not to vote.

---

[34] *Globe*, p. 84. It is to Lincoln's credit that he did not "skulk" the vote on the Gott resolution. The two eminent Northern Whigs, Truman and Caleb Smith, were in their seats when the vote was taken, but did not vote. When this was called to the Speaker's attention Winthrop said that the House rules required every member present to vote, but there was no means of enforcing the rule.

Something of the scene is suggested by Giddings' letter to Sumner (December 22, 1847, Julian, p. 260): "It was a curious spectacle to look at the members and witness their various emotions. Some were cursing, some looked daggers, some left the hall in disgust, and some were laughing."

Julian commented on Lincoln's vote: "To vote [as Lincoln did] would have been regarded as a direct support of the slave trade. This, few northern men were willing to do. . . . Among other surprises, revealed by this vote . . . is the fact that Abraham Lincoln . . . voted to lay the resolution on the table, voted against its adoption, and then voted for the successful motion to reconsider the vote on its passage, which finally disposed of the question. Unlike several of his northern brethren, he showed no disposition to dodge the question, but placed himself squarely on the side of the South."

[35] Quaife, *Polk's Diary*, IV:280-309.

[36] Henry W. Hilliard, *Politics and Pen Pictures at Home and Abroad* (1892), p. 199.

[37] Richard K. Crallé (editor) Calhoun, *Works* (1851-56), VI:290-313. The reference to Lincoln's proposed bill is on p. 306.

At this juncture Lincoln entered the debate.[38] He had an amendment to offer, and, as it proved, his amendment was a substitute for Gott's resolution. It was a bill to abolish slavery in the District. He moved to omit everything after the word "Resolved," and that with a suitable preamble a bill be inserted which may be thus summarized:

Sec. 1. No person within the District shall ever be held in slavery within it.

Sec. 2. No person now within the District, or anyone owned by anyone in it, or hereafter born within it, shall be held in slavery; except that officers of the Government who are citizens of slave-holding States many bring their personal slaves there temporarily while the owners are on Government service.

Sec. 3. All children born of slave mothers now within the District shall be free after January 1, 1850. They shall be maintained and educated by their mothers' owners until they shall have reached —— years of age. The municipal authorities of Washington and Georgetown shall make provision for the enforcement of this Section.

Sec. 4. Owners of present slaves may emancipate their slaves with compensation, after which such slaves shall be forever free. The President, Secretary of State, and Secretary of the Treasury shall be a board to determine the value of such slaves to be freed. They shall hold a meeting on the first Monday of each month to discharge these duties.

Sec. 5. The municipal authorities of Washington and Georgetown are required to provide active and efficient means to arrest and deliver up to their owners all fugitive slaves escaping into the District.

Sec. 6. The foregoing provisions are to be placed before the free white male citizens of the District over 21 years of age for a referendum vote; if a majority votes to adopt this Act it shall be placed into effect by proclamation of the President.

Sec. 7. Involuntary servitude in punishment of crime shall not be affected by this Act.

Sec. 8. For the purposes of this Act, the jurisdiction of Washington is extended to all parts of the District except Georgetown.[39]

Lincoln, holding the floor by courtesy of Wentworth, said that he was authorized to state that about fifteen of the leading citizens of the District had been shown his proposed bill, and that all had approved it; everyone had desired that some such bill should be passed. He was interrupted with the demand, "Who are they?" "Give us their names." He did not reply.

---

[38] *Globe,* pp. 211 f.

[39] *CW* II:20-22.

The reference to about fifteen leading citizens invites a query. On December 21, 1847 Giddings had offered a petition praying that the slave trade in the District be abolished.[40] The petition carried the signatures of twenty-one residents of the District. One of the signers, Thomas Fitnam, was employed by the House. The following day the *National Intelligencer* printed "A Card" in which Mr. Fitnam stated that he had signed the petition without reading it. He did not endorse it. He opposed it. He had never been an abolitionist. What was more, he said, the man who asked him to sign the petition had afterward erased his own name. "There must have been," Mr. Fitnam reasonably concluded, "A design somewhere to deceive." Were Lincoln's "about fifteen" citizens some of the persons who had signed this petition?

The problem of Lincoln's substitute is further complicated by his giving notice, on January 13, of leave to introduce a bill to abolish slavery in the District "by the consent of the free white people . . . and with compensation to owners." Perhaps his substitute for the Gott resolution was the bill he referred to; the manuscript copy in his writings contains that document, but no copy of a second bill on the subject. No bill was offered by him.[41]

In view of Lincoln's "yes and no" position, how is this more positive act to be understood? Giddings claimed some credit. His *Diary* entry of January 8, 1849 notes that "Mr. Dicky of Pa and Mr. Lincoln of Illinois were busy preparing resolutions to abolish slavery in the D C this morning. I had a conversation with them and advised them that they thereto draw up a bill for that purpose and push it through. They hesitated and finally accepted my proposition. . . . Mr. Lincoln called on me this evening read his bill and asked my opinion which I freely gave." Lincoln then talked with Mr. Seaton, Mayor of Washington. This he reported to Giddings next day, mentioning that Mr. Seaton assumed that Giddings would be opposed to the bill. Lincoln, Giddings wrote, "Thinking that such an idea may be useful, did not undeceive him." Lincoln read his bill to Giddings as he had amended it. Dickey also discussed it. On the eleventh, Giddings wrote "This evening our whole mess remained in the

40 *Globe*, p. 60.
41 *Globe*, p. 244.

dining room after tea and conversed upon the subject of Mr. Lincoln's bill to abolish slavery. It was approved by all. I believed it as good a bill as we could get at this time and was willing to pay for slaves in order to save them from the southern market as I suppose nearly every man . . . would sell his slaves if he saw that slavery was to be abolished."

Some of Giddings' statements must be discounted. If, as he said, the whole mess was present it is incredible that it was approved by all. Mrs. Sprigg's mess housed five Pennsylvanians (Dickey, Blanchard, McIlvane, Pollock, and Strohm), Giddings, and Lincoln. Pollock and Giddings were anything but congenial, and although all members were Whigs there was wide disagreement among them. Busey, a nonpolitical resident, says in his *Reminiscences* that, particularly in heated discussions of slavery, Lincoln was the one who eased strained situations by telling one of his apt stories.[42] But Giddings did not get along with anyone who differed from him on slavery. He described in a letter to his son what one hopes was the worst example of hostility among the Whigs at Mrs. Sprigg's. In a discussion of the proposed admission of California and New Mexico as states, Giddings

denounced it at the breakfast table . . . and it kicked up a row such as we never had at our boarding house. Pollock denounced me as an agitator, and that all I desired was to keep up an excitement. I replied that I was unwilling to have my motives impugned by a miserable Doughface who had not mind enough to form an opinion nor courage enough to avow it. He sprang from the table as he sat opposite and marched around to where I was. I was however on my feet and he cooled down. Dicky and McIlvane interfered, but it is not pleasant living with a scamp & were it not for the name of quarreling I would not stay with the miserable scamp.[43]

One hopes that Lincoln had an especially good story at that juncture.

Giddings wrote presently that his fellow boarders showed more kindness, adding that "Mr. Dicky in particular defends me and quarrels with my persecutors." [44] It does not seem that in such an atmosphere there would be full agreement on a bill which contained the features which distinguish Lincoln's. Quali-

---

[42] Busey, *Recollections*, pp. 25-27.

[43] Giddings, letter to his son, Ohio Archaeological and Historical Society.

[44] Giddings, *Diary*, January 18, 1818.

fied approval was possible only because Tompkins of Mississippi, resident in the first session, lived elsewhere then.

Giddings himself could not have fully approved Lincoln's bill. It contained two features to which he was unalterably opposed: limiting the referendum to adult white males and a fugitive slave clause. Giddings had earlier proposed a referendum, but his idea was that all adult males, including free Negroes and slaves, should vote; he vigorously defended their inclusion. It is impossible that he would countenance the fugitive slave clause. His words show how qualified was the approval which he gave; he accepted the bill by default only because it was "as good a bill as we could get," and he acquiesced in the compensation clause (which was utterly against his principles) only for the practical good that thus liberated slaves would be kept off the Southern market.

The obvious point is that Giddings had been cultivating Lincoln, doubtless hoping to attach him to his coterie of free-soil associates, as he succeeded in doing with Dickey. Dickey and a few others worked loyally and persistently with Giddings throughout the Thirtieth Congress. Lincoln did not. It cannot be other than significant that from the time that Lincoln voted in favor of reconsidering the adoption of Gott's resolution, and then made no effort to push his substitute for it (as Giddings had advised him to do), there is not another reference to Lincoln in the extant writings of Giddings until long after the time of the Thirtieth Congress.

The probable reason may be suggested why Lincoln, after this brief excursion into antislavery legislation, resumed his former moderate position. Giddings failed to attach Lincoln to his group, but Lincoln continued his association with such Southern Whigs as Stephens and Preston, and with moderates among Northern Whigs such as Thompson and Embree. He closely followed the position of the moderates of the party in issues directly and indirectly involving slavery. Taylor was soon to be inaugurated, and Lincoln took no position which might embarrass the incoming administration. This is doubtless why he voted "Nay" on California and New Mexico territorial bills. This is probably why he did not push to a vote his or other bills against slavery in the District.

In any event Lincoln's bill added nothing to his stature as a legislator or as an antislavery man. As Wentworth had said, no bill on that subject could have passed the Thirtieth Congress, and Lincoln's was impossible of passage. That was perhaps as well. It was not a masterpiece of law. It was of doubtful constitutionality; although recent cases sustain the constitutionality of boards in the executive department it is certain that the Supreme Court, under Taney, would have objected to the delegation to the President and two cabinet secretaries the duty of valuing slaves, without acts of Congress for guidance. The bill would have been unworkable; its fugitive slave section would have made the District a paradise for runaways, and would have required an army of police to apprehend and return fugitive slaves.

Lincoln got some publicity in Illinois for his bill. The *State Journal* reported and printed it on January 31, and the Galena *Gazette* had a report (erroneous in detail) of it on January 16: "Mr. Lincoln presented a resolution asking the cost of liberating all the slaves in the District after 1850, and have the government purchase the slaves of Maryland and Virginia."

That there was a desire on the part of citizens of the District to have action became more evident when Gaines of Kentucky presented a petition of members of the Washington City Council, two of whom were named, requesting Congress to empower the authorities of Washington and Georgetown to pass ordinances abolishing the slave trade.[45] Wentworth became the advocate of this petition, but Southern members, led by Alexander Stephens, blocked its reception.

A significant turn in the tenor of the slavery debate occurred in a speech by R. W. Thompson.[46] Its point of view exactly coincided with Lincoln's. It was first of all irenic—Thompson's purpose was to soothe the exacerbated feelings on both sides of the question. But he was severely taken to task by Brown of Pennsylvania. Brown also referred to the expiring Gott resolution.[47]

Buried though it was, the Gott resolution was having indirect effect by forcing bills such as it recommended. Edwards of Ohio, a member of the Committee on the District of Columbia, presented one on January 31, and again John Wentworth

---

[45] *Globe*, p. 323.

[46] *Globe*, pp. 367-70.

[47] *Globe*, p. 403.

defended it. This time he minced no words. For several years past, he said, bills of this sort were presented. The people had the impression that progress was being made toward the abolition of slavery in the District. But they did not know, he said, that when a bill of this type was referred to the Committee of the Whole it was the end of it, as though it had never been introduced. But Wentworth was powerless. Another long debate ensued, with heightened emotional tension, in which Gott's resolution was attacked and defended.[48]

Certainly no one could complain that any member's liberty to speak was abridged. An example of the proslavery viewpoint and an illustration of the latitude in debate was furnished by Wallace of South Carolina. He presented a series of resolutions against the Wilmot Proviso which had been adopted by the legislature of his state. Under the House rules, debate of such resolutions was not permitted. But by unanimous consent Wallace made an hour long speech on them and on slavery. When he finished Ashmun tried to get the floor, but was stopped by the Speaker, now applying the rule.[49] Next day Northern members forced a correction of the House *Journal*, to show that the courtesy extended to a Southern member was denied to a Northern.[50]

Wentworth's patience boiled over on February 16, when (as was told in a previous chapter) an attempt was made to amend the House rules so as to expedite business. Wentworth reminded his colleagues of their responsibility. Under the present rules, he said,

the yeas and nays are not called upon seconding the demand for the previous question. Members who are afraid to vote . . . can vote against rescinding the previous question. This is often done. . . . They can get the proposition in such a position on the Speaker's table, or in the Committee of the Whole . . . that it will never be reached in the regular order of business, and can never be taken up out of order, save on Mondays, and then only by a vote of two-thirds. In this latter condition are Mr. Gott's resolutions, which the House cannot reject, and dare not pass. They sleep the sleep of death upon your table, with a majority in this House professing to be in their favor.[51]

---

[48] *Globe*, pp. 415 ff.

[49] *Globe*, pp. 519 f.

[50] *Globe*, p. 527.

[51] *Globe*, pp. 548 f.

Wentworth was right. There lay the Gott resolution when the session ended. And there Lincoln had voted to lay it.

The implications of slavery in the attempts to provide territorial government remain to be considered. Two factors were involved in the opposition: the slavery issue and purely party interests. Many Whigs did not want legislation which would have placed patronage appointments at the disposal of the Democratic President. Both factors were equally reprehensible. Polk justly noted in his *Diary*: "I fear that for all my efforts to induce Congress to provide some government for California and New Mexico they will adjourn without doing so. Should this be the result theirs and not mine will be the responsibility. . . ." [52] And as was pointed out, the patronage issue became quite irrelevant; the bills came so late that if passed (as they were not) appointments would have been made by Taylor.

Lincoln voted for the passage of a territorial bill on February 27, and this vote is to be understood as in line with the principle of excluding slavery in the territories, for the House bill contained a prohibitory clause, and the antislavery men favored it.[53] The same principle is implied in his vote against a Senate amendment to the Civil and Diplomatic Appropriations Bill (the Walker amendment extending the Constitution and laws of the United States over the territories).[54] It was considered that their extension made it possible for slavery to exist there. Such interpretation was straining possibilities to the breaking point, and the whole episode illustrates the extreme sensitiveness of the slavery issue.

Throughout the short session Douglas in the Senate had made every effort to frame a bill or bills providing territorial government. Seeing the implacable opposition of the ultra-Southern members of both Houses, Douglas despaired of having the Senate adopt any bill from his Committee on Territories; he then tried to induce the Senate to adopt the House bill, unsatisfactory as it was. He pointed out that opponents of territorial government did not care what happened to the people in those territories so long as office holders might obtain their salaries.[55]

---

[52] Quaife, *Polk's Dairy*, IV:348 f.

[53] *Journal*, p. 539.

[54] *Globe*, pp. 695 f.

[55] *Globe*, p. 685.

It is unpleasant to observe that Lincoln, by following his party on the question, was doing exactly what Douglas said. True, he voted for the territorial bill which the House committee offered, but the Whig majority in the House shared responsibility with the ultra-Southern Senators in refusing to pass it, or any of the legislation which Polk had so urgently requested. It was one of the tragedies of the Thirtieth Congress that, rather than permit California to enter the Union as a free state, all territorial government there and in New Mexico was withheld. As Polk said, Congress, not he, was responsible, and in that responsibility Lincoln shared.

It is difficult to make a correct estimate of Lincoln's Congressional career with reference to the slavery question. As was pointed out, he was consistent in the matter of antislavery petitions, and he was almost consistent in voting against tabling resolutions or motions whose purpose was the shutting off of debate on slavery. Beveridge and Thomas generalize that Lincoln was consistent in voting for bills and resolutions looking to the prevention of the spread of slavery into the new territories.[56] They note his votes on bills to establish territorial government. Thus Beveridge identifies five occasions on which Lincoln supported the Wilmot Proviso (or its principle). Neither he nor Thomas notes Lincoln's vote on receding from the rejection of the Walker amendment. Nor do they take into account the factor of the Whig party's willingness to delay territorial government which so disastrously played into the hands of the proslavery politicians. It would seem that Lincoln, as an antislavery man, might have voted for the admission of California as a free state. A more accurate estimate than Beveridge's or Thomas's is that Lincoln maintained the principle that there should be no extension of slavery into the areas where it did not then exist. But his votes show that he had no clear conception how this was to be accomplished. He had expressed this principle in his campaign speeches, and some of his votes bore it out. But there were other instances in which he did not demonstrate clear-cut, consistent, logical ideas. He did not make any attempt to advocate or support antislavery or abolitionist measures. When, later on, in speaking against the Kansas-Nebraska Act

[56] Thomas, *Lincoln 1847–1853*, pp. xxv–xxviii; Beveridge, I:435-37, 480-86.

he declared that he had voted for the Wilmot Proviso at least forty times he was claiming much more than the record shows.[57]

The most conspicuous feature of Congressman Lincoln's course with reference to slavery is his discreet silence. In the first session of his term the slavery issue brought out many speakers in the House, both pro- and antislavery. In the short session the volume of speeches increased as the tension heightened—there were thirty-six full-length speeches on slavery. There was none by Lincoln. The Lincoln, who in the long session presented the polemical Mexican War speech, expounded his party's views on internal improvements and spoke persuasively for his party's Presidential candidate, in the short session engaged in no controversial subject, least of all slavery. This contrasts sharply with John Wentworth's outspokenness; Wentworth's antislavery attitude in the Thirtieth Congress was much more aggressive than Lincoln's. Even Lincoln's colleagues Turner and Ficklin were among the thirty-six speakers on slavery, and McClernand participated in debate. But Lincoln remained silent.

What is revealed by the sources bears out the generalization implied in Lincoln's remark to Seward. His experience in Congress gave him the opportunity to see, as though in an arena, the ominous development which the slavery question was taking. Slavery was first of all a moral problem, and, as many a slaveholder (it suffices to cite Washington and Jefferson) testified, it was morally indefensible. Slavery was an economic problem; it had disappeared in the North, where it was economically unprofitable. But slavery became a political question; temporarily quiescent after the adoption of the Missouri Compromise, it flared up again with the Wilmot Proviso. Resurgent in the Twenty-ninth Congress, the conflict increased in the Thirtieth, when all the arguments appeared that were advanced in the debates of the Compromise of 1850 and erupted in the secession crisis. While Lincoln was in Congress, Southerners were demanding their "rights," in debate and in the Conference of Southern Representatives where Calhoun presented in radical form the position which was to be reiterated until the ultimate break came.

Sectionalism contributed to the tension over slavery. Polk

---

[57] In the Peoria speech, October 16, 1854, *CW* II:252.

foresaw this, and did his best to obviate it. But the deluded idealism of Giddings did not prevent him from playing upon sectional economic interest to further antislavery feeling. He demanded "Are the liberty loving democrats of Pennsylvania ready to give up their tariff . . . in order to purchase a slave-market for their neighbors . . . ? Are the mechanics and manufacturers of the North prepared to abandon their employments, in order that slave markets may be established in Texas?" [58] The North, as the dean of American historians pointed out, was uniting hostility to slavery with the fear of Southern hostility to the tariff and internal improvements.[59] The politicians were blind to the danger of the sectional appeal. Men of those days cannot be blamed for not seeing what is apparent today, and they cannot be blamed for failing to realize that a question which ought to be settled on moral and economic grounds is not likely to be properly settled as a political issue. But that was the fate of the slavery question. Lincoln saw something of this while he was in Congress. He saw that the question must be dealt with, and that he and other politicians had "got to give more attention to it hereafter than we have been doing." Hereafter. . . .

---

[58] Giddings, *Speeches in Congress*, pp. 104-06.
[59] Turner, *The United States, 1830–1850*, p. 558.

14

"AND GET THE PLACE FOR YOUR HUMBLE SERVANT"

"To the victor belongs the spoils" was a political maxim attributed to Polk's Secretary of War.[1] The so-called spoils system was current when Lincoln was in Congress.

The patronage was always an unwholesome aspect of government. It reached its lowest level with a change of party administration. Then the scene reminds one of nothing quite so much as hogs with their feet in the trough.

To get government jobs for people of one's party was a politician's obligation. Lincoln accepted it, and did his best to discharge it. When he entered Congress there was little that he could do because the Democrats held the executive offices and controlled the Senate. As his term ended the inauguration of the Whig administration enormously stimulated the number of patronage applications. His efforts increased correspondingly, for Lincoln took his patronage obligation seriously. He applied to it the great effort which the onerous task involved. In it he maintained a standard of political ethics which merits the highest praise.

No more instructive picture of the evils of the patronage

---

[1] *Register of Debates*, 22nd Congress, 1st Session, p. 1832. See Leonard D. White, *The Jacksonians* (1954), pp. 307-24.

can be found than that in Polk's *Diary*. In those days the President saw many more visitors than are now admitted, so that the number of office seekers who came to him was enormous. So arduous was his task, and so costly of his time and energy, that Polk planned to write a book exhibiting the evils of the system.[2] It is a pity that he did not live to write it.

But his *Diary* contains much that is instructive. For example,

An unusual number of hungry office seekers greatly importuned and annoyed me. . . . Judging from their appearance and conduct and what I knew of some of them, scarcely one who called was worthy of the place he sought or was fit to fill it. . . . One . . . placed his papers of recommendation in the hands of Judge Mason to present to me. No particular office was specified in the papers; and the Judge reported to me that he enquired of him what office he wanted; to which he answered that he thought he would be a good hand at making Treaties, and that as he understood there were some to be made soon he would like to be a minister abroad.[3]

It is no wonder that Polk defined office seekers as persons who study to live off the public without relying upon their own resources and exertions, and came to the conclusion that they were the most useless and least deserving portion of society.

He certainly encountered some who warranted so harsh an estimate. One such was a lady who came to ask that a man, then a government clerk, be made Paymaster of the Army. They were in love, she said, and were anxious to marry, but they could not live on a clerk's salary. "As a rule," the disillusioned President noted, "those people who are the most importunate are the least deserving." [4]

A revealing episode occurred when Paymaster Dix died. Within less than an hour of the mere rumor of his death a man managed to get access to the President and asked to be appointed. Next day there were many applicants. One entire delegation of a state in Congress—the two Senators and all the Representatives—called and urged the claims of one of their constituents.[5]

This incident did not stand alone. The Marshall of the Dis-

---

[2] Quaife, *Polk's Diary*, III:422.

[3] *Diary*, III:422.

[4] *Diary*, IV:274.

[5] *Diary*, IV:275.

trict fell ill. Immediately Polk had half a dozen applications for the job in the event that the incumbent died.[6]

When a bill whose terms created patronage jobs was introduced—long before it could possibly pass—a swarm of office seekers always descended upon the President.[7]

The lowest point, in Polk's estimation, of this deplorable aspect of government was the intercession of Congressmen on behalf of office seekers. "I must say that some of the worst appointments I have made during my administration have been made upon recommendation of members of Congress. Indeed, many members sign all papers & recommend all persons who apply to them, without seeming to reflect that they [are] misleading the President, and without considering that they have any responsibility for such appointments as they recommend."[8] Lincoln was a conspicuous exception.

Lincoln's patronage duties began soon after he took his seat; December 7, 1847 he signed a petition for the appointment of one McRaub, to a position of minor importance.[9] Next day, aware that as a Whig he would not be welcomed by the Democratic President, he wrote to Polk recommending the appointment of one of his constituents, Franklin F. Rhoades of Pekin, to a commission as Second Lieutenant in the Army.[10] He wrote again December 11; Col. Baker wrote through Lincoln supporting Rhoades' application, and Lincoln forwarded Baker's letter to Polk.[11] He joined the other members of the Illinois delegation (thus making it a nonpartisan appeal) in recommending to the President, Francis B. Thompson of Edwards County for the position of Assistant Surgeon in the Army.[12]

Lincoln busied himself with matters of financial interest to his constituents although these matters were not of the patronage category. He followed through his petition for reimbursing his friend Dr. Henry.[13] He tried to get for John Dawson (one of

---

[6] *Diary*, III:331.

[7] *Diary*, III:330.

[8] *Diary*, IV:240, 271, 273, 277, 295.

[9] *CW* I:417.

[10] *CW* I:417 f.

[11] *CW* I:419.

[12] Thomas, *Lincoln 1847–1853*, p. 52.

[13] DNA RG 233, HR 30 AF3 (7); *Globe*, 398, 535.

his oldest Illinois friends and a former colleague in the state legislature) compensation for work which Dawson had done as pension agent in the Tyler administration.[14]

He cheerfully ran errands for constituents. A. L. Merryman of Pekin asked his aid in getting a passport. Lincoln went to the State Department, got the information, and sent it to Merryman.[15] Several times he went to the Land Office to ascertain the status of applications for land grant pensions made by people back home. He visited the Pension Office on behalf of a Mrs. Pearson.[16] In such efforts he left nothing undone for the people whom he represented.

So long as the Whigs were out of office there was little that Lincoln could do in securing patronage jobs. The one field of some promise was the Post Office. Before the Taylor administration came into power, Lincoln's friend Diller (whom he had recommended for postmaster in Springfield when Hardin was in Congress) wrote asking for an increase in his allowance for clerk hire and for other expenses. Lincoln promised to do what he could.[17] But when the Whigs took over, the Springfield post office became a patronage plum. Diller, a Whig when appointed, had gone over to the Democrats. Consequently he was to be removed. Walter Davis, a leader among the Springfield "Whig mechanics," a friend of Lincoln's and the man who constructed the model of his patented device, wanted the job. Lincoln replied guardedly, promising that he would do his best to get Davis something, but not committing himself to the post office. Caleb Birchall, presently to become bitterly hostile to Lincoln, was an applicant. The Whig who got the job was Abner Y. Ellis, who had known Lincoln since New Salem days and was ever his loyal supporter.[18]

The Chicago postmastership involved Lincoln. Several of the applicants for it wrote to enlist his aid. This job was important enough to appeal to the Lisle Smith faction; Smith went to Washington to promote the cause of Wilson, the editor of the

---

[14] *Journal*, p. 276.

[15] *CW* I:452.

[16] *CW* I:422, 446, 453, 464 f, 499 f, 519.

[17] *CW* II:27.

[18] Smith to Lincoln, February 22, 1849, RTLP; notice of appointment RTLP, *CW* I:464, II:519.

Chicago *Journal*. One of the applicants, J. Wright, wrote to Lincoln to "counteract Lisle Smith's malign influence." Wilson was appointed. This outraged Baker (who, as Congressman-elect, claimed equal voice with Lincoln in patronage matters), and helped to build up an intra-party feud.[19]

Some of the post office applications fully document the cases noted in Polk's *Diary*. The favored candidate at Pekin was recommended because he was poor, out of health, and had a large family; it was against his rival that the latter was rich and a confirmed old bachelor. The poor, sick, but prolific applicant qualified and was appointed.[20] Haza Parsons, of Bloomington, had as qualifications for postmaster the following advantages: he was old, poor, lame, and had a large family and was unable to labor. They sufficed; he was appointed.[21]

In Tremont there was such a swarm of applicants that the unity of the party was endangered. Lincoln's advice was asked. He sagely suggested that a poll be taken, and the winner be recommended. David Roberts won and was appointed.[22]

Many Whigs wrote about post offices. Some asked for them. Others said that the Democratic incumbent should be removed and a Whig appointed, and asked how to go about it. Whigs from northern Illinois wrote for aid, saying that their interests had been referred to Baker, who had done nothing about them.[23] One discerning constituent wrote that "you must find it irksome and troublesome attending to the numerous calls for office." [24]

One letter of application is quaint enough to warrant full quotation. It was from an old friend—an old contemporary in New Salem, Isaac Onstott. Onstott now lived in Havana, Illinois. He wrote:

Hon Lincoln—Dear Sir We are all well and kicking about The German Peas are growing finely And theres been no cases of cholera

---

[19] Dole to Lincoln, March 30, 1848; Wright to Lincoln, April 12, 1849; Morris to Lincoln, April 12, 1849; Baker to Lincoln, April 27, 1849, RTLP.

[20] Thompson to Lincoln, April 19, 1849 (appointment May 15), RTLP.

[21] Funk to Lincoln, March 1, 1849 (appointment March 20), RTLP.

[22] Ball, Briggs, Gill, Perkins to Lincoln, April 19, 1849; James to Lincoln, April 29 (appointment May 11), RTLP.

[23] Proctor, Dills, Wardlaw, Cross, Artz to Lincoln, RTLP. Artz said that "This matter was entrusted to E. D. Baker, but he neglected it with many others entrusted to him."

[24] Thompson to Lincoln, April 23, 1849, RTLP.

in this vicinity up to the present time I would also state that the Post Office in Havanna is held by an uncompromising Loco Foco—a man that wrote the petition to turn out Mr. Rockwell a Whig postmaster solely because he was a Whig and ought not to hold office under Polk & had himself appointed in his place   you once in writing to me said that turn about is fair play So I think it would be fair to turn him out of the postoffice Mr. J. Dearborn in this town and appoint a Whig in his place.

I would most respectfully ask you to use your influence to have him turned out & get the place for your humble servant.[25]

The documents in the Robert Todd Lincoln Papers show that Lincoln was successful in getting postmasterships for several of his constituents, including Onstott.

One of Lincoln's tasks was to help E. D. Baker to get a cabinet appointment. Baker had been elected to Congress, but he aspired to higher things. He wanted nothing less than a place in President Taylor's cabinet, specifically the War Department.[26] Baker was not a retiring man, nor was there any limit to his ambition. He is said to have wept because his foreign birth precluded his becoming President, but he did not hesitate to aspire to any office from which he was not constitutionally disqualified. He was mentioned as a suitable candidate for the Vice Presidency; even the Chicago *Democrat* thought him eligible.[27] He was favorably regarded as Whig candidate for governor, but Baker was no man to sacrifice himself in a hopeless cause. He worked for a cabinet appointment.

His groundwork was the assertion that the West, and Illinois in particular, ought to be so recognized. He induced the legislatures of Illinois, Iowa, and Wisconsin to adopt resolutions to that effect, naming him as the proper person for the place. He attempted, without success, to get similar action in other states. Then influential people in Washington were to represent this popular demand to President-elect Taylor. Of course Baker assumed that his war service would appeal to Taylor. He assumed also that his having been an early promoter of Taylor's nomination, and his campaigning for his election, would help.

---

[25] Onstott to Lincoln, May 30, 1849, RTLP; *CW* II:166.

[26] *Illinois State Journal*, January 2, 1849; Beardstown *Gazette*, January 10, 1849; Galena *Gazette*, January 16, 1849; *Illinois State Journal*, January 17, 1849. According to the *State Journal* (January 20), the Baltimore *Post* had mentioned Baker for a cabinet position.

[27] The Charleston *Courier* was so quoted in the *Illinois State Register*, April 21, 1848.

Lincoln did everything he could. While looking out for
Baker's interests in Washington he tried to enlist the aid of the
press. He wrote to Schouler, the Boston editor, sending him an
item from the *Illinois Journal* with one of the Baker recommendations. He reported the resolutions adopted by the three states,
and made the point that the West was entitled to a cabinet
place. He asked Schouler to reprint the newspaper item, with
or without comment, as Schouler chose.[28]

But Baker was pitted against impossible odds. He did not
command the support of key people, in Congress or elsewhere.
That shrewd operator, Caleb B. Smith, who with Truman Smith
worked under cover, wanted appointment as Postmaster General.[29] Even if Baker could have overcome this serious handicap
he was doomed by the effective influence of none other than
Jefferson Davis. Davis, although a Democrat, had great influence upon Taylor. He had been the General's son-in-law, and
he had won Taylor's unstinted admiration by his gallantry in the
capture of Monterrey. And Jefferson Davis held Edward D.
Baker in utter contempt. He expressed himself in a letter to ex-
Senator, then Governor-elect Crittenden, of Kentucky: ". . . the
Englishman Baker, who came from the Rio Grande to draw pay,
mileage, and a year's stationery as a member of Congress is
here, with recommendations from legislatures for the post of
Secty. of War. What would General Taylor say to such impu-
dent dictation and indelicate solicitation?"[30]

The Galena *Jeffersonian* (of course hostile to Baker) purported to reveal what Taylor thought (April 2, 1849): "A distinguished ex-colonel of volunteers from the North-West, who
was recommended for the War Department called upon Gen.
Taylor and commenced a speech about his (the Col's) claims
to office, and his great influence in the North-West. The Presi-

---

[28] *CW* II:25.

[29] Washburne had been apprised of the Baker movement by a Galena
friend, John F. Drummond (Washburne Papers). He quickly took steps to
block it. He knew that Caleb Smith desired a cabinet place (Postmaster
General), and he assumed that no more than one person would be appointed to the cabinet from Indiana and Illinois. He aided Smith to foil
Baker.

Schuyler Colfax wrote to Smith (February 20, 1849, Smith Papers) that
Truman Smith "goes on to comment upon Baker's fitness for a cabinet
officer about as you wrote me Mr. Toombs did." Obviously the odds against
Baker were insurmountable.

[30] Davis to Crittenden, January 30, 1849, Crittenden Papers.

dent stopped him in the midst of his harangue, saying—'Don't make that speech to me—make it to the Department where you present your application.'" Of course this was but a canard. Baker's references were presented to Taylor by Lincoln through the mail, with a suitable covering letter in which Lincoln made his own recommendation.[31] But the irreverent *Jeffersonian* had more to say: "DISappointments.—We condole with 'an ex-Colonel of volunteers' for not having received an appointment in the War Department. After all his useful services, and in consideration for his 'tremendous influence in the North-West;' he certainly had *pretensions* to a lion's share of government pap. We shall now have his invaluable services in Congress. What a pity it is, however, to have to 'chain a dog to keep him home.'" [32]

Disappointed in his desire for a cabinet post, Baker sought other means of avoiding service in the Congress to which he had been elected. Early acquiescing in the view that California should be admitted to the Union, he wrote to this effect to Secretary of State Clayton. He suggested that he be sent to California as an emissary to organize the movement for statehood. Lincoln supported Baker's application for this position, saying that Baker was exactly the man for it if the administration sent such a representative.[33] Taylor did send someone, but not Edward D. Baker.

Baker perforce resigned himself to the lesser role of Congressman. Before he took his seat he became active in dispensing jobs. In doing so he was not scrupulous in political ethics. He was like those Congressmen deplored by Polk for recommending anyone who applied, without ascertaining the candidate's fitness.

He did not scruple to ask Lincoln to do something which he knew to be wrong. He wrote to Lincoln, enclosing a sheet,

---

[31] Appointment Papers, DNA FR RG 59. With Lincoln's letter (*CW* II:30) is his endorsement of a document signed by all Whig members of the Illinois legislature recommending Baker.

[32] The Galena *Jeffersonian* items were reprinted in the Chicago *Journal*, March 29, 1849; this shows the rupture between Baker and Wilson (the editor). Normally a Whig newspaper would not reprint a Democratic newspaper's attack upon a fellow Whig. Wilson had been friendly to Baker as late as December 20, 1848, when he wrote to Washburne favoring Baker for a cabinet appointment. (Washburne Papers.)

[33] Baker to Clayton, March 20, 1849, Clayton Papers; *CW* II:38; Wiltse, *John C. Calhoun, Sectionalist*, pp. 396, 542 note.

blank except for Baker's signature, asking Lincoln to write the recommendation. The applicant was Dr. Wallace, Lincoln's brother-in-law. In his letter to Lincoln explaining the case, he admitted, "I think, nay I know it is wrong for you to do it." In other words, Baker did not have the nerve to say "No." It became noised about that Baker and Lincoln had jointly recommended Wallace for the position of Indian Agent. This led Dr. A. G. Henry—whose judgment was seldom questioned by Lincoln— to write in sharp protest. A mutual friend had sworn that if Lincoln did this after the abuse Wallace had heaped upon Lincoln he would never forgive him for it. Henry more mildly said that "I should feel a little sore about it myself, for he [Wallace] and Butler are going it bitterly against me." Nevertheless on Baker's and Lincoln's recommendation Wallace was appointed pension agent at Springfield.[34]

Lincoln, when untrammeled by requests from Baker, was honest with all applicants, candid, tactful, and zealous to advance the cause of the worthiest man. An example is his handling of applications for the job of Marshall of Illinois. Before January 27, 1849, John Murray of Belleville had written for it; Lincoln answered his letter on that day. He assured Murray of his strongest friendship, told him that there were several applicants, and promised to give his claim that consideration due to impartiality, fairness, and friendship.[35] Of the six others interested, one was Benjamin Bond, who was supported by petitions from some two hundred people. Most of the Whigs who were or had been in the legislature sent letters. Forty-six Democrats in the current legislature endorsed him, as did many other good citizens. Lincoln wrote to Clayton, who controlled the appointment. He was bound to be influenced by Bond's recommendations. He certified that Bond was in every way worthy of the office. He forwarded the papers, and solicited full and fair consideration for his claims. But he closed, "Having said this much, I add that in my individual judgment the appointment of Mr. Thomas would be the better." [36] Bond was appointed.

---

[34] Baker to Lincoln, April 27, 1849; Henry to Lincoln, June 15, 1849; RTLP; DNA NR RG 48; Department of the Interior Appointments, Pension Agents Ala-Ill 1849-1878, Box 89.

[35] *CW* II:24.

[36] Lindsay to Lincoln, February 21, 1849; *CW* II:36-38; Appointments RTLP.

Land Offices provided many jobs, and they were eagerly sought. Some presented no problem: local citizens would write to Lincoln making a recommendation, Lincoln would recommend as requested, and the applicant would be appointed. In this way Lincoln secured the appointment of Matthew Gillespie, brother of his friend and supporter, Joseph Gillespie, to the office at Edwardsville.[37]

But some Land Office vacancies were so hotly contested that Lincoln was greatly troubled. There were several candidates for the two jobs (Register and Receiver) at Shawneetown. Hunger for office bore no relation to the ability of the job seekers. Henry Eddy wanted to be Receiver. A letter in his support stated that he "has a large family, has been sick all winter, and is in very straitened circumstances." [38] The jobs at Vandalia presented an even more difficult problem. Among the several applicants were Dr. Stapp and Col. Remann. Another, J. B. Herrick, also wanted the place, and did his worst to undermine favorable consideration of Stapp and Remann. He caused copies of the poll books of recent elections to be made and certified, thus showing that neither of his rivals was a good Whig; both in the past three elections had voted for more Democrats than Whigs. After careful study Lincoln recommended Stapp.[39]

Of all the Land Office jobs to which Lincoln recommended appointments the most troublesome were the two at Springfield. He had no doubt of one of the applicants: it was for this, not the post office, that he recommended Walter Davis.[40] He nominated for the other Turner R. King, a resident of the northern part of Tazewell County, who was not well known to him. Soon recriminations against King were made, both to Lincoln and to Secretary Ewing, in whose department jurisdiction lay. King was said to be a drunkard, a gambler, and an abolitionist. Lincoln was exasperated. He had recommended King at the request of fellow Whigs. Now they must either stand by their

[37] *CW* II:31.

[38] Eddy to Lincoln, March 22, 1849; Marshall to Lincoln, April 6, 1849, RTLP.

[39] Herrick to Lincoln, April 20, 1849, Eccles to Lincoln, May 29, 1849, Stapp to Lincoln, May 31, 1849, Herrick and others to Lincoln, June 9, 1849, RTLP; *CW* II:52.

[40] *CW* II:40.

recommendation, or admit that they had made a poor one.[41] The faithful Dr. Henry wrote to Ewing, explaining the circumstances of the imbroglio, and saying that in his recommendations Lincoln was serving the best interests of the party and of the Interior Department.[42] Richard F. Barrow, of Springfield, who thought that Lincoln had been imposed upon in the case of King, agreed that Lincoln was honest and was trying to do the right thing.[43]

Lincoln requested that action be suspended until he could ascertain the facts. Then he wrote to several trusted constituents for information. He became convinced that King was a proper candidate. Next he suggested that several residents of Tazewell County secure testimonials of King's fitness and send them to Washington. This procedure Herndon later indignantly characterized as a specimen of low politics, adding that in recommending King, Lincoln turned down the application of William O. Butler, who had been one of the first to befriend Lincoln when he moved from New Salem to Springfield.[44] Henry's letter alluded to the passing over of Butler and said that part of the turmoil against Lincoln was caused by this fact and by the further fact that he had rejected the application of a brother-in-law.[45] All this amply bears out Lincoln's statement to Ewing that the people who were objecting to King's appointment were trying to stab him.[46] There is no reason to conclude that Lincoln was playing an unworthy part in this instance. But it is plain that he added to the number of disappointed office seekers, who, because he did not recommend them, formed a grudge against him.

Lincoln was asked to find clerkships in the General Land Office for three of his friends,[47] and his inability to get a place

---

[41] *CW* II:40-42, 44, 45-47; Certificate of the Character of Turner R. King, RTLP.

[42] Henry to Ewing, May 10, 1849, Ewing Papers.

[43] Barrow to Ewing, May 6, 1849, Ewing Papers.

[44] Herndon and Weik, I:277 f.

[45] See R. S. Todd to Lincoln, February 20, 1849, David Todd to Lincoln, Februry 3, 1849, Ann E. Todd Campbell to Lincoln, April 20, 1849, RTLP. Lincoln sent R. S. Todd's letter and recommendation to Ewing.

[46] *CW* II:44 f.

[47] *CW* II:46 f; unsigned memorandum enclosed in a letter from Herrick to Lincoln, March 22, 1849, RTLP.

for one of them led to a sad bit of personal criticism. This was the case of a former Tremont merchant, John M. Morrison, who had been of some influence in Lincoln's nomination to Congress: it was Morrison who wrote, "it is Abraham's turn now." Morrison had failed in business, and removed to Wyoming (in Stark County, outside the Seventh District). He sought a government job, and sent recommendations.

The record does not show what Lincoln did, but Morrison's application was rejected. He blamed Lincoln, and complained:

> But Lincoln . . . I know . . . that patronage is bestowed on those who are supposed to be able to repay with usury.
> Had my claims been pressed I know I might have obtained *something*. As the matter now stands I consider it a mockery to present my name with others, for places which will not be regarded or noticed when *you* leave the city. Accept my thanks for the interest you have manifested in my favor, and have my name withdrawn as an applicant for any government patronage—It appears that neither you nor Mr. Baker consider *me* as one of *your constituents*. Consequently I can have the pleasing consolation left, that my *friends* have not overlooked me.[48]

Lincoln was asked to endorse patronage applications in several departments. There were two Illinois applicants whose requests seem not dissimilar to Polk's story of the man who thought himself a good hand at writing treaties. C. H. Constable, of Charleston, wrote a long letter asking help in getting a diplomatic appointment somewhere in South America.[49] His reason for seeking it was that he needed financial relief. Another such request was from Stephen A. Hurlbut, of Belvidere. Significantly Hurlbut did not address his request to Lincoln, but to Caleb B. Smith, which shows that he had cut his eye teeth politically. He had asked for appointment as "chare" (so he spelled the word) to one of the South American republics. "Lincoln, I believe," he wrote, "is pledged to Dr. Henry, one of my electoral colleagues, and Baker is too busy fishing for himself to do anything without a quid pro quo." Hurlbut did not get what he wanted. He accepted a job which was doubtless more commensurate with his abilities, as postmaster.[50]

---

[48] Morrison to Lincoln, March 13, 1849, RTLP.

[49] Webb to Lincoln, April 8, 1849, Harlan to Lincoln, May 3, 1849, Dills to Lincoln, April 10, 1849, Constable to Lincoln, May 3, 1849, RTLP; *CW* II:48.

[50] Hurlbut to Lincoln, February 1, 1849, C. B. Smith Papers; Chicago *Journal*, July 20, 1849.

Other seekers of diplomatic posts sought Lincoln's aid. A Congressional colleague, Moses Hampton of Pennsylvania, applied for the mission to Brazil. Incidentally, Hampton's letter reflects the exchange of off-color jokes in which Lincoln indulged.[51] Later, unsolicited, Lincoln wrote to Secretary of State Clayton warmly urging the appointment of his Indiana friend, Richard W. Thompson, to a diplomatic office.[52] E. P. Oliphant wanted to become *chargé* (he knew how to spell it) *d'affaires* in Denmark; Lincoln recommended him.[53]

Of the extremely varied kinds of requests which came to Lincoln, one of particular interest was made by Nathaniel Pope, who asked him to introduce John Cook to President Taylor.[54] The young man was the son of Daniel Pope Cook, who had been the first Congressman from Illinois; he was son-in-law of the first governor, Ninian Edwards. Young Mr. Cook was after a patronage job.

In the wide range of recommendations, not of the patronage category, were those to cadetships at West Point. Lincoln recommended three.[55]

The many requests which besought Lincoln to use his influence as Congressman include one concerning the public printing. George T. M. Davis, formerly editor of the Alton *Telegraph*, now editor of the *New Era*, had long been a hardworking Whig. His views did not closely coincide with those of Lincoln. He had been a last ditch supporter of Hardin against Lincoln in 1846, and he had supported the Mexican War without reservation. Perhaps because of their differences his request was put indirectly through Elihu Washburne: "I want you to see Mr. Lincoln for me & ask him if he will not unite with Mr. Yeatman to aid in securing the publishing of the laws and the printing for the 'New Era.' I have no office to ask for myself and would not get one if I did. . . . Mr. Lincoln can do a great deal for the New Era in this respect if he would, and I will take it as a great personal kindness if you will see him Early upon the subject." [56] The outcome is not known, but Lincoln did complain to a cabi-

---

[51] Hampton to Lincoln, March 30, 1849, RTLP; Mearns, I:169.

[52] *CW* II:56.

[53] Oliphant to Lincoln, May 8, 1849, RTLP; *CW* II:48.

[54] Pope to Lincoln, February 20, 1849, RTLP.

[55] DNA WR RG 94 Letters of Recommendation, File 160; *CW* I:466.

[56] Davis to Washburne, February 1, 1849, Washburne Papers.

net member because so large a share of the public printing went to Democratic papers.

The newspapermen for whom Lincoln fought the hardest to get jobs were his two friends, Simeon Francis, editor of the *Illinois State Journal,* and Dr. Anson G. Henry. Lincoln tried tenaciously to get Francis appointed Secretary of Oregon Territory,[57] but in spite of his best efforts the place went to another. He worked even more assiduously for Dr. Henry.

It must have been most vexatious to Lincoln that his unceasing efforts on behalf of Dr. Henry went so long unrewarded. He had long felt obligated to this great and good friend. Henry first came into the Lincoln story when, as a physician in Springfield, he was helpful to Lincoln in that break in health which followed the "fatal first of January," when Lincoln's engagement to Mary Todd was broken; he went so far as to say that Dr. Henry was necessary to his existence. He besought John Todd Stuart, then in Congress, to get Henry appointed postmaster in Springfield. But Henry was not appointed. He became active in Whig politics, and without deviation he loyally supported Lincoln.[58] Never was his support more valuable than while Lincoln was in Congress. Although he deprecated Lincoln's Mexican War stand he was one of the few who upheld and defended him.[59] As the following chapter will show, he was a tower of strength in looking after Lincoln's interests.

It was no wonder, then, that Lincoln went all-out to do something for Henry. Stephen Hurlbut was in error when he supposed that Lincoln was trying to get a diplomatic post for Henry; in fact he was trying to get him appointed Secretary of the newly organized Minnesota Territory:

On the other half of this sheet is a copy of a recommendation, that Anson G. Henry of Springfield, Illinois, be appointed Secretary of the Teritory of Minesota. In their confidence and kindness in and for Col. Baker and myself, fortynine of the Whig members of the H. R. have signed it, they being nearly all to whom it was presented. I am

---

[57] *CW* II:61, 64, 65; Ewing Papers.

[58] See Harry E. Pratt, "Dr. Anson G. Henry, Lincoln's Physician and Friend," *Lincoln Herald,* 45 (1943), 3-17, 31-40 (reprinted as a monograph); Pratt, *Concerning Mr. Lincoln.*

[59] Henry's letter to Ewing (p. 227) explained that the opposition of Butler and Wallace to him was because he had defended Lincoln's course as Congressman, referring obviously to his defense of Lincoln's Mexican War stand.

exceedingly anxious, the appointment of Dr. Henry shall be made; and fearing the place may be filled before I can see you personally, must be my excuse for troubling you in this way. On other matters I am anxious to a common degree; but on *this*, my solicitude is extreme.[60]

In that letter to Secretary of State Clayton, Lincoln's sincerity and commitment are apparent.

George W. Rives, of Paris, Illinois, wrote to Lincoln asking his help for appointment to a position in Minnesota or Wisconsin.[61] Rives claimed that Henry, Baker, Judge Logan, and others would back him. Possibly he assumed that they would, but Rives was ignorant of essential facts. In any event his request was insincere and unrealistic. He was a Democrat, and unless he was the merest tyro in politics he must have known that a member of his party would not get a job from a Whig administration which was just coming into power.

However, Lincoln replied courteously and frankly. Saying that Rives overestimated his power in the matter, he added: "Besides this, at the very inauguration I commenced trying to get a Minesota appointment for Dr. Henry, and have not yet succeeded; and I would not now, lessen his chance, by recommending any living man for any thing in that Teritory." [62]

The matter had gone on until May 1 without a decision. Then Lincoln bethought himself of a tactic which might have been decisive if attempted earlier. He wrote to the very influential Caleb B. Smith:

You remember my anxiety that Dr. A. G. Henry . . . should be appointed Register of the Land Office at Minesota.

Since I left Washington, I have heard nothing of the matter. I suppose Mr. Evans of Maine, and yourself are constantly together now. I incline to believe he remembers me, and would not hesitate to oblige me. . . .

Now I will do twice as much for both of you, some time, if he and you will take some leisure moment to call on Mr. Ewing, and, in as graceful a way as possible, urge on him the appointment of Henry. I have always had a tolerably high hope that Mr. Ewing will appoint Henry, if he does not forget my peculiar anxiety about it.[63]

---

[60] *CW* II:31.

[61] Rives to Lincoln, June 3, 1849, RTLP.

[62] *CW* II:46.

[63] *CW* II:46.

Smith did not reply for some time. When he did he said that he would have written earlier but had waited until he had definite information. Directly after receiving Lincoln's letter he had seen Ewing, who gave him no encouragement. Then a Mr. Lester of Iowa received the appointment which Lincoln had tried to get for Henry; Smith learned this from a newspaper. He went again to Ewing, who explained that a complication of affairs in Iowa made it necessary to do as he had done. Ewing added that the Receiver in Minnesota would not be removed. There was no job for Henry.[64]

But the ways and means of getting patronage jobs defy rationalization. On June 19, knowing that Henry would not be appointed, Lincoln recommended N. G. Wilcox for Receiver in the Land Office at Still Water, Minnesota, and Wilcox got the job.[65]

Lincoln's interest in Henry did not wane, nor did his efforts flag. More than a year after his Congressional term was over he worked to get the doctor appointed to an Indian Agency, saying to Ewing that "Dr. Henry was at first, has always been, and still is, No. One with me." [66] This time Henry received the appointment. Lincoln never forgot him; one of his Presidential appointments was an office for him.

It is difficult to generalize the effectiveness of Lincoln's work in the patronage. His frequent lack of success in getting what he asked is obvious, but it is easier to state the fact than to account for it. What seems to be indicated is that Lincoln had slight influence with key people of that element in the Whig party who controlled much of the patronage. There is one exception, which bears out the point. Lincoln had formed a fine friendship with Jacob Collamer of Vermont, who became Taylor's Postmaster General. The Post Office was the department in which Lincoln had the greatest success with his recommendations. But as has appeared and will appear further, he had little influence with the powerful Ewing. This stands in contrast to the greater influence, power, and effectiveness of Truman and Caleb Smith.

There is another factor, which operated negatively. It had

---

[64] Smith to Lincoln, June 3, 1849, RTLP.

[65] *CW* II:55.

[66] *CW* II:78.

been expected that Senator Crittenden would be a member of Taylor's cabinet. But he generously sacrificed that prospect to aid his party by running for governor of Kentucky. If he had become Taylor's Secretary of State Lincoln's recommendations would have been given greater and more sympathetic consideration, for Crittenden thought highly of Lincoln.[67] But Lincoln did not have access to Clayton, and Ewing repeatedly rebuffed him.

One thing can be said with assurance. When Lincoln was President, despite the pressure of problems more serious and more difficult than any predecessor had faced, he devoted the closest personal attention to major and minor patronage appointments. He viewed the patronage as a highly important means of political control, and as such he used it as a means to save the Union.[68] Lincoln's experience with the patronage as a member of Congress, meager in result as it was at the time, was invaluable to him later, when the single term Congressman occupied a more exalted position.

---

[67] Lincoln had his friend, Joshua F. Speed, who lived in Louisville, sound out Crittenden as to his estimate of Lincoln, Baker, and Hardin (although Hardin was dead at that time). Speed reported that Crittenden thought highly of Lincoln, but had a low opinion of Baker. Speed to Lincoln, February 13, 1849, RTLP; Mearns, I:161 f.; CW II:28.

[68] Harry J. Carman and Reinhard Luthin, *Lincoln and the Patronage* (1943).

15

"HE'S FOR AN OFFICE BOUND"

The Whig victory in 1848 made it certain that the Democratic Commissioner of the General Land Office would be removed and replaced by a Whig. The doomed Commissioner was Judge Richard M. Young, of Illinois. He had been appointed by Polk, and had carried out his work acceptably. His removal would be made on political grounds only—a normal procedure when there was a change in party administration. As early as December 20, 1848, the Quincy *Whig* demanded the place for an Illinois Whig, alluding to Archibald Williams, a Whig residing in Quincy, as a suitable person.

Even earlier than this Illinois had an active candidate for the position: Cyrus Edwards, of Alton, who looked to Lincoln to promote his appointment. Edwards and Lincoln were friends of long standing. Cyrus Edwards was the brother of Ninian Edwards, Sr., and the uncle of Ninian Edwards, Jr., Lincoln's brother-in-law. Cyrus Edwards had a creditable record of political activity and public service, although he was only twice elected to office (as state representative in 1832 and 1840). His greatest achievement, even though it did not result in victory, was the vote which he polled for himself and the Whigs in the gubernatorial election of 1838; he received only 926 votes less than the Democrat who was elected, carrying 34 of the 71 counties of the state. This was much the nearest the Whigs

ever came to a majority in an election for a state office.[1] So far
as political standing was concerned, Edwards merited the support of his party.

He was by far the earliest applicant for the place; on November 23, 1848, a letter signed by three Edwardsville Whigs,
led by Joe Gillespie, recommended him.[2] The earliest extant
reference of the matter to Lincoln was in a letter of January 27,
1849, from William Thomas of Jacksonville. Nathaniel Pope wrote
in the same vein to Lincoln on February 3. The Edwards candidacy was made public by the *Illinois State Register* on February 5, in an item clipped from the St. Louis *New Era*. This report
named three Illinois Whigs as seekers of the office: Edwards,
J. L. D. Morrison, and Martin P. Sweet.

An interesting turn in the Edwards candidacy came on
February 8, when members of the Kentucky legislature endorsed
him. Back of this was Governor Crittenden, who on several occasions gave his wholehearted support to Edwards. The files
contain a long letter, signed jointly by Governor William Pick-
ering and Crittenden, dated March 5. It is noteworthy that Edwards and Lincoln both looked to Crittenden for support; the
significance is the greater because of the peculiar turn which
presently appeared: the rivalry between Crittenden and Ewing
in the party patronage, the outcome of which was the emergence,
so fateful to Lincoln, of the greater power of Ewing.

Gillespie wrote to Lincoln on February 7, explaining why
the petition of members of the Illinois legislature in favor of
Edwards did not contain more names. The petition had been
entrusted to a man who negligently left it in his room while the
similar petition for Sweet was actively circulated and was signed
by several who, had they known of the Edwards petition, would
have signed it.

But this was not the only snag which the Edwards candidacy encountered in Illinois. Edwards had written to Lincoln
on February 14, asking his aid in securing the Land Office job,

---

[1] Pease, *Illinois Election Returns*, pp. xxix, lii, 112, 264 f, 399, 454.

[2] In this chapter, in order to keep documentation to a minimum, it is
to be assumed that unless otherwise specified source documents are to be
found in the National Archives, Department of the Interior, Appointment
File. When the date appears in the text citation will not be made; the date
plus the assumption sufficiently indicate the place of the document referred to.

and Lincoln worked hard to help him get it.[3] But Baker asserted his claim to a share in the Illinois patronage, and Lincoln was obliged to recognize it. Lincoln had written to the new Secretary of the Treasury on March 9, requesting that he and Baker be consulted about Illinois appointments, and stating that the Whigs of the state held Baker and him responsible, to some extent, for them.[4]

Baker's claim was an evident embarrassment to Lincoln, and nowhere more so than in the commissionership of the General Land Office. It became the decisive factor in the whole matter, for Baker advanced the candidacy of Col. J. L. D. Morrison. This was not merely unfortunate; it was fatal in result both to Edwards and to Lincoln. What is more, it was based upon an unworthy motive: Baker was jealous of Edwards.[5] It was not long until Edwards learned of Baker's interference. He wrote to Lincoln on April 15 that Baker was making desperate exertions to defeat him.[6]

Baker's opposition to Edwards was complicated by a further detail which reflects no credit: Baker's hostility toward Elihu Washburne, who would probably have been nominated for Congress in the Sixth District had Baker not horned in. Because he had, the group including Washburne, Sweet, Lisle Smith, and Justin Butterfield was opposed to anything that Baker favored. It was because of this factious bickering that the candidacy of Sweet for the Land Office was advanced by Lisle Smith. The upshot was that there were three rival candidates for the job in Illinois, with a dangerous weakening of the case for any one of them.

The files contain a total of eleven letters in favor of Edwards. They reflect the worthiness of the candidate and dignity of his support. Duff Green, recommending Edwards, wrote to President Taylor that "You must be aware that generally a long list of

---

[3] Edwards to Butterfield, June 11, 1849.

[4] This was followed, on March 11, by a joint letter of Lincoln and Baker to Ewing, stressing their interest in the General Land Office appointment (Ewing Papers).

[5] Edwards to Butterfield, June 11, 1849.

[6] Edwards to Lincoln, April 15, 1849. This letter reveals the cause of Baker's jealousy of Edwards: Baker was inordinately vain of his oratorical prowess, and Baker thought that he had been outdone by Edwards at the funeral of Col. Hardin.

recommendations proves want of merit or a want of self respect. No man of proper feeling conscious of his own claims on his party of fitness for the office will permit his name to be bandied about as an applicant for office." Green recounted Edwards' qualifications, and referred to the unfortunate effect of Baker's promotion of the claims of Morrison. He informed the President that Lincoln and Baker had agreed to return to Illinois to consult Whig leaders there so as to prevent a contest between the two rival candidates. Lincoln, Green wrote, had done this in good faith, while Baker, making no attempt to resolve the differences, had made extraordinary efforts on behalf of Morrison—all this, Green averred, because Baker aspired to supersede Edwards as the prominent man of the Illinois Whigs.[7]

In the meanwhile the assumption that the office would go to an Illinoisan had been challenged. As early as January 16, John J. Cooper of Alabama was after the job, supported by Lincoln's colleague in the House, H. W. Hilliard. Since the latest of the Cooper letters was dated March 8 (there were only six letters) it would seem that his candidacy was abandoned soon after it began. Only one day behind the first Cooper letter came one in support of Col. Samuel R. Curtis, of Keokuk, Iowa. There are five letters in his interest, continuing his candidacy until the end of April. There is no indication that Curtis was seriously considered. Some unavailing effort was made on behalf of James Collins of Indiana, whose candidacy was endorsed in a letter jointly signed by R. W. Thompson and Caleb Smith.[8] Still less effective was the application of Jesse Conrad, of Indiana, who, however, had the gumption to enlist the aid of Caleb Smith.[9]

A candidate who was anything but modest, and, in his own estimation extremely versatile, was General Eugene Hamilton of Portsmouth, Ohio. This office seeker, who strongly suggests some of the cases in Polk's *Diary*, appeared late. He first asserted himself in a letter of May 22 to Secretary Ewing, asking for a job in the Land Office, the Indian Agency, or the Pension Bureau —any job. His friend, Charles O. Tracy, wrote to Senator Corwin a week later that Hamilton was on his way to Washington seeking "some position under the government." With that ir-

---

[7] Duff Green to Taylor, April 27, 1849.

[8] Letters dated March 8 and 29, April 15, 1849.

[9] Conrad to Smith, May 5, 1849, C. B. Smith Papers, Library of Congress.

responsibility of which Polk rightly complained, Corwin endorsed the letter and sent it to the Land Office. So able a man as Congressman Vinton also lent his name to Hamilton's cause, in response to Hamilton's solicitation. Needless to say, Hamilton was disappointed in his attempt to get the Land Office job or any which he specified, but he was easily gratified by appointment to a minor office, as shall be related.

Several others sought the Commissionership. Lincoln's friend, Orville H. Browning of Quincy, was "mentioned," and Lincoln said that Browning wanted it.[10] Wyatt B. Stapp was also mentioned.[11] Lincoln said that ex-Congressman McGauhey of Indiana was in Washington after the job early in 1849.[12] Josiah M. Lucas, a clerk in the Land Office who kept Lincoln closely informed, told him that Alabama, Florida, and Mississippi had aspirants.[13] The crassest of all was D. A. Whitney of Belvidere, Illinois, who applied directly to Ewing for the job and closed his request with the blunt offer that if appointed "I will do as much, with interest, for you in '52." [14]

A few words suffice for Martin P. Sweet. His candidacy was merely the role of stalking horse for the purpose of foiling Baker. The files contain thirty letters in his favor.[15] Oddly enough, one of them was signed by the same D. A. Whitney, who must have given up his own candidacy as hopeless. The decisive factor ending Sweet's prospects was the transfer of his group's support to Justin Butterfield. However, the effort for Sweet had the desired effect of weakening the case for Morrison.

Morrison's case was damaged, also, by protests against him that he was interested in many land claims that would be handled by himself were he appointed.[16] He was said to have bought many old French land claims, extremely speculative but

---

[10] CW II:29.

[11] Stapp to Lincoln, April 13, 1849, RTLP.

[12] CW II:29.

[13] Lucas to Lincoln, April 12, 1849, RTLP; Mearns, I:171.

[14] Whitney to Ewing, April 26, 1849.

[15] Numbers 184-212 inclusive, in File; withdrawn June 22, 1849; Bracken to Washburne, February 20, 1849, Washburne Papers.

[16] Morrison's recommendations are numbered 214-229. Except for Orville H. Browning, no Whig of dominant influence lent his name to the Morrison candidacy. The paucity of letters indicates clearly that Baker did not work hard for Morrison.

very profitable if sustained, and he was an active speculator in lands near Peoria.[17] Former Governor John Reynolds later said of Morrison that if he managed to stay out of the penitentiary for twenty years he would be the richest man in Illinois. A remonstrance against his appointment alleged that "putting a land speculator in this office would cause large depreciation of real estate in the city" of Peoria.[18] But Baker did not hesitate to endorse him.

Thus the issue was joined, to the great detriment of the Whig party in Illinois. Edwards rightly deemed that having been first in the field, with the unqualified support of such eminent Whigs as Governor Crittenden and Duff Green, and with Lincoln's sponsorship he should be the sole Illinois candidate, and that Morrison should withdraw. Edwards wrote to Lincoln, outlining the situation and stressing Morrison's refusal to withdraw. Lincoln in reply pointed out his inability to do anything until the two rivals settled the matter by the withdrawal of one of them.[19]

The continued impasse between Edwards and Morrison threatened the loss of the office to Illinois. After long and careful consideration Lincoln came to the conclusion that the only way to keep it for the state was to get it himself.

In working out the details of this episode, chronology is of essential importance, especially because Edwards later questioned Lincoln's probity in the matter. It must be remembered that Edwards was the first candidate, and that he had early called on Lincoln for aid. It was Lincoln's judgment that at any time up to February 20, 1849, so far as the Whigs in Congress were concerned, he might have had the office for himself by common consent. He was later assured by President Taylor and Ewing that he might have had it up to the time (May 10) when Ewing decided in favor of Justin Butterfield.[20]

During that period Lincoln had been under considerable pressure to seek the office for himself. The earliest known instance of such urging is a letter of Judge David Davis to Lincoln

---

[17] Letter signed by C. Ballance for himself and "diverse other citizens of Peoria" to Taylor, March 7, 1849.

[18] Ballance to Meredith, March 7, 1849.

[19] Edwards to Lincoln, April 15, 1849, RTLP; Edwards to Butterfield, June 11, 1849, refers to Lincoln's reply on April 19.

[20] *CW* II:28 f, 57-59.

(dated February 21) in which the Judge said flatly: "were I in your place, could I Get it, I would take the Land Office." [21] By April 6 the situation had become sufficiently well known in Illinois that Dr. Henry and others wrote Lincoln in the strongest terms. These loyal Whig leaders feared that the office would be lost to the state, and since Lincoln was the only man who could get it, it was their earnest desire that without delay he should press his claims upon General Taylor. Recognizing the delicacy of Lincoln's position with reference to Edwards and Morrison, they undertook to "take care that no misapprehensions on the part of friends [who were then] soliciting the appointment shall render [him] in their estimation obnoxious to the suspicion of having acted in bad faith towards them personally." [22]

In view of Edwards' charge that Lincoln had acted in bad faith, Lincoln's reply to this appeal is important. On April 7 he wrote that if the office could be secured to Illinois by his consent and not otherwise, he gave his consent that his friends request it for him. He pointed out that some months earlier he had promised to get the place for Edwards if it were in his power to do so, and that more recently he had stipulated with Baker that if either Morrison or Edwards would withdraw in favor of the other he and Baker would jointly recommend the remaining candidate. Then he said: "In relation to these pledges, I must not only be chaste but above suspicion. If the office shall be tendered to me, I must be permitted to say 'Give it to Mr. Edwards, or, if so agreed by them, to Col. Morrison, and I decline it; if not, I accept.' . . . It must also be understood that if at any time, previous to the appointment being made, I shall learn that Mr. Edwards and Col. Morrison have agreed, I shall at once carry out my stipulation with Col. Baker." [23]

Less than a week later, the Land Office clerk, Josiah Lucas, informed Lincoln of a dangerous new development: the candidacy of Justin Butterfield. [24]

Butterfield was that New England Federalist who, when the Mexican War broke out, remembering his disastrous opposition to the War of 1812, said that he was for "war, pestilence, and

---

[21] RTLP; David C. Mearns, *The Lincoln Papers* (1948), I:166.

[22] Henry and others, April 6, 1849, RTLP; Mearns, I:169 f.

[23] RTLP; Mearns, I:170 f; *CW* II:41.

[24] RTLP; Mearns, I:171 f.

famine." He had done well in his Chicago law practice, specializing in land law, and he was well qualified professionally for the Land Office Commissionership. But Lincoln's judgment that Butterfield was not entitled to the place was well founded. Patronage appointments should be given to people who have worked for the party, to reward them and to encourage others. Butterfield had taken no active part in Whig politics, yet he had received a patronage appointment from President Tyler. In the campaign of 1848 he had been a Clay man and had opposed the nomination of Taylor to the very last.

The numerous documents endorsing Butterfield show that he first applied for the position of Solicitor in the Treasury Department.[25] This is why, in the early stage, the story concerned only Edwards and Morrison. But presently Butterfield's testimonials recommend him for either the Treasury or the Land Office, and one dated April 16 states that his friends favored his appointment to the Land Office. Yet as late as May 25 he sought an office. He had been rejected by the Treasury.

It was Butterfield's entrance upon the scene that decided Lincoln to go after the office for himself. Again chronology is important. Lincoln later said that he had first "determined to be an applicant, unconditionally, on the 2nd of June." [26] Between April 15 (when Lucas reported the candidacy of Butterfield) and June 2 Lincoln received a perfect barrage of letters urging him to apply for the office as the only means of saving it for Illinois, and warning that if he did not it would go to Butterfield. Lucas wrote on May 7 that Young, the incumbent, was to be removed, adding that there was no chance for Morrison, and that General Taylor and Postmaster General Collamer were for Lincoln. Lucas did not overlook Lincoln's obligation to Edwards; he was sure that Edwards would be reasonable and would do what was right. Lucas stressed the immediacy of the situation and the necessity for Lincoln to come to Washington and press his case in person.[27] So urgent was the crisis that only three days later Lucas wrote two letters about it.[28] The first literally pleaded that Lin-

---

[25] The recommendations of Butterfield, and other documents in Butterfield's interest, are numbered 1-63 in the File.

[26] *CW* II:58.

[27] RTLP; Mearns, I:174.

[28] RTLP; Mearns, I:176-78.

coln pocket his modesty. The second stated a fact of grave import: "Ewing *insists* on Butterfield—and that he *is his man*." Young, the Commissioner, wrote to Lincoln in corroboration of what Lucas had reported; he warned that Butterfield, having lost the appointment as Solicitor of the Treasury, was now out for the Land Office. Like Lucas, Judge Young urged Lincoln to "lay modesty aside and strike out" for himself.[29]

Still Lincoln hesitated because of his commitment to Edwards. He immediately opposed Butterfield. But it was some time before he decided to go after the place for himself. Soon after the receipt of Lucas' two letters of May 10 Lincoln wrote to Duff Green. He reported that he had heard from Washington that Butterfield would probably be appointed Land Commissioner, and advised against it. He mentioned Butterfield's inactivity for the party, and that his only effort was to oppose Taylor's nomination.[30] Next day Lincoln wrote to Joe Gillespie, asking him, if he agreed that Butterfield's appointment would be a blunder, to write to Governor Crittenden to that effect.[31] This letter shows that Lincoln was then aware not only that Ewing was unfavorable to his own appointment, but that Ewing was the key man: he warned that if Gillespie wrote to Ewing the President would never hear of his letter. Lincoln was right: it was Taylor's practice to delegate to cabinet heads all appointments within their departments, and to transmit to them, unread, any applications and recommendations which came directly to him. But Lincoln was mistaken in supposing that Crittenden could control the matter. Crittenden could do nothing. Ewing could make the appointment, and he did make it. Had it not been for an unprecedented action by the President, an exception to his otherwise uniform practice, the case would have been disposed of as soon as Ewing decided upon Butterfield.

Lincoln's letter to Duff Green contains a further significant item. Edwards, he wrote, had written to him offering to decline. In view of Edwards' later accusation of bad faith on Lincoln's part, this assertion is important. Edwards' own letter to Butterfield, in which he made the accusation, bears out Lincoln's statement to Green. Edwards accurately stated his understand-

[29] Mearns, I:176-78.
[30] *CW* II:49 f.
[31] *CW* II:50.

ings with Lincoln, and (referring to the letter which Lincoln had mentioned to Green) went on to say that "I wrote to Mr. Lincoln . . . that as I was at all times, unwilling to burden my friends on my account, and never disposed to pursue the dog in the manger policy, I hoped he would feel himself entirely untrammeled and take such a course as he might think best—and that I should be gratified at his success over Baker's nominee whoever he might be, if I could not obtain the appointment for myself." [32] Further, Lincoln's statement that Edwards had withdrawn in his favor had outside support. In one of his letters Lucas had said that Chambers, of the St. Louis *Republican,* was in town and had told him that Edwards had withdrawn. Lincoln had ample ground for writing to Green in the terms which he used.

The amazing fact is that even when Edwards wrote to that effect Lincoln did not actively seek the appointment. He told Edwards that his withdrawal did not add to his perplexity, and advised him not to withdraw even if it were a matter of indifference whether he received the appointment or not.[33] So long as there was any hope Lincoln tried to secure the position for Edwards. The end of any hope was when Butterfield, rejected by the Treasury, went after the Land Office against both Morrison and Edwards.

When Butterfield did decide to seek the Land Office he went after it like a tornado. There are in the files of the Interior Department 63 documents in support of Butterfield's candidacy, several having multiple signatures, so that the number of recommendations exceeds 130.

An analysis of these recommendations is revealing. The central core reflect the Chicago group which Butterfield controlled: J. Y. Scammon, J. J. Brown, James Wilson, and Lisle Smith. Associated with these are the anti-Baker leaders of northern Illinois, Martin P. Sweet and Elihu Washburne. But Butterfield, wiser in this particular than Lincoln, saw the value of other than local support. He sought and secured recommendations from several bar associations, and—of great value—resolutions from the legislatures of Wisconsin, Iowa, and Michigan. Not overlooking the influence of politicians he secured recommendations from

---

[32] Edwards to Butterfield, June 11, 1849.
[33] *Ibid.*

ex-Senator Breese of Illinois, Congressmen R. W. Thompson and Caleb Smith of Indiana, and Truman Smith of Connecticut. Illustrating the truth of Polk's *Diary,* Breese had signed a similar letter for Morrison, and Thompson and Caleb Smith had as cheerfully petitioned in favor of James Collins; Caleb Smith had also supported Jesse Conrad, thus distinguishing himself by supporting three candidates for the same office. Butterfield went to Washington with a letter of introduction signed by Thurlow Weed.

Unquestionably the shrewdest move which Butterfield made was to enlist the support of Caleb Smith. There was much political maneuvering behind this. The letters of Schuyler Colfax, who at that time was hardly more than an undercover man for Caleb Smith, but an amazingly effective organization man in Indiana Whig politics, are an instructive source of information of how things were handled.[34] One sees why Smith was so powerful a man in Indiana, and how he was able to bring to bear at a moment's notice testimonials to this or that man's usefulness to the national organization. Such an instance appears in this correspondence as early as February 19, when Colfax wrote to Smith:

. . . Mr. Wilson editor of the Chicago Journal is the fidus achates of J. Lisle Smith. . . . They are as twin brothers in politics and friendship. . . . When I wrote to Mr. Smith, asking for a letter recommending you in case Baker was not appointed to a Cabinet position, his reply was one strongly and *unconditionally* in your favor, with an inferential back stroke at Baker. As Smith and Wilson always consult together, this was doubtless done at Wilson's suggestion. You will remember also the editorial articles in your favor which appeared in the Journal, & the others, the publishing of which Wilson procured in the papers of Mineral Point and Galena, Ills., around Baker's own home. . . .[35]

Thus is explained Caleb Smith's quick and effective response to Butterfield's candidacy when requested by J. Lisle Smith. This plus the decisive factor of Caleb Smith's access to Ewing, makes it easy to see why Lincoln's claims were undercut before they were even made.

The union of the Wilson-Smith forces with Elihu Washburne, basically motivated by mutual hostility to Baker, was

---

[34] Colfax letters in the C. B. Smith Papers, Library of Congress; Colfax Papers.

[35] C. B. Smith Papers, Library of Congress.

effective in itself and had the further formidable result of con-
solidating the anti-Baker strength of northern Illinois. It was
simple and easy to bring this powerful consolidation to bear in
the promotion of Butterfield's candidacy.

And Butterfield was acute enough early to see the necessity
of lining up all the support he could get from central and southern Illinois. First Baker's own district in northwestern Illinois
was canvassed, and (it must have been greatly to Baker's dis-
comfiture) a petition signed by the mayor and postmaster of
Galena, the sheriff of the county, the chairman of the Whig
Central Committee, and the president of the Galena Rough and
Ready Club was secured—this in the face of Baker's presence
and his appeal to each one not to sign.[36] Then the campaign
turned southward. Residents of Peoria, members of the LaSalle
County bar, and people from the extreme southern area petitioned for Butterfield.

Then when the contest was at its hottest, early in June,
Butterfield boldly invaded Lincoln's own bailiwick, with results
most disconcerting to Lincoln. Butterfield effectively appealed
to elements predisposed toward him: to those who resented the
control of Whig affairs by the small group of leaders (including
Lincoln) in Springfield, to the disgruntled office seekers who
blamed Lincoln because they had not got patronage jobs, and—
fatal weakness— to the critics of Lincoln's Mexican War course
in Congress. Even Butterfield was surprised that there were so
many who were against Lincoln. He wrote to Caleb Smith June
6:

> I found Mr. Lincoln' boasted "overwhelming majority" like Fal-
> staff's men "in Buckram," they have vanished into thin air. So far
> from his being the choice of a majority of the Whigs I find the leading
> Whigs here opposed to him, and in my favor. . . . The Whigs of this
> city [Springfield] without any solicitation on my part tendered me the
> enclosed petition signed by the clerk of the circuit court, the clerk
> of the county court, Judge of Probate and sheriff of the county, being
> all the Whig county officers elected by the people, and also signed
> by the leading Whigs of the county. They offered to provide for me
> . . . the petition of a majority of all the Whig voters in the county. . . .[37]

That petition is extant, and the signers include some names
well known in the Lincoln story. To be sure, one of them was a

---

[36] Washburne to Ewing, May 15, 1849; Butterfield to C. B. Smith, May
20, 1849, C. B. Smith Papers.

[37] C. B. Smith Papers, Library of Congress.

disappointed office seeker, but another was James H. Matheny, whose friendship with Lincoln was of long standing, and close enough that Matheny had been best man at Lincoln's wedding. Butterfield took the petition for notarizing, and it must have been galling for the notary, A. Y. Ellis, a firm friend and supporter of Lincoln, to have to certify that the signers were leading and respected Whigs.

Another anti-Lincoln petition which Butterfield managed to get in Lincoln's home town reflected the still current repudiation of Lincoln's Mexican War policy. The prime mover was Caleb Birchall, who also stressed the point in a personal letter. No doubt Birchall's hostility to Lincoln was caused by Lincoln's refusal to recommend Birchall for the postmastership at Springfield. Nevertheless his efforts were damaging. His name headed the list of twenty-eight signers of a petition in his handwriting: "The undersigned Whig mechanics of the City of Springfield, Illinois, represent to your department that your petitioners are dissatisfied with the course of Abraham Lincoln as a member of Congress from this Congressional District. Your petitioners recommend Mr. Justin Butterfield as a suitable person to occupy the Office of Commissioner of the General Land Office." [38]

As though this were not enough, Birchall wrote the letter to Ewing which has already been quoted. He offered his judgment that "of these two applicants Mr. Butterfield would be decidedly the most acceptable." Explaining his preference by reference to Lincoln's war stand and its results, he concluded, "Is it strange, then, that we should desire that the appointments should fall upon some other man. a Man in Whome the Whigs would take greater pleasure to honor." [39] This letter must have been extremely damaging to Lincoln's chances, for however much it was to be discounted because of Birchall's being a disappointed office seeker it spoke a political language that bore a powerful argument to a patronage dispenser, one of whose functions was to bestow favors with a view of building up party strength and solidarity. [40]

---

[38] The document is undated. It is filed with the Butterfield recommendations.

[39] Birchall to Ewing, June 6, 1849; see above, p. 122.

[40] Birchall's letter, numbered 42 in the file, is endorsed (for President Taylor's reference) "see this letter." Evidently Ewing desired Birchall's letter to do all the harm it could.

Butterfield overlooked nothing. Someone had said that he had once had an apopleptic stroke, which had impaired his mental health. He countered this by dint of more letters and documents. He got the doctor who had bled him to relieve "a determination of blood to the head" to certify that he had no mental defect from apoplexy. He secured the certification of three other physicians to the same effect. Then—he seemed never to know when to stop—he induced the mayor of Chicago to certify that the doctors were professors in a medical college and were eminent and scientific practitioners.[41] This must have been highly edifying to Secretary Ewing.

Nor did Butterfield scruple to descend to devious tactics. He, or perhaps his friends (one looks for the hand of the editor of the Chicago *Journal*) inspired the false announcement that he had been appointed. Apparently this spurious news first appeared in the Chicago *Commercial Advertiser* on May 21. The report was quoted in the *State Register* on the twenty-eighth, in the Rockford *Forum* on the thirtieth, and in other Illinois newspapers. Some of them mentioned the purported appointment with approval, and these Butterfield rushed to Caleb Smith, knowing that they would get to Ewing. With characteristic exaggeration he claimed that the statement was "immediately" copied in "most" Illinois newspapers, "both Whig and Locofoco in the most cordial and complimentary terms of approval." Washburne, presumably by request, at the same time wrote to Ewing congratulating him for having made the appointment, saying that it would be most cordially approved by the Whigs of Illinois. Butterfield did not neglect to send a copy of the newspaper item to Ewing, and the pro-Butterfield secretary obligingly put it in the file to be shown to Taylor.[42]

On June 2 the President did an unprecedented thing. Shortly before this Dr. Henry had written to him, and on this occasion the President read the letter before referring it to the secretary. Evidently Henry had told Taylor that the appointment of Butterfield would ruin the party in Illinois, and had made a strong enough case to convince the President that, at the very least,

---

[41] Documents 12, 17.

[42] Butterfield to C. B. Smith, May 28, 1849, C. B. Smith Papers, Library of Congress. The erroneous report got as far afield as the New York *Herald*, June 3, 1849.

the whole matter should receive further consideration. Dr. Henry received a telegram from President Taylor stating that the appointment would be postponed for three weeks.[43] The postponement was made in Lincoln's interest.

Dr. Henry immediately wrote to Joe Gillespie and in similar vein to others, stating the new facts, quoting Navy Secretary Preston (one of Lincoln's particular friends in Congress) to the effect that only Lincoln could beat Butterfield, and that to do so Lincoln must come to Washington immediately. When Henry wrote, Lincoln was returning to Springfield from Coles County; he was expected on the third. Henry asked Gillespie to write to the President explaining to him the sentiment of his county. In his letter Henry took it upon himself to say (it is important to bear in mind that Lincoln was not a party to this) that with Lincoln in the Land Office men of Illinois would be sure to obtain a fair share of patronage appointments and that "our friend Edwards will not be overlooked."

Fortunately the record contains facts of the background of Taylor's decision. Some of them appear in a letter of Josiah Lucas to Henry, dated May 22.[44] Lucas saw that Lincoln, because of his faithfulness to Edwards and his understanding with Baker, would do nothing in his own interest. Lucas called upon the President on the twenty-first and had a good talk with him. He showed Taylor some letters, which Taylor read with much astonishment. (It is easy to see that until Lucas made his personal appeal Taylor had only Ewing's reports of the situation.) Taylor expressed "great partiality for Lincoln and was astonished to find that Butterfield was not their [i.e., the Illinois Whigs'] choice." Lucas reiterated that Collamer was for Lincoln and so was President Taylor. Then with many words underlined Lucas warned Henry that the time was now; immediate action must be taken. A satellite of C. B. Smith's had telegraphed Butterfield to come to Washington. The incumbent commissioner would refuse to resign until the very last moment to secure more time for Lincoln.

It is not difficult to see why Dr. Henry was convinced, and

---

[43] Henry to Gillespie, June 2, 1849, Photostat in the file of the Abraham Lincoln Association.

[44] RTLP.

why he acted as he did in Lincoln's absence. To reinforce the information which Henry had received from Lucas, a telegram awaited Lincoln when he reached home.[45] W. A. Henderson, another clerk in the Land Office who was friendly to Lincoln's cause, warned him that Butterfield was expected, and, making a final appeal, closed with the words, "Use your discretion," i.e., use the release which Edwards had given.

Additional information is found also in a letter from Ben E. Green, son of the redoubtable Duff, who had acted in his father's absence. This was a fortunate move; Duff Green had instructed Ben to turn over all data to Ewing, but Ben, knowing what would happen in that event, used his own judgment and saw President Taylor instead. Green's letter established the fact of Taylor's normal procedure: ". . . to read no letters and listen to no explanations on the subject of appointments unless presented to him through the Secretaries of the respective departments." [46] Ben Green made another shrewd move: he laid the whole case before Col. W. W. Bliss, who had been Taylor's Chief of Staff in the Mexican War, and who, having proved himself indispensible in that capacity, had been retained by Taylor in Washington on his secretarial staff. Bliss already knew something of the story, and agreed to intercede with the President. Green learned that it was commonly understood that Butterfield was to be appointed on June 1.

Thus the strenuous efforts of Lucas, the valuable aid of Ben Green, and the strong appeal of Dr. Henry, all brought to bear at approximately the same time, succeeded in inducing Old Zach to modify his usual procedure and to take the extraordinary step of ordering a postponement of the decision for three weeks in Lincoln's favor. It is obvious that Butterfield's receipt of the same news was what stimulated his hectic efforts and caused him to invade Lincoln's area at that precise time.

This was the situation when Lincoln arrived in Springfield. He accepted it and went feverishly to work. His tactic was to send copies of the same brief letter to numerous people: "Would you as soon I should have the Genl. Land Office as any other Illinoian? If you would, write me to that effect at Washington

---

[45] Henderson to Lincoln, May 26, 1849, RTLP.
[46] Ben E. Green to Lincoln, May 26, 1849, RTLP.

where I shall be soon. No time to lose. Yours in haste." [47] This form, or a similar variant, was copied by others, including Mrs. Lincoln, signed by Lincoln, and sent. Friends, in addition to Dr. Henry who did special work at this time, included B. F. James, Judge David Davis, Robert Boal, R. H. Constable, Jesse K. Dubois, Richard Yates, and Pierre Menard.[48]

Lincoln sent his form letter to several of his Congressional colleagues, and their response was gratifying. R. W. Thompson wrote a personal letter to Ewing, stating that before Lincoln was a candidate he had joined with Caleb Smith in recommending Butterfield, but now that Lincoln wanted the place he desired to say that Lincoln was his decided preference.[49] Schenck wrote that Lincoln was "the very man." Tariff Andy Stewart responded. Amos Abbott was but one of the Massachusetts delegation to write. Speaker Winthrop supported Lincoln. Rockwell, Dixon, and Hubbard of Connecticut recommended him; one wonders whether their influence had any effect against that of Truman Smith. The Democrat, C. J. Ingersoll, was for Lincoln. So were other Pennsylvanians: Brady, McIlvane, Butler, and Nes. White, Greeley, Putnam, Rumsey, Duer, Rose, and Gott of New York responded suitably. Still others were Evans and Fisher of Ohio, Cranston of Rhode Island, and Evans of Maryland. Lincoln solicited and received the endorsement of the Native American, Levin, willing then, as later, to accept Native American aid although he repudiated the party principles. Noteworthy, too, is the fact that Caleb Smith wrote in Lincoln's favor—an insincere and worthless endorsement, since he had already recommended three other candidates for the office, and was actively working against Lincoln and for Butterfield when he wrote his letter.[50]

---

[47] Numerous examples of this message are extant. One copy is in *CW* II:53. Others can be identified by the language of replies, e.g., Pollock of Pennsylvania would "as leave, or a little liever," and Evans of Maryland had "as lief . . . but a little liefer," that Lincoln should have the job: letters June 18, 23, 1849, RTLP; Mearns, I:186.

[48] James to Lincoln, June 3, 1849, Davis to Lincoln, June 6, 1849, Boal to Lincoln, June 7, 1849, Constable to Lincoln, June 10, 1849, Dubois to Lincoln, June 11, 1849; Endorsement and document numbers 113, 117, 147, 171 in Ewing file.

[49] Document 1 in Ewing file.

[50] Ewing file, Endorsements.

Only one Senator is listed as a Lincoln supporter: Tom Corwin. Lincoln asked for a letter of Willie Mangum, but there is no evidence of Mangum's response. The record shows that Douglas favored Lincoln's appointment, although Butterfield claimed him as one of his supporters.

Of the members of Congress who aided Lincoln, only R. W. Thompson did more than write as requested. Thompson not only wrote, but used his influence to circulate a petition in his home county.[51]

It took some time to circulate the county petitions, but soon they were forthcoming, from Sangamon, of course, and from Lawrence, Putnam, White, Vermilion, Schuyler, Morgan, Macoupin, and Tazewell. The Tazewell County petition was circulated by Pierre Menard, and its 180 signatures bear out the claim of "Old Tazewell" to be the strongest Whig county in the state. Of Indiana counties, Thompson's Wabash and also Vincennes were represented.

Strong as these petitions were, they had an obvious weakness: they bore eloquent testimony to Lincoln's strength in central and southern Illinois, but not one of the northern counties petitioned. The utmost that could be done in that area was to secure letters from individuals; these were channeled through the faithful Dr. Henry. What they lacked in quantity they had in vehemence; Henry wrote Lincoln of the indignation which they expressed, and sent one sample which was mild in comparison with others.[52] But the Baker-Washburne feud, and Baker's unpopularity because of his tactics in seeking a cabinet appointment, had done such damage that this part of the battle was lost before it began.

Lincoln and his workers did not overlook the press. A strong editorial appeared in the Lacon *Illinois Gazette,* and the *Illinois Journal* at Springfield was at Lincoln's service as needed. Dr. Henry assured Lincoln that the Whig papers in Quincy, Danville, Rockford, and Rock Island were ready to "cut loose," and added that the papers in Galena and Chicago were already boiling over.[53] The editorials were sent with other supporting documents.

The local campaign for Lincoln coincided with Butterfield's

[51] Thompson to Lincoln, June 14, 1849.
[52] Henry to Lincoln, June 15, 1849, RTLP.
[53] *Ibid.*

efforts in the same area. The Lincoln canvass eclipsed the Butterfield. By June 10, it was reported to Lincoln, all local opposition to his candidacy had ceased, "utterly," his informant said. Dr. Henry, who, although a biased witness, was entirely credible, assured Lincoln that almost every name on the Butterfield petition circulated in Springfield had been obtained through misrepresentation, adding that "I have yet to see the first man who does not regret having signed it." [54]

Of course Butterfield continued his feverish efforts. He overlooked nothing. One of the curious documents in the file is a certification that he was not an abolitionist.[55] Someone may have asserted that he was, and it is an indication of the opprobrium of the epithet that Butterfield gratuitously disclaimed it. Apparently he could induce his supporters to swear to anything; he forwarded a sworn statement that he had never opposed Taylor's nomination. That oath did not alter the fact; Butterfield in a letter to Lincoln had said that he favored Scott and opposed Taylor.[56]

While seeing to it that documents continued to pour into Washington, Butterfield perceived that Lincoln was getting the better of him. So on June 9 he sent an emissary to Lincoln (while Butterfield was combing Indiana for support) proposing that neither of them go to Washington. Of course Lincoln did not accede. Failing in that too obvious tactic, Butterfield determined to go to Washington, and Lincoln also set out for there. Butterfield had a slight advantage, because he was closer at the start. This time there was no taking a longer route for the sake of the mileage.

The *Illinois State Register* saw some humor in the race. On June 14 it carried the following parody:

A Steeple Chase, For the Spoils Cup

Away went Justin, neck or naught
Away went hat and wig;
He little dreamed when he set out
Of running such a rig.

---

[54] Henry to Lincoln, June 11, 1849, RTLP. This petition had been circulated by William O. Butler, a disappointed office seeker.

[55] Petition dated June 9, 1849, signed by Wilson and four others (Ewing file).

[56] Butterfield to Lincoln, April 10, 1848, RTLP.

Away went Lincoln, who but he;
His fame soon spread around;
He carries weight! He rides a race;
He's for an OFFICE *bound.*

The contest among the "hungry" in this state for the office of Commissioner of the General Land Office, has been narrowed down between Messrs. Lincoln and Butterfield. In the "training" heretofore had preparatory to the great race, Edwards could not overcome the stiffness peculiar to old horses, while Morrison's service as *war-horse* had seriously impaired his powers in a race for the spoils; both were therefore withdrawn. On Sunday evening last after several ineffectual efforts at a "good start," Lincoln and Butterfield "went off hand-somely," the former having a slight advantage in the start, though Lincoln had the "inside track," (in the opinion of his friends); it being a "steeple chase," after the *British fashion,* the goal being the federal capital. We will be unable to give any account of their respec-tive paces, until we hear from the result at the "outcome." Bets run high, though the backers of Lincoln give slight odds. They contend that their horse has more *wind,* although the opposing nag has the best *bottom,* and for a "single dash" the wind is bound to win. Be-sides, they say that Lincoln is in better condition, owing to his anti-war training, while Butterfield had favored "war, pestilence, and famine" during the Mexican war, to the injury of his racing powers, having abandoned his British training, which he adopted during the War of 1812.

Some of "the friends" express doubts of fair dealing by the judges in Washington. They doubtless think that the jockey club who presides there, from their known juggling propensities, will not be impartial in their decision of the race. Their fears are well founded, doubtless.

What Lincoln and Butterfield did in Washington is not known, but Butterfield was appointed on June 21. Beginning with the next day notices of the appointment appeared in several newspapers, such as this in the Baltimore *Patriot*: "Appointments by the President: Justin Butterfield of Illinois, to be commissioner of the General Land Office, from and after the 30th inst., vice Richard M. Young, resigned."

Apparently President Taylor, despite his unprecedented intervention, reverted to his army pattern and accepted the recommendation of the department secretary. It is certain that Ewing arranged the documents in Butterfield's favor. Ewing received them all, arranged them under the name of each applicant, and prepared (or caused to be prepared) a blanket endorsement consisting of a list of the documents, identifying each by reference to its writer or sponsor, giving some idea of its contents, and noting the more important ones. This list was doubtless made for the President's use in making his final decision. The whole file is so voluminous that it was not expected that the President would read all the documents, and Ewing clearly took advantage of that fact: here and there the endorsement (by Ewing) advised the reading of one and another letter —and without exception those so indicated were particularly antagonistic to Lincoln. Prominent place, by filing it last and thus out of its sequence, was given Cyrus Edwards' letter to Butterfield in which he accused Lincoln of having acted in bad faith.

The appointment is thus readily explained.[57] The marplot in the whole affair was Baker. Had he not asserted his claim to a share in the disposal of Illinois appointments the Land Office would certainly have gone to Cyrus Edwards. Ewing's estimate was that "from these recommendations it appears that Mr. Edwards is a man of high character and standing, and fully qualified." Baker's interference was the more reprehensible because it was motivated by his personal jealousy of Edwards. To defeat Edwards he sponsored a man of questionable ability for the office, succeeding only in weakening the likelihood of either being appointed.

Then the (for Butterfield) fortunate link between Caleb B. Smith and Ewing was decisive. The record shows clearly that Smith was for Butterfield, and Smith had access to Ewing. Thus Baker's interference played directly into Butterfield's hands by giving him time to cultivate Smith, and thus get his case presented to Ewing. While this was going on Lincoln had to depend upon Governor Crittenden and Duff Green, who, although they were more eminent in Whig party circles than Smith, had no access to Ewing.

The supporting documents show that Lincoln and Butterfield were equally qualified for the position. Those favoring Lincoln are the more impressive; they are relevant to the considerations of qualification and fitness, while Butterfield's contain several which hectically assert that he had never had apoplexy,

---

[57] The traditional explanation was offered by Butterfield's daughter, Elizabeth Sawyer, in a letter to Jesse W. Weik, October 12, 1888. She stated that her father was preferred over Lincoln because of "the paramount influence of his friend Daniel Webster." This may have been Butterfield's formal explanation. The facts do not bear it out. See Herndon and Weik, I:301 note.

was not an abolitionist, had not opposed Taylor's nomination, and that character assassins were conspiring against him.[58]

There is no evidence, direct or indirect, that Lincoln was guilty of or responsible for misrepresentation. Baker may have, on his own initiative, violated ethical proprieties. It may have been he, or one of his friends, who started the whispering campaign about Butterfield's infirm health. Elihu Washburne associated Lincoln with Baker's alleged untruthfulness ("Baker, while in Washington, backed up in a measure, I am sorry to say, by Lincoln, lied about Butterfield most outrageously to Mr. Ewing") but there is not a shred of evidence to substantiate his statement.[59]

As a matter of fact, Lincoln's earliest reference to Butterfield acknowledged his ability: "he is my personal friend, and is qualified to do the duties of the office." The same statement was made by Lincoln to a cabinet secretary. The same evaluation appears in the last heat of the struggle: "Nothing in my papers questions Mr. B's competency or honesty." [60]

Lincoln's case for himself was very simply and quite correctly based: he and Butterfield were equally qualified; Lincoln deserved the place because of his efforts for the Whig party from the beginning, because of his political achievements, and because of his labors for the nomination of Taylor and for the success of the party in the recent election. Butterfield did not deserve the office because (although he was a regular Whig) he had been inactive as a party member and had opposed the majority in the party's presidential nomination movements. Beyond this Lincoln proceeded upon curiously mistaken assumptions: that central Illinois, where the Whig strength was concentrated, deserved the recognition which it would receive by his appointment, and that northern Illinois, lacking Whig strength, did not merit it.

It was Cyrus Edwards' charge of bad faith which disturbed

---

[58] Butterfield was no mean hand at character assassination himself: "Col. Baker . . . is a vain supercillious Englishman . . . holding out the most corrupt and dishonorable inducements to editors of newspapers to give him their support" (Butterfield to Hunter, June 4, 1849); Young, the Commissioner, "has a fair exterior but is in fact the most treacherous whining sniveling creature that ever existed" (Butterfield to C. B. Smith, June 6, 1849, C. B. Smith Papers, Library of Congress).

[59] Washburne to C. B. Smith, Library of Congress, May 7, 1849, C. B. Smith Papers.

[60] *CW* II:43, 49, 54.

Lincoln most. Lincoln's letter to Joe Gillespie, dated July 13, reviews the matter in some detail.[61] As has been shown, a complete examination of all extant source materials completely vindicates Lincoln. Nevertheless there was a break in the friendship of Edwards and Lincoln. Happily Edwards came to recognize Lincoln's honesty, and friendship was resumed.

As for the new Commissioner, Butterfield soon demonstrated the characteristics which some of his opponents suspected and predicted. At this point an example of Lincoln's thoughtfulness appears. During the contest one of Lincoln's supporters, James Berdan, wrote a glowing endorsement of Lincoln. Lincoln learned that Butterfield was trying to secure Berdan's service in the office. When Lincoln withdrew the documents submitted for him he took pains to insure that Berdan's letter would not remain in the file and incite Butterfield's hostility when he took over.[62] But Lincoln did not know that a list of the letters, with Berdan's name on it, remained in the file. Lincoln's informant in the office, Josiah Lucas, was retained for a while and then dismissed. So was W. H. Henderson, who had worked for Lincoln's appointment. Butterfield was an unconscionable nepotist; he placed on the payroll two of his sons, his brother, three nephews, and four other relatives.[63] Unfortunately the doubt of Butterfield's physical condition proved to be well founded. He was frequently away from Washington because of illness, and bad health necessitated his resignation before the end of the Taylor-Fillmore administration.[64]

Lincoln was bitterly disappointed when he lost the patronage position which, once his for the asking, was given to another because Lincoln sacrificed his own chance while trying to favor a friend. Nevertheless he felt no rancor toward his successful rival,[65] nor, strangely enough, toward Secretary Ewing.[66] Indeed, the time came when Lincoln's silence in regard to a manifest injustice was of great value to the department head who had

---

[61] *CW* II:57 f.

[62] *CW* II:55, 59 f.

[63] As to Butterfield's nepotism, see statement with other documents in the Archives.

[64] Butterfield resigned with effective date September 16, 1852 (Archives).

[65] *CW* II:91 f.

[66] *CW* II:67.

done the injustice; Lincoln valued party harmony above personal vindication. The time came when all soreness was healed, and Lincoln could say that he would not take the place if it were offered to him.[67] His fairness to his rival and his consideration for Ewing are the measure of unstinted magnanimity.

---

[67] *CW* II:92.

16

"I CANNOT CONSENT TO ACCEPT IT"

Beveridge, emphasizing Lincoln's humiliation in the loss of the Land Office commissionership, and under the impression that the only appointment offered him was that of Secretary of Oregon Territory, said that "this position was the measure of the Whig Administration's estimate of Lincoln's political importance in the autumn of 1849." [1] Beveridge was mistaken.

It is true that Lincoln was offered the Oregon secretaryship. Although he was never an applicant for it and several others sought it, he was the first to whom the post was offered. Early in August of 1849, to his great surprise, Lincoln received a letter from Secretary of State Clayton, offering the appointment and enclosing the commission for it. [2] Evidently some one, or some group, in the administration, aware that Lincoln deserved recognition for his efforts on behalf of Taylor and the party, made him this offer. It was made by cabinet recommendation. Ewing must have realized that Lincoln had been unfairly treated in the Land Office matter, and perhaps he hoped to make amends.

Nevertheless Beveridge's inference that so poor an offer (the salary was only $1,500 per year) represented the measure of the administration's value of Lincoln and his services, was in error.

---

[1] Beveridge, I:493.

[2] *CW* II:61.

It is refuted by the fact that the governorship of Oregon Territory was offered him, on the direct interposition of President Taylor. It is important to note, too, that Ewing was forced to make this offer by direction of the President.

The only formidable candidate for the secretaryship of Oregon Territory was Eugene Hamilton of Portsmouth, Ohio, who, even before Taylor was elected, was in the forefront of Whig office seekers as soon as the prospect of a Whig victory seemed bright. He had written to Ewing on May 22, 1849, applying for a job in the Land Office, the Indian Agency, or the Pension Bureau—a job in any of these, or elsewhere, would suit him.[3] He presently narrowed the scope of his aspirations to the Land Office, and managed to get Congressman Vinton and other Ohio Whigs to recommend him. Ewing evidently consigned his recommendations to the wastebasket, for in the file of documents for the President's inspection he noted below Hamilton's name merely, "His own letter of application." But since any job would be acceptable, Hamilton did not cease trying, and he presently sought the Oregon position.

He had competition. L. D. Stickney of New Harmony, Indiana, sought the place, and Lincoln's friend and Congressional colleague, Elisha Embree, went to his aid. Embree wrote to Lincoln asking him to support Stickney. Lincoln replied that before he received the request he had recommended another for the office (his candidate was Simeon Francis), but that he had written to Clayton, endorsing Stickney in the highest terms.[4]

As Lincoln's correspondence shows, he had vigorously championed the appointment of his friend Simeon Francis, who, ever since 1832, had done so much for Lincoln through the columns of his newspaper. In his own message declining the secretaryship of Oregon Lincoln urged that the place be given to Francis. But again his recommendation was disregarded.

Lincoln had been appointed Secretary of Oregon Territory on August 10, 1849; the Domestic Letters of the State Department contain copies of the commissions issued on the same day to Marshall as governor, and Lincoln as secretary. Lincoln de-

---

[3] National Archives, Interior Department, Appointments.

[4] Charles O. Tracy to Thomas Corwin, May 30, 1849 (Archives); B. T. Kavanaugh to Ewing, September 4, 1849, Wm. D. Defrees to Ewing, Ewing Papers; Wm. Sasscer to Embree, September 7, 1849, Embree MSS; *CW* II:61.

clined the offer by mail, as did Marshall, but for some un-
explained reason Clayton did not receive Lincoln's letter; he
failed also to receive other letters written later to him by Lincoln. News of Lincoln's appointment had been published locally,
in the Chicago *Democrat* on August 24, in the Indiana *State
Sentinel* on the same date, and in the Vandalia *Yeoman* next
day. In these news reports doubt was expressed that Lincoln
would accept.

When Lincoln declined the appointment, the way was open
for Hamilton, since neither Francis nor Stickney was given
serious consideration. The appointment was offered Hamilton
and he accepted it with alacrity: on September 18 he telegraphed Ewing (not Clayton—again the departmental confusion) in jovial terms, "In reply to your dispatch of yesterday as
I never was thought hard I have only to say Yes siree," and his
letter of the same day (also sent to Ewing despite the fact that
the commission had been sent by Clayton) formally accepted the
appointment. The final word from the new territorial secretary
was a wire to Meredith, Secretary of the Treasury, asking him
to "Send me immediately Bond Blank." [5] He was eager to get
going.

Of all these developments Mr. Stickney was uninformed.
He still worked to secure an office which was already filled.
Letters of two Indiana Whigs recommended him on September
4. A letter to Embree from Washington dated the seventh quoted
Col. Fitz Henry Warren to the effect that the office had been
offered Lincoln, and stated that if Lincoln declined Warren
would refer Stickney's case to Ewing. Stickney learned from
Embree that Lincoln had declined, and he thereupon continued
his campaign. Dunn, another Indiana Congressman, was supporting him. Dunn advised Stickney to cultivate Truman Smith,
and this Stickney proceeded to do. Letters from two supposedly
prominent Kentucky Whigs were sent to Truman Smith. Finally
Stickney went to Washington to cinch the job in person, only to
find, on November 21, that Hamilton had been appointed more
than two months before.[6]

The offer to Lincoln of the worthwhile office of Governor of

---

[5] Telegram and letters in Ewing Papers; copy of commission in Vol. 37,
Domestic Letters, State Department, p. 322; telegram to Meredith, *ibid.*
[6] Dunn to Ewing, August 20, 1849, Ewing Papers; Stickney to Embree,
November 21, 1849, Embree MSS.

the Oregon Territory must be placed in its setting. It was a good appointment, carrying prestige and a salary of $3,000 per year (the same as that of the Commissioner of the General Land Office).[7] It had valuable perquisites, and under normal conditions such an appointment was of value to an astute politician, especially as a steppingstone to higher office.

Oregon Territory was organized early enough in the Polk administration so that inevitably its first governor would be a Democrat. Doubtless anyone offered the post would consider its probable tenure, and when the territory was organized there was an appreciable fraction of the Polk administration remaining and a reasonable possibility that a Democrat would hold the executive branch for another four years. Consequently Polk had no difficulty in finding a suitable person for the office.

However, the man who was his first choice did not accept the offer. This was Lincoln's contemporary of long standing, James Shields,[8] whose availability was enhanced by the military reputation which he had won at Cerro Gordo and Cherubusco. With years of political experience he was in a strategic position for advancement. What he desired materialized at this juncture: he became a candidate for United States Senator against the aging Sidney Breese and he was elected. He telegraphed his resignation of the Oregon appointment.

Polk wrote in his *Diary* that he had already made up his mind that if Shields declined the Oregon office it would be offered to General Joseph Lane, of Indiana.[9] When Shields resigned Polk immediately sent Lane his commission and wrote him that he was appointed. This appointment, too, was a political reward for Mexican War service; Lane had emerged as one of the outstanding officers, with rank of brevet Major General. He accepted the offer. Reaching Oregon by way of Santa Fe, in his brief incumbency he gave the territory an excellent administration, winning well deserved popularity.

---

[7] *Register of All Officers and Agents in the Service of the United States,* pp. 135, 271.

[8] Polk, *Diary,* IV:91; *Dictionary of American Biography,* XVII:106 f; William H. Condon, *Life of Major General James Shields* (1900); New York *Herald,* August 18, 1848; *Illinois State Journal,* August 26, 1848.

[9] *Dictionary of American Biography,* X:579 f; Sister M. Margaret Jean Kelley, *The Career of Joseph Lane, Frontier Politician* (1942); New York *Herald,* June 5, 1849, Chicago *Democrat,* June 9, 1849; *Indiana State Journal,* September 2, 1849; Galena *Gazette and Advertiser,* July 10, 1849; New York *Tribune,* December 13, 1849.

When the appointment of a governor of Oregon fell to the succeeding Whig administration, the place was first offered to Joseph G. Marshall of Indiana. Apparently Marshall did not seek the place, but a commission was sent to him with a covering letter by the Secretary of State.[10] In the same mail Clayton sent a commission as secretary of Oregon to Lincoln.

Marshall's appointment received some publicity. The Indiana *State Sentinel* quoted the Democratic national organ, the Washington *Union,* on August 23: "The chivalrous and heroic Gen. Lane—the Marion of the Mexican War—has been removed from the office of Governor of Oregon, and a Mexican Whig by the name of J. H. Marshall, of Indiana appointed to succeed him." To the *Union's* complaint the *Sentinel* added, "through the President of their *outside* cabinet, Truman Smith." Next day the Galena *Gazette* published the news of the appointment, and the Vandalia *Fayette Yeoman* noted the appointment of both Marshall and Lincoln.[11] The Vandalia paper expressed doubt that Lincoln would accept. The Indiana *State Journal* defended the appointment of Marshall and denied injustice to Lane. The *State Sentinel* on September 6 published the intelligence that Marshall had declined. Marshall wrote to Clayton a few days later, declining the place on the ground that circumstances made it impossible to accept.[12]

The next Whig to be offered the governorship of Oregon was Lincoln. It is true that the extant sources do not enable the exhibit of the actual commission nor the citation of an official document explicitly stating the fact of the offer. But the highest degree of probability that the offer was made can be established.

Beveridge came to his erroneous conclusion, first, because he assumed that the appointment was at the disposal of the State Department, and second, because when he was making his investigation the records of the State Department were restricted and not available to him. He was satisfied, or had to be satisfied, by having the Secretary of State, Frank B. Kellogg, search the records for him. Mr. Kellogg found no record of the appointment in the department, and so informed Beveridge. So far as Mr. Kellogg's statement went it was correct, but it did not go far enough.

---

[10] Domestic Letters, State Department, p. 270.

[11] Vandalia *Fayette Yeoman,* August 25, 1849.

[12] State Department Archives.

In the early months of the Taylor administration there was confusion about the specific functions of the recently established Department of the Interior, especially as to what functions it took over from the State Department. Previously territorial appointments had been handled by State. But Ewing, as the first Secretary of the Interior, proceeded upon the view that his new department was the proper one to make appointments to territorial administrations. He soon saw to it that it made them. If Beveridge, instead of going only to the State Department for information, had also searched the records of Interior, doubtless he would have reached a different conclusion.

These records of the Interior Department, when considered with certain facts well established in the published writings of Lincoln, clearly indicate two things. First, that Ewing, acting as Secretary of the Interior and by direction of President Taylor, offered Lincoln the governorship of Oregon Territory. Second, that Clayton, acting through the State Department upon cabinet recommendation, had previously offered him the secretaryship of the same territory.

The earliest Interior Department source is a letter of that faithful friend of Lincoln's, Dr. Henry, to Secretary Ewing.[13] The body of that letter has nothing to do with Lincoln and the governorship of Oregon; it concerned the still sore feelings about the handling of the Land Office appointment. It was only when the doctor got to a postscript that his letter shed light on the Oregon matter: "I have just learned by a letter received by Mr. Lincoln's brother-in-law (Mr. Lincoln being from the city on Professional business) that he has declined the office of Governor of Oregon, and for reasons I presume entirely personal to himself and *certain friends* whose claims he early pressed upon Gen. Taylor for appointment to office. I know Mr. Lincoln is disposed to yield the administration his most cordial support notwithstanding his refusal to take office for *himself* so long as his friends are unprovided for." Correlating with this letter is the text of a telegram of the same date:

Hon: Thos Ewing
Mr. Lincoln is absent, will be home tonight
Wm. Pope [14]

---

[13] Henry to Ewing, August 21, 1849, Ewing Papers.
[14] *Ibid.*

But Lincoln did not reach home at the time he was expected. His absence was protracted for several days; before his return a most revealing telegram was sent:

> Telegraph Office
>> cor 4th St. & Pa Ave.
>> Is Mr. Lincoln in Springfield? The President wishes to hear from him immediately.
>>> T. Ewing
> Charge dispatch and answer to Dept of Interior [15]

There are two documents by Lincoln which pertain to this phase of the story. The first is a telegram which he sent from Springfield on September 27:

> Hon. Thomas Ewing
>> I respectfully decline Governorship of Oregon; I am still anxious that Simeon Francis shall be Secretary of that Territory.[16]

The second is Lincoln's letter of the same date to Ewing: "Some discrepancy may appear between my letter of the 23rd. and my Telegraphic dispatch of today, to explain which I write this. As I told [y]ou in that letter, I sent a dispatch the same [d]ay to a friend at Springfield to be forwarded [to] you; but that friend and some others, supposing [I] had decided hastily, withheld the dispatch, and [w]rote me again. On receiving your letter, I came to Springfield, and now Telegraph you myself." [17]

From these several documents the essential background of the story can be reconstructed. Ewing's communication to Lincoln, whether a letter or telegram, reached Springfield before September 21. Lincoln was in Tremont. The message being from a government official, it was delivered to someone close to Lincoln, who very properly read it. Its content offered Lincoln the appointment as governor of Oregon. So important a message was taken to Lincoln. While the courier was on his way to Tremont, William Pope notified Ewing of Lincoln's absence from the city. On the twenty-third Lincoln sent to these friends in Springfield a copy of a telegram, declining the appointment, which he instructed his friends to put on the wires. Springfield

---

[15] Department of the Interior, Letter Book, Miscellaneous, No. I, 1849-50, p. 12.

[16] *Ibid.*

[17] *CW* II:66

then had telegraphic connection with the East; Tremont did not. But these friends, convinced that he was acting hastily, did not send it. On the same day (September 23) Lincoln wrote to Ewing, presumably declining the offer. Consequently no reply reached Ewing for several days.

While Ewing was waiting for Lincoln's reply, President Taylor became insistent, and Ewing sent his telegram on the twenty-fifth, inquiring whether Lincoln was in Springfield and saying that the President desired to hear from him at once. Taylor had favored the appointment of Lincoln to the Land Office position; he had appointed Butterfield only in accordance with his policy of following the recommendation of the department secretary. Now he wanted to make amends. "The President," not "The Secretary of the Interior," wished to hear from Lincoln. The President was taking the responsibility.

But Lincoln did not reach Springfield until the twenty-seventh, and then found that his directions had not been followed. No doubt his friends, who had thought that he was acting hastily, tried to convince him that he should accept the offer. But he did not change his mind because of any pressure which they brought to bear. Forthwith he sent his telegram of declination and wrote his letter explaining the circumstances.

Even before the date of the first primary source materials (Dr. Henry's letter of September 21 to Ewing), the appointment of Lincoln had been announced in the press. The earliest reference which has come to light contains a curious misprint. The Baltimore *Clipper*, which because of its nearness to Washington was frequently the first to print national political news, carried this item on September 19:

Wash. Sep. 18—1849
Appointment of Governor of Oregon
Yesterday the Hon. Mr. Sinclair, ex-member of Congress, of Illinois, was appointed Gov. of Oregon, in the place of Mr. Marshall, of Indiana, who, before he left the city last week, declined the tendered honor; Col Hamilton, of Ohio, was appointed Secretary of State.[18]

Next day the *Clipper* corrected its "error of the type," not "of the pen," (so it said) and made clear that the offer was to Mr. Lincoln, "a clever, go ahead, good natured, and proper person for the station."

---

[18] Baltimore *Clipper*, September 19 and 20, 1849.

By the twentieth the news had reached Horace Greeley's
New York *Tribune,* and Lincoln's colleague in Congress published the following:

Oregon: We are informed that Hon. Abraham Lincoln, a member of
the last Congress, from Illinois has been tendered the appointment of
Governor of this Territory.[19]

On the twenty-first the *Illinois Journal,* whose editor knew
well what was transpiring in Springfield, printed the

Summary News

We learn by dispatch from Washington that the Governorship
of Oregon, declined by Mr. Marshall of Indiana, has been tendered
to the Hon. A. Lincoln of this city. Mr. Lincoln being absent from
home, we have no means of knowing, for a certainty, whether he will
accept it or not. Judging from what we know of Mr. Lincoln's present
position, we are inclined to the opinion that he will *decline the appointment.*

The following day a fuller account appeared in the New
York *Tribune.* The fact that newspapers of national importance
carried the report gives greater corroboration than newspaper
reports of only local origin. Greeley's *Tribune* story, which came
by "the midnight southern mail" said:

Governor of Oregon Appointed

Hon. Abraham Lincoln of Ill. has been appointed Governor of
Oregon. Mr. Lincoln was conspicuous in the last Congress, especially
during the last session, when he attempted to frame and put through
a bill for the gradual Abolition of Slavery, in the District of Columbia.
He is a strong but judicious enemy of Slavery, and his efforts are
usually very practical, if not always successful. He is a man of sound
judgment, good though not brilliant mind, and capable, mentally and
physically, of great endurance,—qualities very essential to the position
he is about to assume.

The Indiana *State Journal* on September 24 republished an
item by "Ashland," the Washington correspondent of the Louisville *Courier.* It explained in some detail, and expressed regret
for, the declination of the Oregon governorship by Mr. Marshall,
and added that "Abraham Lincoln, Esq., of Illinois, another
wholesouled Whig, is spoken of in connection with that place,
he having been previously offered the Secretaryship of the Territory under Mr. Marshall." This was rumor, but it has value as

---

[19] New York *Tribune,* September 20, 1849.

indicating the status of the matter at the time the offer was made to Lincoln. Time in itself is significant: the reprinting in an Indianapolis newspaper of an item derived from a Louisville paper, which item had first been transmitted from Washington, puts "Ashland's" rumor, in point of time, some days earlier than September 21.

On September 25 the Quincy *Whig* carried a report, to which attention was directed by a "printer's fist," that "The office of Governor of Oregon has been offered to Hon. A. Lincoln of Springfield." It cited the *Illinois Journal's* doubt that Lincoln would accept. On the same day John Wentworth demonstrated his regard for Lincoln in the notice:

Good for Abraham.—Hon. A. Lincoln has been appointed Governor for Oregon. The Whigs of the Galena District are anxious that Col. Baker should have a foreign appointment.[20]

And on the same day the Louisville *Courier* had in its regular feature from Washington, another letter of "Ashland's" with interesting detail:

The Cabinet at its last meeting agreed upon the selection of A. Lincoln Esq. of Illinois, as Governor of Oregon, in the place of Mr. Marshall, of Indiana, who declined the appointment. Major Gaines was the choice of several members of the Cabinet, but arriving here in Washington most opportunely he peremptorily refused to allow his name to be brought in conflict with Mr. Lincoln's under any circumstances whatever. It is problematical whether Mr. Lincoln will accept the appointment, although his friends here are exceedingly anxious that he should do so.[21]

"Ashland's" letter is of more than ordinary value. As his letters show, he was accurate and well informed. His statement that the cabinet had agreed upon Lincoln, although some of its members favored Major Gaines, carries great weight. As the story of the Land Office appointment had demonstrated, Collamer and Preston were loyally in Lincoln's favor. Always President Taylor was appreciative of him.

The press reports continued. The *Illinois Journal* on September 28 said that "We have understood that Hon. Abraham Lincoln has declined the office of Governor of Oregon." Next day

[20] Chicago *Democrat*, September 25, 1849.

[21] Louisville *Courier*, September 25, 1849. The date of "Ashland's" dispatch was September 20.

the Indiana *State Journal* carried the following: "Governor of
Oregon.—The Washington correspondent of the Baltimore
Clipper, of the 18th Inst, says that the Hon. Mr. Lincoln, ex member of Congress, of Illinois, has been appointed Governor of
Oregon in place of Mr. Marshall of Indiana, who, before he left
the city, last week declined the tendered honor; and Col. Hamilton of Ohio was appointed Secretary of State." The New York
Tribune in its main editorial column on October 1 stated that
Lincoln had declined the Oregon governorship. The Baltimore
Clipper was heard from again three days later: "It seems a
difficult matter to provide a Governor of Oregon, in place of
Gen. Lane, whose doom is sealed. First, Mr. Marshall, of Indiana,
was designated, and he declined; next Mr. Lincoln, of Illinois,
was named, and he begged to be excused, and now Major J. P.
Gaines is appointed. Perhaps he may not desire to go to Oregon,
and a fourth gentleman may have to be tendered the situation."
But the Indiana *State Journal* on October 4 was not so well informed as the *Clipper.* Under "News of the Day" it stated that
"We learn from the Cincinnati *Enquirer* that Mr. Lincoln late
representative in Congress from the Springfield District, Illinois,
has been appointed Governor of Oregon by President Taylor."
But by the ninth the Indiana *State Sentinel,* which seemed to
prefer to get its news from other papers but disdained to cite its
local contemporary, the *State Journal,* quoted the Washington
Republic to the effect that Lincoln had declined and Gaines had
been appointed. On that date the Quincy *Whig* noted Lincoln's
declination, and on October 10 the *Illinois Journal* quoted the
St. Louis *Republican* with one fact and one utterly erroneous
statement: "Martin P. Sweet of Illinois is named for governor of
Oregon in place of Hon. A. Lincoln who declined appointment."

Lincoln's war record was rehashed in some of the newspaper
references to the Oregon appointment. Since the motive was
political the stories are not to be taken seriously except as evidence of how tenaciously the reputation gained by the Spot
Resolutions and the war speech remained in memory. On October
11 the Indiana *State Sentinel* had the following:

> The Hon. Mr. Lincoln of Illinois, has been appointed Governor
> of Oregon. "Spotty" has at last received his reward and has found
> out the "exact spot" to which he would like to go.—St. Louis *Union.*
> At any rate Indiana has been punished, for not responding favorably to Truman Smith's propositions. By the way; it is said that
> "Spotty" *declines* the appointment. . . .

Again on October 25 the *Sentinel* carried a similar note, this time quite wide of the truth: ". . . Lincoln, who was offered [the Governorship of Oregon] was one of the fourteen who in Congress voted against granting supplies of men and money to the American Army in·Mexico. . . ." On that note of the eagle's scream it will suffice to close the account of newspaper publicity given Lincoln's appointment.

One item of Lincoln's correspondence indicates something of the interest which his friends took in advancing his appointment to the Oregon office. John Addison (whom Lincoln had tried to get placed in a clerkship in the Land Office) and others are referred to in a letter to Addison. Addison wanted to become secretary of Oregon Territory, apparently overlooking the improbability that both governor and secretary would be appointed from the same state. Lincoln thanked Addison and the others (G. T. M. Davis is specifically mentioned) who had interested themselves in his behalf, and told Addison candidly that he was already committed to the promotion of Simeon Francis for the second office. "On as much reflection as I have had time to give to the subject [of his own appointment as Governor] I cannot consent to accept it," he wrote.[22]

Lincoln nowhere in extant sources stated his reasons for declining the appointment. A. G. Henry had assumed that his reasons were "entirely personal to himself," and the *Illinois State Journal* implied much the same.[23] Herndon offered the opinion that Lincoln had some inclination to accept, but was overruled when "his wife put her foot squarely down upon it with a firm and emphatic No."[24] Thus began the tradition that a domineering wife determined the event. This is most unlikely. Lincoln made his own decisions, and there is no evidence in the primary sources to indicate other than that Mrs. Lincoln was a loyal wife, proud of her husband, and cooperative in his political career.

However, if it were true that Mrs. Lincoln was opposed to the removal of the family to Oregon her judgment was sound and deserving of approval, not censure. Both the Lincoln children were small, and Eddie was in such delicate health that he died less than six months from that time. Any route to Oregon was

[22] *CW* II:65.
[23] *Illinois State Journal*, September 21, 1849.
[24] Herndon and Weik, I:306.

difficult. Major Gaines, who accepted the appointment, went to Oregon by what was supposed to be the easiest mode of travel, by ship around the Horn, and on the voyage two of the Gaines' daughters died of yellow fever.[25]

One reason for Lincoln's refusal can readily be surmised. Of course the offer was considered, among other reasons, with reference to its advantage for his political future. The next goal of Lincoln's aspiration in his political career was election to the Senate. It is highly probable that he scrutinized the Oregon appointment with this in view, and one may hazard the guess that if the office of governor of Oregon would have served as a steppingstone to election to the Senate Lincoln might have accepted it. But the prospects were exactly the opposite. There was no certainty that the tenure of office would extend beyond the incumbent administration. If the Whigs remained in power there would be another four years of prospective tenure. But that was quite uncertain, and at that time improbable.

And Oregon was overwhelmingly Democratic. This was well known at the time. The Chicago *Democrat* on September 27 noted that a recent census of Oregon showed a population of 8,900, with about 2,500 voters. In another item on the same page it said that Oregon was Democratic and that "whigery is growing less every year." The Indiana *Sentinel* a week later cited a letter written from Oregon City, then the territorial capital, which reported that the Democrats had triumphed in a recent election; four Democrats had received 887 votes to a lone Whig's 106. The *Sentinel* succinctly summed up the Oregon political situation by saying that there were not enough Whigs in the territory to make mile posts. As a matter of fact Oregon remained Democratic until 1860.

Lincoln was sagacious enough to know that he would have been committing political suicide had he gone to Oregon. He was aware, too, that while governor of Oregon he could not advance himself in the law. Whatever other reasons he had for declining the office, these were enough.

Lincoln had received many rebuffs in his efforts to influence party patronage. He had experienced a bitter disappointment

---

[25] The *Indiana State Sentinel*, February 24, 1849, has an interesting and highly illustrative letter relating conditions of travel to Oregon. Bancroft, in his *History of Oregon*, II:139, tells of the hardships and misfortunes of the Gaines family traveling to Oregon.

when he was rejected after seeking the General Land Office commissionership for himself. But now he had some satisfaction that his efforts on behalf of his party and his party's President were recognized and appreciated by the President and some of the administration leaders. He must have been grimly pleased when those cabinet officers who had treated him and his recommendations in so cavalier a fashion had, willingly or unwillingly, united with his friends in the cabinet to recommend that he be offered one of the highest paid offices within the power of the government to bestow. The governorship, not the minor and poorly paid secretaryship, of Oregon Territory, was the measure of the Taylor administration's value of Lincoln. Even though the position offered was not acceptable to him, he had the consciousness of the recognition which the offer implied. His judgment not to remove to Oregon was sound. His future lay not in the far West, but in the growing and changing Prairie State.

17

"HEREAFTER"

It was the opinion of A. T. Bledsoe, once a friend and political associate, that Lincoln, after his one term in Congress, was "in such low repute among his neighbors, and with his former political friends, that he could not have been elected a constable or a justice of the peace." [1]

Lincoln himself put it differently. In the Fell "autobiography" he said merely, "In 1846 I was once elected to the lower House of Congress. Was not a candidate for re-election. From 1849 to 1854, both inclusive, practiced law more assiduously than ever before. Always a whig in politics, and generally on the whig electoral tickets, making active canvasses. I was losing interest in politics, when the repeal of the Missouri Compromise aroused me again. . . ." [2] In the material written for use in the 1860 Presidential campaign he made a fuller statement. Writing in the third person, he said, "In 1846 he was elected to the lower House of Congress, and served one term only, commencing in Dec. 1847 and ending with the inauguration of Gen. Taylor. . . ." Apparently conscious of the criticism of his Congressional career ("Much has been said of his course in Congress in regard to the

---

[1] Harry E. Pratt, "Albert Taylor Bledsoe: Critic of Lincoln." *Transactions of the Illinois Historical Society*, 1934, pp. 153-83.

[2] *CW* III:511 f.

[Mexican] war.") he made a fairly long statement of his record in voting supplies and in explanation of his vote on the Ashmun amendment, but said nothing of the Spot Resolutions or of his speech. Then he continued:

> Mr. L. was not a candidate for re-election. This was determined upon, and declared before he went to Washington, in accordance with an understanding among whig friends. . . .
>
> Upon his return from Congress he went to the practice of the law with greater earnestness than ever before. . . .
>
> In 1854, his profession had almost superseded the thought of politics in his mind, when the repeal of the Missouri Compromise aroused him as he had never been before.
>
> In the autumn of that year he took the stump with no broader practical aim or object [than] to secure, if possible, the re-election of Hon. Richard Yates to Congress. His speeches at once attracted a more marked attention than they had ever before done.[3]

Bledsoe's estimate was exaggerated and colored by the bias and enmity which existed at the time of his writing. Lincoln's own estimate was a rationalization. Only the backward look from a time interval of several years could have seen in his lesser participation enough to warrent the words, "I was losing interest in politics." The qualifying "almost" in the second statement is eloquent. From his New Salem days until his death Lincoln never lost interest in politics. Lyman Trumbull, who knew him well, wrote that "From the time when, at the age of twenty-three, he announced himself a candidate for the legislature from Sangamon County, till his death, he was almost constantly in office, or struggling to obtain one. Sometimes defeated and often successful, he never abandoned the desire for office till he had reached the presidency the second time." [4]

Lincoln did not retire from politics at the close of his Congressional career. He was involuntarily retired, by reason of the widespread and lasting unpopularity of his record with reference to the war. Naturally he gave more time and effort to the practice of law. Between 1849 and 1854 he devoted himself the more to the law because during that period he was in forced retirement from politics. Throughout that period he was as ambitious for political office as ever he had been. His ambition was

---

[3] *CW* IV:65-67.

[4] In a letter to his son, quoted in Horace White, *The Life of Lyman Trumbull* (1912), p. 429.

to be elected to the United States Senate, and he awaited only the opportunity to become a candidate. He was sufficiently acute to sense that he was politically unavailable until he had lived down the unpopularity caused by his Mexican War stand. As soon as the opportune time brought an issue he was again in politics.

A problem of harmony within the Whig ranks emerged early in Lincoln's period of "retirement." The local resentment at the way he had been treated in the Land Office appointment simply would not down. Ewing's role and tactics became known, although Lincoln did his best to prevent discussion. He knew that Ewing was guilty of chicanery, and apparently he revealed his knowledge, in confidence, to some friends.[5] Evidently his confidence was betrayed, for the story got around. Lyman D. Stickney, the unsuccessful candidate for the secretaryship of Oregon, wrote to Elisha Embree that there was great indignation among the Illinois Whigs over Butterfield's appointment, and that it would take but little to call forth a public expression against Ewing.[6]

That public expression was made by Lincoln's friend, Usher F. Linder, who made it from the floor of the lower house of the Illinois legislature. It was a hot speech. Linder began by saying that although the state legislature was not an appropriate place to discuss national matters, he could not refrain from protesting the acts of a national officer, Thomas Ewing, minister of the "Home Department." Ewing was unsuited to wield the immense patronage which had been placed in his hands. He was hostile to all that was popular. He had no sympathies with the people. He disposed of offices more like a prince than a servant of a republican people. Linder waxed warm as he addressed the speaker: "I speak plainly, sir, for I want what I say to be published, that it may reach the individual for whom it is intended— the man who could disregard the almost unanimous wish of . . . the Whig people of Illinois—and overlook the claims of such men as Lincoln. . . ." Amid the cheers of the Democrats in the house, who enjoyed the exposure of cracks in the Whig edifice, the indignant Linder continued: "Such a man as Ewing has no right to

---

[5] For one example, see Lincoln's letter to Joe Gillespie, June 13, 1849 (CW II:59).

[6] Stickney to Embree, September 7, 1849, Embree MSS.

rule the cabinet of a republican president. He is universally odious, and stinks in the nostrils of the nation. He is a lump of ice, an unfeeling, unsympathetic aristocrat, a rough, imperious, uncouth, and unamiable man." Linder closed with the prediction that if President Taylor retained Ewing in his cabinet the Whig membership in Congress would not amount to a corporal's guard.[7]

Of course this episode had repercussions. The Chicago *Journal* felt obliged to take Linder to task. It must be acknowledged that the editor's and the paper's support of Butterfield was no reason why it should not do so. To be sure, the *Journal* in its rejoinder defended Ewing from the personal viewpoint of the editor, but its point that Linder's remarks must be disavowed was valid in the interest of party harmony. The *Journal* summarized Linder's speech, and denounced it in a long editorial. It noted with concern that while the speech was received with tremendous applause from the floor of the house, the lobby, and the galleries —the only spontaneous outburst during the session—not a word of censure had been uttered by Whigs in the House nor in the press. What was most remarkable was that a clerk in Butterfield's office, who was a member of the house, was present. His silence bore out the truth of Linder's assertions. Of course the *State Register* made the most of the incident.[8]

But it was inconceivable that Lincoln would let the speech go without disavowal; "the generous Lincoln, successively offered by the President the offices of Secretary and Governor of Oregon," would not countenance such an assault, least of all justify it, the *Journal* insisted.

The *Journal* was right. Its editor sent a marked copy of the issue to Lincoln. He wrote to the editor promptly. He explained that he had been away from Springfield the whole time the legislature was in session, so that his first acquaintance with the episode was a reference in the *Illinois Journal.* Had he known of the intention of any Whig to make such a speech he would have done his utmost to prevent it. Lincoln made a graceful remark about Butterfield, spoke of the great difficulties which Ewing met in the discharge of his duties, and said that he believed

---

[7] An extract from Linder's speech appears in Nicolay and Hay, *The Complete Works of Abraham Lincoln* (1890), II:132 f. A longer report of the speech appeared in the Chicago *Journal,* November 14, 1849.

[8] *Illinois State Register,* November 8, 1849.

Ewing to be an able and a faithful officer. He closed by remarking that a more intimate acquaintance with Ewing would probably change the views of most of his opponents.[9]

But Lincoln could not quiet the matter. The suspicion of
fraud in the Land Office appointment persisted. The suspicion
was substantial enough to cause a Congressional investigation.
Lincoln's former colleague, William A. Richardson was named
chairman of the committee.[10] The New York *Herald* (clipped in
the Chicago *Democrat* of June 18, 1850) said of its work:

> The Richardson Committee have waded through the pile of
> papers furnished by Secretary Ewing, and will, tomorrow, commence
> examining witnesses, commencing with Justin Butterfield, Mr. Ewing's
> man Friday. . . . It may be that the Committee will ascertain whether
> there was not frand and deception practiced to get Butterfield ap-
> pointed instead of Abraham Lincoln . . . and whether there was not
> papers of note in Lincoln's favor, which were carefully and designedly
> excluded from the abstract which was made up in the Department of
> the Interior, and taken to the President for his decision as to what
> man he would appoint.

The committee found that a clerk in the Interior Department
had suppressed some of the Lincoln documents. It was not difficult to read between the lines. It has been related that Ewing prepared, or caused to be prepared, a dossier for each applicant, and
that in the whole collection the documents supporting Butterfield were given favorable and prominent place, while the materials recommending Lincoln were placed inconspicuously—and
the documents *against* him were pointedly displayed, with advice
to the President to read them. It was true that two Lincoln documents were suppressed. Lincoln mentioned this in a letter to
Josiah Lucas, who had worked so hard in his interest.[11] Apparently Ewing made one of his clerks responsible for the suppression. The Richardson committee was forced to absolve Ewing.
Yet, said the New York *Herald* on August 2, 1850, "there is so
much opposition making its appearance in Washington just now,

---

[9] *CW* II:68.

[10] Although the New York *Herald* emphasized the alleged fraud involved
in the Butterfield appointment, the Richardson committee's investigation
was of alleged misuses of public funds and of alleged control of appointments in the Pension Office and the General Land Office. The committee's
report contains no reference to the Lincoln-Butterfield incident.

[11] *CW* II:67.

to the continuance in office of Mr. Commissioner Butterfield. . . . The manner in which he received his appointment . . . is much talked of here."

The details which were not publicly known were given Lincoln by his friend Addison, still in the Land Office as a clerk.[12] It is most unfortunate that Lincoln did not retain Addison's letter, for his reply suggests something of its content, and implies that the full information would be revealing. It appears that Lincoln had known these things for a long time, and had contemplated making them public. He goes so far as to characterize someone's act as "villainy," and to refer to the "original villain," and the act fills him with indignation. It is not clear whether the original "villain" was Butterfield or Ewing; probably it was Ewing. At all events, Addison had been persecuted for his support of Lincoln. Nor was he the only one persecuted: Henderson, the Land Office clerk, who as a member of the legislature had heard Linder's speech without protesting it, was discharged.[13] Yet, Lincoln wrote to Addison, a public exposure would do no good. It might confound the guilty, but it would disparage a good cause. Certainly Lincoln's bitterest opponent would have to admit that he sacrificed his own interest for the sake of his party's welfare. Heartily sick of the Land Office affair, Lincoln said to Addison that if the Land Office place were now offered him he would not take it. He held no grudge.

Busy though Lincoln was in the law in those days, a decision whether or not to run for Congress in 1850 had to be made. There were those who wanted Lincoln to run. Pierre Menard had urged his candidacy. The Pekin *Mirror* advocated his nomination. Without doubt the *Illinois Journal* and other Whig papers would have done so had not Lincoln formally withheld his name. In the *Illinois Journal* of June 7 he published a letter in which he said that he would have peremptorily forbidden the use of his name if he had been at liberty to do so. He offered his opinion that there were several other Whigs in the district who might be elected and who could be elected as easily as he might be. He invited all those who preferred him to hold a convention

---

[12] *CW* II:91 f.

[13] Document filed in Interior Department, National Archives, unsigned, undated, but obviously written after Butterfield's appointment and before the New York *Herald* items cited.

and nominate another. He predicted that in the election the district would again appear right side up.[14]

In this Lincoln was undoubtedly acting in accordance with the desire of Richard Yates of Jacksonville. Thomas L. Harris, who was certain to be the Democratic nominee, expected to be opposed by Yates, and he estimated the relative strength of Yates and Lincoln. Yates, he thought, could carry Morgan (his own) County, and Scott, which Lincoln could not do. Lincoln and Yates would be about equal in Sangamon, and Lincoln would be stronger than Yates in the northern counties. But in his opinion Lincoln was not as strong as Yates in the district as a whole. He added that Yates was much less assailable than Lincoln on slavery and the Wilmot Proviso.[15]

Harris' estimate and Lincoln's statement are the best contemporary indications of Lincoln's political standing at the aftermath of his term in Congress. They must be viewed in the light of the disastrous defeat of Logan in 1848. Lincoln's unpopularity as a result of his record in Congress continued until well after 1850.

The Congressional campaign of 1850 was interrupted by the death of President Taylor. Lincoln was in Chicago on law business at the time, and he was invited to speak at a memorial service. With little time to prepare, he made an excellent, though restrained, eulogy which is notable for its omission of political reference, especially to the compromise measure then being debated in Congress.[16]

Yates was nominated in August, undoubtedly with Lincoln's active support. Lincoln certainly controlled the Sangamon County convention, whose delegates to the District convention were instructed for Yates. The Tazewell County delegates were instructed for Lincoln, but in the face of the formal withdrawal of Lincoln's name and the instruction of the Sangamon delegates for Yates, they acquiesced. Yates was nominated by acclamation.[17]

The record does not show any campaign activity of Lincoln

---

[14] CW II:79.

[15] Harris to Lanphier and Walker (Editors of the *Illinois State Register*), August 1, 1850, Lanphier MSS, Illinois State Historical Library.

[16] CW II:83-90.

[17] *Illinois State Journal,* August 2, 1850; Lacon *Illinois Gazette,* August 10, 1850.

for Yates, but on November 5 the Whig candidate brought the Seventh District back into the Whig column, defeating Harris by a 954 vote margin.[18] This, too, must be taken as an indication of the effect of Lincoln's record. There is no escaping the fact, or the meaning of the fact, that a Whig of much less eminence but of much greater availability recaptured the Whig stronghold.

That Lincoln had by no means withdrawn from politics is indicated by the presence of his name on the call of a Whig District convention which appeared in the *Illinois Journal* on November 29, 1851. The convention met December 22, and Lincoln was made a member of the Committee on Resolutions and a member of a committee of seven who were to nominate four delegates to the Whig National Convention and to select the Whig Central Committee.[19]

As became a shrewd politician, Lincoln was as much interested in local as in state and national affairs. Thus the degree of his loss of interest in politics is to be measured in the fact that on April 7, 1852, he was one of 175 Whigs to sign a call for a meeting to nominate candidates for city offices. This meeting also took action concerning Ninian Edwards, Jr., who had astounded his associates by renouncing Whiggery and joining the Democratic party. The Whig meeting, with Lincoln present, adopted a resolution denouncing him, and demanding that he resign from the Legislature, to which he had been elected as a Whig.[20] Edwards did resign, and a Whig was nominated to succeed him.[21]

The *National Intelligencer* in Washington reported on June 26 that Lincoln had been appointed as Illinois member of the Whig National Committee, but there is no evidence that he took any part in the committee's deliberations.

On July 6 he delivered a political eulogy, this time on the occasion of the death of Henry Clay.[22] Next day he undoubtedly

---

[18] Blaine B. Gernon, *Lincoln in the Political Circus* (1936), p. 202. In 1850 the Democrats recaptured the Sixth District, which Baker had carried for the Whigs in 1848.

[19] *Illinois State Journal,* December 24, 1851. Lincoln's name headed the "Call" of this convention. (*CW* II:113).

[20] *Illinois State Journal,* April 9, 10, 1852.

[21] *Illinois State Journal,* April 27, 1852.

[22] *CW* II:121-32. Lincoln had presided over the planning meeting of local Whigs on June 29 and 30 (*Illinois State Journal,* July 1, 2, 9, 1852).

attended the session of the Whig State Convention in Springfield and the ratification meeting which was held in the evening.[23] The National Convention had been held in Baltimore and the Illinois Convention was deliberately timed to meet afterward because of the unpopularity of Scott, the Presidential nominee, in Illinois. Liking neither the candidate nor the party platform, the apathy of the Illinois Whigs was at its lowest point when the state convention met. Orville H. Browning, presiding, made no attempt to dispel the apathy; in his keynote speech he acknowledged that the party did not hope to elect its candidates for state offices nor to carry the state for Scott.[24]

As Lincoln wrote, he made some speeches as a Scott elector, but the hopelessness of the situation made him exert himself much less than he had done in earlier national campaigns.[25] However, the party did have one success in the state. Heretofore the Whigs had never had more than one Illinois Congressman. In 1852 they elected four, among them Yates, in Lincoln's district. They won in the north central, and in the west central areas, and in the Galena district Elihu Washburne succeeded in attaining the place for which Baker had defeated him in 1848. These Whig victories were due chiefly to two things: the denser settlement of the northern rural areas, with a high population of emigrants from New England and the Middle States, and a more advantageous distribution of Whig strength by the redistricting of the state. But while gaining in the Congressional elections, the party sustained a disastrous loss in the state legislature, and lost all state offices while losing the electoral vote for the Presidency.[26] Oddly enough, in view of his explicit statement that he was not a candidate, Lincoln received some votes on the first ballot of the Sangamon County convention nominating candidates for the legislature.[27]

It is revealing that in his campaigning for Scott the substance of Lincoln's speeches was criticism of Douglas. It could not have

---

[23] *Illinois State Journal*, July 6, 1852; Theodore C. Pease and James G. Randall, *The Diary of Orville Browning* (1925, 1933), I:56 f; *Quincy Whig*, July 19, 1852.

[24] Alexander Davidson and Bernard Stuvé, *A Complete History of Illinois from 1763 to 1873* (1874), p. 600.

[25] *CW* IV:67.

[26] Analysis based upon manuscript election returns, Illinois State Library.

[27] *Illinois State Journal*, August 11, 1852.

added to Lincoln's happiness that Douglas was a contender for
the Democratic nomination for President in 1852. In any event
it is evident that Lincoln was fully aware of the importance of
Douglas and his policies. Further, he was building himself up by
attacking them, while advocating the cause of Scott and the Whig
party. He solicited the opportunity to attack Douglas' Richmond
speech, and did so in Springfield on August 14 and 26. He spoke
in Peoria on September 17 and in Pekin on the twentieth.[28] When
Douglas campaigned in Illinois Lincoln replied to his Springfield
speech on October 28 and 30.[29] Whatever Lincoln did for himself
he did little for Scott, who was beaten in Illinois by 16,000 votes.

It should have been evident to Lincoln that the Whig party
was dying. In the death of Clay it had lost its great national
leader. Webster in decline could not fill Clay's place, nor could
Seward, as yet, although his potential ability was by then indicated. The party had lost its issues—one might almost say that
it had lost its celebrated "principles." There was no longer a
bank question, and the lower tariff of 1846 was generally accepted. So long as an orthodox Democrat was President a reversal
of his party's stand on internal improvements was improbable,
but emphasis upon that single issue could not revive the declining Whig opposition. The Compromise of 1850 appeared to have
quieted the slavery and disunion debate which was so rampant
in 1848 and 1850. A discerning Whig, like Lincoln, could take
but cold comfort in the fact that the "Clay Compromise," with
the several measures presented in one omnibus bill, had failed of
passage, and that the several measures, presented singly, had
been adopted principally because of the valiant efforts of Douglas
supported by the other Democrats.[30] There was little political
advantage in the compromise for a Western Whig. Lincoln seems
to have sensed this, for in his eulogy of Clay he praised the Ashland Sage's achievement in securing the Missouri Compromise,
but said little of the Compromise of 1850.

How, then, was an aspiring and ambitious Whig to achieve
election to the Senate in a Western state whose Whig strength,

---

[28] *Illinois State Journal*, August 17, 30, September 22, 1852. Democratic
allusions to these speeches are found in the *Illinois State Register*, August
29, 1852, the Peoria *Democratic Press*, September 22, 1852, and the Pekin
Reveille, clipped in the *State Register*, September 25, 1852.

[29] *Illinois State Journal*, October 30, November 1, 1852.

[30] Hamilton, *Zachary Taylor, Soldier in the White House*, pp. 270-339.

never formidable, and decisive only where it was locally concentrated, was steadily and now rapidly diminishing? It was not difficult for Lincoln to find the answer. If one had no hope of getting elected on the internal improvements issue, one other issue offered opportunity. "I reckon you are right, Senator. We have got to deal with this slavery question, and got to give it more attention hereafter than we have been doing."

The year 1853 was a quiet one, politically, for Lincoln. So it was for everyone else. The Pierce administration was, without brilliance or display, pursuing its steady way, with little difficulty from the opposition. There seemed to be no cause, no burning question which could be utilized as the occasion for Lincoln's long deferred re-entry into politics. The lapse of five years was, perhaps, sufficient for people to have forgotten their indignation against his Spot Resolutions and his war speech. The time was ripe, or would be ripe, when the issue presented itself.

The explosive reaction to the presentation by Douglas of the Kansas-Nebraska Act was precisely the occasion which Lincoln needed. Nothing could have been better adapted for his political revival than this bill in its final form, innocent though it was in intent and purpose. It was, of course, the duty of Douglas as chairman of the Senate Committee on Territories to present organization bills as they were needed. His success with the Utah and New Mexico bills was apparent. It was now time for the organization of these two areas. To exhibit here the whole of the complicating factors would be irrelevant. Railroad building and land speculation were involved. The legislation was needed, and it was forthcoming.[31]

The detail of the bill which, more than any other, became a political and emotional firebrand—the very thing that Lincoln needed and wanted—was the repeal of the Missouri Compromise. This, incidentally, was not the contribution of Douglas, nor of any other Democrat, but of a Kentucky Whig, Senator Dixon. But no one would ever have learned this fact from anything that Lincoln said. Enough for him that the bill, as it passed the Senate on March 3 and the House on May 22, 1854, contained the repeal. He had his issue. "Hereafter" had become now. From that time Lincoln gave more attention to slavery than he had ever given it before.

---

[31] Milton, pp. 97-154.

In this, again, he was not leading. He was following. The free soil Democrats had long since been out in front, and the first public protest against the putative wrongs of the Kansas-Nebraska Act was not by antislavery Whigs but was the "Appeal of the Independent Democrats." [32] It mattered not that Douglas proved that the same politicians who assailed him for the repeal had, until 1848, strenuously opposed the compromise, and in 1848-49 had refused to extend the compromise line to the Pacific. It mattered not that Lincoln was one of the latter group. By his enemies Douglas was made a symbol of the proslavery power. His way from Washington to Illinois was lighted by burning effigies of himself, and abolitionist enthusiasm burned brighter than the fires. Illinois went with the other free states.[33] Whig newspapers carried anti-Nebraska messages which were blazoned from Maine to Iowa. Significantly, a few Democratic papers in Illinois joined them. Anti-Nebraska meetings were held in several Illinois cities, as they were in other states. Out of these meetings grew the Republican party. From the complex of forces was to emerge that sectional break which Polk had foreseen and dreaded, and, incidentally, the final collapse of the Whig party.

But Lincoln was far behind the van in these struggles. Indeed, even in advancing his own interests, he made haste slowly. Nor did he admit that the Whig party was dead; in speaking against Douglas and the Kansas-Nebraska Act in 1854 he expressly denied it.[34] But the defeat of Yates by the same Thomas L. Harris, that year, in spite of Lincoln's efforts for Yates, might have enlightened Lincoln as to the vitality of his party. He did presently perceive that there was no longer a simple division between Whigs and Democrats, but that there was a cleavage between free-soilers and conservatives on the slavery issue which cut across the line of Whigs and Democrats. He correctly concluded that the division between the supporters and the opponents of the Kansas-Nebraska Act gave him his long awaited opportunity to run for office, and gave him the issue to run upon.[35]

---

[32] Craven, pp. 326 ff.

[33] Milton, pp. 171-86; Moses, *Illinois*, II:587 ff.

[34] Wilson to Lincoln, October 20, 1854, RTLP; Mearns, I:188 f.

[35] This point was made by Herndon: "Lincoln saw his opportunity and Douglas's downfall." "This repeal was his opportunity and he seized it and rode to glory on the popular wave." (Herndon to Weik, October 28, 1885, February 11, 1887, Herndon Papers.)

Obviously his own interests, as well as those of Yates, had been served in his campaigning in the Congressional election of 1854. For in the discussions with Douglas in Springfield and in Peoria he was bent upon enhancing his own political standing by opposing Douglas.

The famous Peoria speech was clearly so pointed.[36] Shrewdly omitting a fair estimate of the purpose of the Kansas-Nebraska Act, Lincoln centered attention upon the repeal of the compromise, and painted in the darkest colors the evils which he claimed would result from it. The provision of the act for "popular sovereignty" as the means of settling the slavery question in Kansas Lincoln characterized as *declared* indifference, but as I must think, covert *real* zeal for the spread of slavery." [37] The act, he said, was an aggravation of the one thing which endangered the Union. The compromise line, he now insisted (although in Congress he had voted against its extension to the Pacific), must be restored. That would restore the national faith, the national confidence, and the national feeling of brotherhood. But, he charged, the authors of the act want even more than the destruction of the compromise: "That future use is to be the planting of slavery wherever in the wide world, local and unorganized opposition cannot prevent it." [38]

Plainly the Peoria speech marks a great advance in Lincoln's literary and forensic power; it is easy to see that when he made use of this power he had passed across the dividing line, from the ordinary to the superior in the composition and delivery of his speeches. But not much can be said for the logic of the speech, nor for Lincoln's fairness. Douglas' alleged "covert real zeal" for slavery extension was soon to be convincingly denied: when President Buchanan recommended the admission of Kansas as a slave state under the Lecompton Constitution it was Douglas who led the fight against it and defeated the administration in the Senate. When Douglas ran for re-election in 1858, Buchanan in retaliation used every means to encompass his defeat, taking away from him every vestige of patronage. In his re-election victory Douglas defeated both Buchanan and Lincoln, winning a triumphant vin-

---

[36] *CW* II:247-83.

[37] *CW* II:255.

[38] *CW* II:273.

dication of his popular sovereignty principle.[39] As has been stated, there were but two slaves in Kansas in 1860, and Kansas was admitted to the Union as a free state on the basis of the Kansas-Nebraska Act, without supplementary antislavery legislation.[40] In his Peoria-speech, with its specious arguments against popular sovereignty, Lincoln was not fighting for a cause. He was using the slavery issue, conveniently presented by the Kansas-Nebraska Act, to advance his own political standing. He was using the act to run for office.

He was, indeed, running for office in 1854. Unmentioned by him in his autobiographical sketches, and difficult to understand until its implications are perceived, is the fact that in that year Lincoln was again a candidate for election to the state legislature.[41] He was elected. To be sure, he did not desire to be a member of the legislature again, and he had no intention to act as a member of it when he became a candidate and was elected. He saw, by the time of the summer of 1854, that the Kansas-Nebraska Act was a heaven-sent opportunity for him—the issue upon which he would run for election to the United States Senate. Without the Kansas-Nebraska Act there was not the slightest likelihood of his election, for as between Whig and Democratic candidates the Democrat, probably James Shields, would probably have been elected. This was evident from the fact that Whig membership in the legislature, the body which then elected Senators, had fallen to so low a point that no Whig could be elected. But after the furor over the Kansas-Nebraska Act there were not only two parties in Illinois; on the simplest analysis there were three: Whigs, Nebraska (Douglas) Democrats, and Anti-Nebraska Democrats. With Whig support alone no one could be elected, but a Whig who could effect a coalition of Whigs and Anti-Nebraska Democrats might be. The crux of the question was

---

[39] Milton, pp. 294-369.

[40] Randall, *Lincoln the President,* I:127.

[41] Beveridge, II:143. Lincoln offered an explanation at the time: "I only allowed myself to be elected, because it was supposed my doing so would help Yates." (*CW* II:289.) This is not fully convincing. Yates was defeated, and any help that Lincoln's election could have given was confined to Sangamon County. If his election was a help to the county ticket, why was a Democrat elected when he resigned? In the Scripps autobiographical materials Lincoln emphasized his campaigning in Yates' interest in 1854, but in that statement, where such an explanation would have been relevant, he is silent.

whether the combined number of Whigs and Anti-Nebraska Democrats would be greater than the number of Nebraska Democrats. To make sure of one additional Anti-Nebraska member, and one less Nebraska, Lincoln himself ran for the legislature and was elected.

But he had made a curious oversight. The new state constitution, adopted while Lincoln was in Congress, made a newly elected member of the legislature ineligible for election to the Senate during the term for which he was elected.[42] As soon as he became aware of the fact, Lincoln resigned his seat. To his great chagrin—and to his disadvantage—a Democrat was elected in his place. This was a particularly humiliating defeat; the election was within Sangamon County, not the Congressional district. The Whigs took for granted that a Whig would be elected, and they did not work at the polls. The election occurred on a rainy day. The Democrats quietly brought out a heavy vote and won.[43]

As soon as the returns were in Lincoln carefully reckoned up the alignment of the new assembly. This required extensive correspondence, since he was not personally acquainted with several of the new members. Incidentally the breach between Lincoln and Washburne was healed; he received much valuable information from Washburne, as well as cordial and hearty support.[44]

While this was going on, Lincoln learned, to his surprise and not at all to his pleasure, that his name had been placed upon a

---

[42] Constitution of Illinois, 1848, Article III, Section 7; Moses, II:1084. Lincoln's ineligibility was pointed out to him by a political friend, E. N. Powell of Peoria (Powell to Lincoln, November 16, 1854, RTLP; Mearns, I:193). This makes it clear that Lincoln's candidacy for the legislature, however much it was done to help Yates, was with the view to his candidacy for the Senate. He had written letters soliciting support before he resigned; it is obvious that a number of political supporters who were also elected to the legislature (which would elect the Senator) knew and approved his plan to be a candidate. Among them was Powell, who reminded him of his of his ineligibility. Note that Lincoln resigned on November 25, *after* he received Powell's letter. Replying to it he said that he resigned "acting on your advice, and my own judgment," (*CW* II:289).

[43] Moses, II:591; *CW* II:303 f.

[44] The correspondence is too voluminous to document. See RTLP of the period. There are representative samples of the letters to Lincoln in Mearns, I:190 ff.; the Lincoln letters are in *CW* II:286-304. In *CW* II:296-98 there is a reproduction of the manuscript pamphlet with a tabulation of members of the legislature and their political affiliations. See Carl Sandburg, *Lincoln Collector* (1949), p. 156.

list of Republican party committeemen in a call for a meeting of the State Central Committee of the new party. Lincoln did not attend the meeting; indeed, he was ignorant of the call until after the time of the meeting.[45] Lincoln was still a Whig; he did not admit that the party was dead, and the nascent Republican party was too much tinged with abolitionism for him to join it.

No, Lincoln was convinced that the Whig party was very much alive, and that a Whig could be elected to the Senate. When he wrote, canvassing for pledges, he said, "I want the chance of being the man." [46] Time was precious. It was used for the writing of numerous letters. Washburne and others reported the attitude toward the Nebraska question held by assembly-men about whom Lincoln inquired. Lincoln quietly ascertained whether others might be rival candidates. He asked Joe Gillespie point-blank whether he intended to run, and inquired of him whether Judge Trumbull intended to be a candidate.[47] Lincoln had difficulty in getting information from Chicago politicians, and in his dilemma he asked Washburne to query John Went-worth and to secure Wentworth's support.[48] Presently he esti-mated (correctly, as it turned out) that the Anti-Nebraska men had a majority, and that he would have the largest number of votes on the first ballot. He calculated that there were 57 Anti-Nebraska men (Whigs and Democrats) and 43 Nebraska men (Democrats, except for one Nebraska Whig) in the legislature, making a comfortable majority of 14.[49] He thought that he had a good chance.

But instead of concentrating upon Shields, the Democratic vote began to swing to Governor Joel Matteson. And, as it turned out, there were five Anti-Nebraska Democrats who could not be induced to vote for a Whig.

The outcome was that Lincoln, needing 51 votes to win, and leading with 45 votes on the first ballot (Shields being second with 41 and Trumbull third with 5) could not increase his lead (which rose to 47) when the Shields' votes shifted to Matteson, because of the intransigence of the five who refused to vote

---

[45] CW II:288.
[46] CW II:288.
[47] CW II:290.
[48] CW II:293.
[49] CW II:296-98, 303 f.

for a Whig. As the Matteson vote increased, Lincoln's vote steadily declined. It became evident that in order that an Anti-Nebraska man might be elected Lincoln must withdraw. This he did on the tenth ballot; the five stubborn men voted for Trumbull, and Trumbull was elected.[50]

Once again Lincoln had suffered the disappointment of defeat. But he was again a politician seeking office. He had lost this election, but he would run again and yet again. Future contests would find him, as this one did, using the one issue certain to be of interest and sure to bring votes. Never before had Lincoln run for office on the slavery issue, but never afterward would he run on any other. He would give more attention to slavery than he had done before. He was "on the track"—to the ordeal of the Union, to his arduous Presidency, to tragic death—and to apotheosis.

---

[50] Beveridge, II:274-90; Moses, II:591-93.

BIBLIOGRAPHY

1. MANUSCRIPTS

Appointment Files, 1849-1878, Department of the Interior, Archives of the Department of the Interior.

Autograph Letters, Chicago Historical Society, Vol. 14 (J. Gillespie), Chicago Historical Society.

Edward D. Baker MSS, Illinois State Historical Library.

John M. Clayton MSS, Library of Congress.

Schuyler Colfax MSS, Indiana State Historical Library.

John J. Crittenden MSS, Library of Congress.

Dedham Historical Society MSS, Dedham, Massachusetts.

Domestic Letters, Department of State, Vol. 37, Archives of the Department of State.

Stephen A. Douglas MSS, Illinois State Historical Library.

Stephen A. Douglas MSS, University of Chicago Library.

Elisha Embree MSS, Indiana State Historical Library.

Thomas Ewing MSS, Library of Congress.

French MSS, Illinois State Historical Library.

Joshua R. Giddings MSS, Ohio Archaeological and Historical Society.

The Diary of Joshua R. Giddings, Ohio State Archaeological and Historical Society.

Joshua R. Giddings and George W. Julian MSS, Library of Congress.

George Saile Gideon Account Book, Library of Congress.

Duff Green MSS, Library of Congress.

John J. Hardin MSS, Chicago Historical Society.

Herndon MSS, Library of Congress.

Anson G. Henry MSS, Illinois State Historical Library.

Lanphier MSS, Illinois State Historical Library.
Robert Todd Lincoln Papers, Library of Congress.
John A. McClernand MSS, Illinois State Historical Library.
Willie P. Mangum MSS, Library of Congress.
John G. Nicolay MSS, Library of Congress.
Caleb B. Smith MSS, Indiana State Historical Library.
Caleb B. Smith MSS, Library of Congress.
Richard W. Thompson MSS, Indiana State Historical Library.
Richard W. Thompson MSS, Lincoln National Life Foundation, Fort
    Wayne, Indiana.
Richard W. Thompson MSS, in possession of his granddaughter, Mrs.
    Charles S. Keene, Terre Haute, Indiana.
Elihu Washburne MSS, Library of Congress.

2. OFFICIAL PUBLICATIONS

*Calendar of Papers in Washington Archives, relating to the Territories
    of the United States,* Washington, Carnegie Institution of Wash-
    ington, 1911.
*Congressional Directory, for the First Session of the Thirtieth Congress
    of the United States of America,* Washington, J. and G. S. Gideon,
    Printers, 1848.
*Congressional Directory, for the Second Session of the Thirtieth Con-
    gress of the United States of America,* Washington, J. and G. S.
    Gideon, Printers, 1849.
The Congressional Globe, New Series, Containing Sketches of the
    Debates and Proceedings of the First Session of the Thirtieth
    Congress, By Blair and Rives, City of Washington, Printed at
    the Office of Blair and Rives, 1848.
Appendix to the Congressional Globe, For the First Session, Thirtieth
    Congress, Containing Speeches and Important State Papers, By
    Blair and Rives, *New Series,* 1847-1848, City of Washington,
    Printed at the Office of Blair and Rives, 1848.
The Congressional Globe, New Series, Containing Sketches of the De-
    bates and Proceedings of the Second Session of the Thirtieth
    Congress, By Blair and Rives, City of Washington, Printed at the
    Office of Blair and Rives, 1849.
Journal of the House of Representatives of the United States: Being
    the First Session of the Thirtieth Congress; begun and held at
    the City of Washington, December 6, 1847, in the seventy-
    second year of the independence of the United States, Wash-
    ington, Printed by Wendell and Van Benthuysen, 1847-1848.
Journal of the House of Representatives of the United States: being
    the Second Session of the Thirtieth Congress . . . 1848-1849.
*Journals of the Convention Assembled at the City of Austin on the
    Fourth of July, 1845, for the Purpose of Framing a Constitution
    for the State of Texas,* Austin, 1846.

Members of the Legislature of the State of Texas From 1846 to 1939, Published by the State of Texas, Austin, 1939.

Oregon Spectator Index 1846-1854, Vol. II, Prepared by WPA Newspaper Index Project, O. P. 665-94-3-60, Sponsored by the City of Portland, Oregon Historical Society, May 1941.

Register of All Officers and Agents Civil, Military, and Naval in the Service of the United States on the Thirtieth September 1851, Prepared by the Department of State, Washington, Gideon & Co., Printers, 1851.

Texas–Abstract of Titled and Patented Lands 1860, Compiled from Records of the General Land Office of the State of Texas (prior to Dec. 1, 1859), Austin, John Marshall & Co., State Printers, 1860.

The University of Texas Bulletin, No. 3324: June 22, 1933, "County Government and Administration in Texas," by Wallace C. Murphy, edited by James L. McCamy, Bureau of Research in the Social Sciences, Study No. 5. Published by the University of Texas, Austin.

3. NEWSPAPERS

The Alton *Telegraph,* Illinois State Historical Library.
The Baltimore *American,* Library of Congress.
The Baltimore *Clipper,* Library of Congress.
The Beardstown *Gazette,* Illinois State Historical Library.
The Belleville *Advocate,* Illinois State Historical Library.
The Bloomington *Western Whig,* Illinois State Historical Library.
The Boston *Atlas,* Library of Congress.
The Boston *Courier,* Library of Congress.
The Boston *Daily Advertiser,* Library of Congress.
The Boston *Evening Traveler,* Library of Congress.
The Boston *Herald,* Library of Congress.
The Boston *Journal,* Library of Congress.
The Carrollton *Gazette,* Illinois State Historical Library.
The Chicago *Democrat,* Chicago Historical Society, Newberry Library.
The Chicago *Gem of the Prairie,* Illinois State Historical Library.
The Chicago *Herald of the Prairies,* Illinois State Historical Library.
The Chicago *Journal,* Chicago Historical Society, Newberry Library.
The Chicago *Western Citizen,* Illinois State Historical Library.
The Frederick (Maryland) *Republican Citizen,* Library of Congress.
The Galena *Jeffersonian,* Illinois State Historical Library.
The Galena *Northwestern Gazette and Galena Advertiser,* Illinois State Historical Library.
The Hennepin *Herald and Bureau County Advertiser,* Illinois State Historical Library.
The Indianapolis *Indiana State Journal,* Indianapolis Public Library.
The Indianapolis *Indiana State Sentinel,* Indianapolis Public Library.

The Jacksonville *Morgan Journal*, Illinois State Historical Library.

The Lacon *Illinois Gazette*, Illinois State Historical Library.

The Little Fort (Waukegan) *Lake County Visiter*, Chicago Historical Society.

The Little Fort (Waukegan) *Porcupine and Democratic Banner*, Chicago Historical Society.

The Louisville *Courier*, Library of Congress.

The New York *Herald*, Library of Congress.

The New York *Tribune*, Library of Congress.

The New York (*Tribune*) *Whig Almanac and United States Register*, Library of Congress.

The Oquawka *Spectator*, Illinois State Historical Library.

The Oregon City *Oregon Spectator*, Portland Historical Society.

The Peoria *Democratic Press*, Illinois State Historical Society.

The Quincy *Whig*, Illinois State Historical Society.

The Rockford *Forum*, Rockford Public Library.

The Springfield *Illinois Journal*, Illinois State Historical Library.

The Springfield *Illinois State Register*, Illinois State Historical Library.

The Springfield *Sangamo Journal*, Illinois State Historical Library.

The Taunton *Daily Gazette*, Library of Congress.

The Vandalia *Fayette Yeoman*, Illinois State Historical Library.

The Washington *National Intelligencer* (Daily), Library of Congress.

The Washington *National Intelligencer* (Tri-weekly), Library of Congress.

4. PRINTED SOURCES

Basler, Roy P. (Editor), Marion Dolores Pratt and Lloyd A. Dunlap (Assistant Editors), *The Collected Works of Abraham Lincoln*, Rutgers University Press, New Brunswick, 1953.

Richardson, James D. (Editor), *A Compilation of the Messages and Papers of the Presidents*, 1789-1902, 10 Vols., New York, Bureau of National Literature and Art, 1905.

Sparks, Edwin Earle (Editor), *The Lincoln–Douglas Debates of 1858*, Springfield, Trustees of the Illinois State Historical Library, 1908.

5. BOOKS, ARTICLES, AND MONOGRAPHS

Abbat, William, *The Magazine of History*, Extra Numbers 89-92, Vol. 23, Tarrytown, New York, 1923.

Ackerman, William K., *Early Illinois Railroads*, Fergus Historical Series, No. 23, Chicago, 1884.

Adams, Charles Francis (Editor), *The Memoirs of John Quincy Adams*, Philadelphia, J. B. Lippincott and Co., 1874-1877.

American Bar Association *Journal*, 34 (1948), 791-894.

Angle, Paul McClelland, *"Here I Have Lived:"* *A History of Lincoln's Springfield, 1821-1865,* Springfield, The Abraham Lincoln Association, 1935.

————— (Editor), "Lincoln and the United States Supreme Court," *Bulletin of the Abraham Lincoln Association,* 47 (1937), 1-9, Supplement, 1-3.

—————, *Lincoln 1854-1861,* Being the Day-by-Day Activities of Abraham Lincoln from January 1, 1854 to March 4, 1861, Springfield, Abraham Lincoln Association, 1933.

Avary, Myrta Lockett (Editor), *Recollections of Alexander H. Stephens,* New York, Doubleday, Page & Co., 1910.

Bailey, Louis B., "Caleb B. Smith," *Indiana Magazine of History,* 39 (1939), 213-39.

Baker, D. W. C., *A Brief History of Texas from Its Earliest Settlement,* New York and Chicago, A. S. Barnes & Co., 1873.

Bancroft, Frederic, *Life of William H. Seward,* 2 Vols., New York, Harper & Brothers, 1900.

Bancroft, Hubert Howe, *History of the North Mexican States and Texas* (The Works of Hubert Howe Bancroft, Vols. 15, 16), Vol. 1, 1531-1800, Vol. 2, 1801-1889, San Francisco, The History Company, 1886, 1889.

—————, *History of Oregon,* Vol. 2, 1848-1888, San Francisco, The History Company, 1890.

Barker, Eugene C., *The Life of Stephen P. Austin,* Nashville and Dallas, Cokesbury Press, 1925.

Barringer, William E., *Lincoln's Vandalia, A Pioneer Portrait,* New Brunswick, Rutgers University Press, 1949.

Bemis, Samuel Flagg, *A Diplomatic History of the United States,* New York, Henry Holt and Co., 1950.

—————, *John Quincy Adams and the Foundations of American Foreign Policy,* New York, A. A. Knopf, 1949.

Beveridge, A. J., *Abraham Lincoln, 1809-1858,* 2 Vols., Boston, Houghton Mifflin Co., 1928.

Bill, Alfred Hoyt, *Rehearsal for Conflict, the War With Mexico, 1846-1848,* New York, A. A. Knopf, 1947.

Binkley, Wilfred H., *American Political Parties: Their Natural History,* New York, A. A. Knopf, 1945.

Binkley, William Campbell, *The Expansionist Movement in Texas, 1836-1850,* Berkeley, University of California Press, 1925.

————— (Editor), *The Official Correspondence of the Texas Revolution,* 2 Vols., New York and London, D. Appleton–Century Co., 1936.

Boggess, Arthur Clinton, *The Settlement of Illinois, 1778-1830,* Chicago, Chicago Historical Society, 1908.

Borome, Joseph, "Two Letters of Robert Charles Winthrop," *Mississippi Valley Historical Review,* 38 (1951), 289-96.

Boucher, Chauncey Samuel, *"In re* That Aggressive Slaveocracy," *Mississippi Valley Historical Review,* 9 (1921), 13-79.

Bracht, Viktor (Charles Frank Schmidt, translator), *Texas in 1848,* San Antonio, Naylor Publishing Co., 1931.

Brown, Mrs. Mary M., *A School History of Texas,* Published by the Author, Dallas, 1894.

Bryan, Wilhelmus B., *A History of the National Capital,* 2 Vols., The Macmillan Co., New York, 1916.

Buck, Solon J., *Illinois in 1818,* Illinois Centennial Commission, Springfield, 1917.

Bullard, F. Lauriston, "Abraham Lincoln and George Ashmun," *New England Quarterly,* 19 (1946), 184-211.

Busey, Samuel Clagett, *Personal Reminiscences and Recollections,* Washington and Philadelphia, Dornan, Printer, 1895.

Calhoun, John C., See Crallé, Richard K.

Carman, Harry J., and Reinhard H. Luthin, *Lincoln and the Patronage,* New York, Columbia University Press, 1943.

Clark, Allen C., *Abraham Lincoln and the National Capital,* Washington, Press of W. F. Roberts Co., 1925.

Clay, Henry. See Colton, Calvin.

Cole, Arthur Charles, *The Whig Party of the South,* Washington, American Historical Association, 1913.

Coleman, Mrs. Chapman, *The Life of John J. Crittenden, With Selections from his Correspondence and Speeches,* 2 vols., Philadelphia, J. B. Lippincott & Co., 1871.

Colton, Calvin (Editor), *The Works of Henry Clay, Comprising His Life, Correspondence, and Speeches,* 10 Vols., New York and London, G. P. Putnam's Sons, Knickerbocker Press, 1904.

Condon, William H., *Life of James Shields,* Chicago, Press of the Blakely Printing Co., 1900.

Crallé, Richard K. (Editor), *John C. Calhoun, Works,* 6 Vols., New York, D. Appleton & Co., 1851-1856.

Craven, Avery O., *The Coming of the Civil War,* New York, Charles Scribner's Sons, 1942.

Dahlgren, Madelene V., "Samuel Finley Vinton," *Ohio Archaeological and Historical Society Publications,* 4 (1896), 231-62.

Darling, Arthur Burr, *Political Changes in Massachusetts 1824-1848,* New Haven, Yale University Press, 1925.

Davidson, Alexander, and Bernard Stuvé, *A Complete History of Illinois from 1763 to 1873,* Springfield, Illinois State Journal Co., 1874.

Dearborn, Jeremiah W., "Sketch of the Life and Character of Amos Tuck," *Transactions of the Maine Historical Society,* Portland, Thurston Publishing Co., 1888.

DeShields, James T. (Matt Bradley, Revising Editor and Publisher), *Border Wars of Texas,* Tioga, The Herald Co., 1912.

DeVoto, Bernard, *The Year of Decision 1846,* Boston, Little, Brown and Co., 1943.

Dodd, William E., *Expansion and Conflict,* Boston, Houghton Mifflin Co., 1915.

———, *Robert J. Walker, Imperialist,* Chicago, Chicago Literary Club, 1914.

———, "The West and the War with Mexico," *Transactions of the*

Illinois State Historical Society, 1912, pp. 15-23, Springfield, Illinois State Journal Co., Printers, 1914.

Douglas, Stephen A., "The Dividing Line Between the Federal and Local Authorities: Popular Sovereignty in the Territories," *Harper's Monthly,* 19 (1859), 519-37.

Edwards, Ninian Wirt, *The Life and Times of Ninian Edwards, and History of Illinois from 1778 to 1833,* Springfield, Illinois State Journal Co., 1870.

Eggleston, Percy C., *Lincoln in New England,* New York, Stewart, Warren & Co., 1922.

Elliott, Charles Winslow, *Winfield Scott, the Soldier and the Man,* New York, The Macmillan Co., 1937.

Ellis, John B., *Sights and Secrets of the National Capital, A Work Descriptive of Washington City in all its Phases,* United States Publishing Co., Chicago, Jones Junkin & Co., 1869.

Fergus, Robert (Compiler), *Chicago River-and-Harbor Convention,* Chicago, Fergus Printing Co., 1882.

Fillmore, Zachary Taylor, *The History and Geography of Texas as Told in County Names,* Press of E. L. Steck, Austin, 1915.

Fish, Carl Russel, *The Rise of the Common Man 1830-1850 (A History of American Life,* Vol. VI), New York, The Macmillan Co., 1927.

Ford, Guy Stanton (Editor), *Essays in American History Dedicated to Frederick Jackson Turner,* New York, Henry Holt & Co., 1910.

Fox, Dixon Ryan (Editor), *Sources of Culture in the Middle West: Backgrounds versus Frontiers,* New York, D. Appleton–Century Co., 1934.

Gambrell, Herbert, *Anson Jones, The Last President of Texas,* New York, Doubleday, 1948.

——, and Lewis W. Newton, *A Social and Political History of Texas,* Dallas, The Southwest Press, 1932.

Garrison, George Pierce (Editor), *Diplomatic Correspondence of the Republic of Texas,* American Historical Association, Annual Report 1907-1908, Washington, 1908-1911.

——, *Texas: A Contrast of Civilization,* Boston, Houghton, Mifflin Co., 1903.

——, *Westward Expansion 1841-1850 (The American Nation; A History,* Vol. 17), New York and London, Harper & Brothers, 1906.

Gernon, Blaine B., *Lincoln in the Political Circus,* Chicago, The Black Cat Press, 1936.

——, *The Lincolns in Chicago,* Chicago, Anacorthe Publishers, 1934.

Giddings, Joshua R., *History of the Rebellion: Its Authors and Causes,* New York, Follett, Foster & Co., 1864.

——, *Speeches in Congress 1841-1852,* Boston, J. P. Jewett & Co., 1853.

Going, Charles Buxton, *David Wilmot, Free Soiler,* New York and London, D. Appleton & Co., 1924.

Graebner, Norman A., *Empire on the Pacific*, New York, Ronald Press Co., 1955.

Greene, Evarts Boutell, "Sectional Forces in the History of Illinois," *Transactions of the Illinois State Historical Society*, 1903, pp. 75-83.

Griffis, William Eliot, *Millard Fillmore, Constructive Statesman, Defender of the Constitution, President of the United States*, Ithaca, Andrus and Church, 1915.

Griffith, James Eveleth, *History of the Washington Monument, from its inception to its completion and dedication*, Holyoke, J. E. Griffith, Printer, 1885.

Hamilton, Holman, "Abraham Lincoln and Zachary Taylor," *Lincoln Herald*, 45 (1951), 14-19.

———, *Zachary Taylor, Soldier of the Republic*, Indianapolis, Bobbs-Merrill Co., 1941.

———, *Zachary Taylor, Soldier in the White House*, Indianapolis, Bobbs-Merrill Co., 1951.

Harper, Robert S., *Lincoln and the Press*, New York, McGraw-Hill Book Co., 1951.

Harris, Alfred G., "Lincoln and the Question of Slavery in the District of Columbia," *Lincoln Herald*, 51 (1949), 17-21, 48; 52 (1950), 2-16; 53 (1951), 11-18.

———, *Slavery and Emancipation in the District of Columbia, 1801-1862*, Unpublished dissertation, Ohio State University Library, 1946.

Harris, Norman Dwight, *History of Negro Servitude in Illinois and of the Slavery Agitation in that State 1719-1864*, Chicago, A. C. McClurg and Co., 1914.

Hatcher, Mattie Alice, *Letters of an Early American Traveler: Mary Austin Holley, her Life and Works*, 1784-1846, Dallas, The Southwest Press, 1933.

———, *The Opening of Texas to Foreign Settlement*, 1801-1821, University of Texas Bulletin No. 2714, Austin, 1927.

Henry, Robert Selph, *The Story of the Mexican War*, Indianapolis, Bobbs-Merrill Co., 1950.

Herndon, William H., and Jesse Williams Weik, *Abraham Lincoln, The True Story of a Great Life*, 3 Vols., Chicago, Belford, Clarke and Co., 1889.

Hertz, Emmanuel, *The Hidden Lincoln, From the Letters and Papers of William H. Herndon*, New York, The Viking Press, 1938.

Hilliard, Henry Washington, *Politics and Pen Pictures at Home and Abroad*, New York, G. P. Putnam's Sons, 1892.

Hinsdale, B. A., *The Old Northwest*, New York, Townsend MacConn, 1888.

Hogan, William R., *The Texas Republic*, Norman, The University of Oklahoma Press, 1946.

Holley, Mrs. Mary Austin, *Texas, Observations Historical, Geographical, and Descriptive*, Baltimore, Armstrong and Plaskitt, 1833.

Holt, Edgar, "Party Politics in Ohio 1840-1850," *Ohio Archaeological and Historical Quarterly*, 38 (1929), 47-182, 260-402.

Horner, Harlan Hoyt, *Lincoln and Greeley*, Urbana, University of Illinois Press, 1953.

Hubbart, Henry Clyde, *The Older Middle West 1840-1880*, New York, Appleton–Century Co., 1936.

———, "Pro-Southern Influences in the Free West 1840-1865," *Mississippi Valley Historical Review*, 20 (1933), 45-62.

Hunt, Gaillard, *Israel, Elihu, and Cadwallader Washburne, A Chapter in American Biography*, New York, The Macmillan Co., 1925.

Johnson, Allen (Editor), *Dictionary of American Biography*, 20 Vols., New York, Charles Scribner's Sons, 1928.

———, *Life of Stephen A. Douglas*, New York, The Macmillan Co., 1938.

Julian, George Washington, *The Life of Joshua R. Giddings*, Chicago, A. C. McClurg and Co., 1892.

Kelly, Sister M. Margaret Jean, *The Career of Joseph Lane, Frontier Politician*, Washington, The Catholic University of America Press, 1942.

Kendall, George Wilkins, *Narrative of the Texan Santa Fe Expedition*, New York, Harper & Brothers, 1844.

Kennedy, William, *Texas: The Rise, Progress, and Prospects of the Republic of Texas*, 2 Vols., London, R. Hastings, 1841.

Kofoid, Carrie Prudence, "Puritan Influences in the Formative Years of Illinois History," *Transactions of the Illinois State Historical Society*, 1905, pp. 261-347.

Lewis, Lloyd, *Captain Sam Grant*, Boston, Little, Brown and Co., 1950.

Linder, Usher Ferguson, *Reminiscences of the Early Bench and Bar of Illinois*, Chicago, Chicago Legal News Co., 1879.

Lubbock, Francis Richard, *Six Decades in Texas*, Austin, B. C. Jones and Co., 1900.

Luthin, Reinhard H., See Carman, Harry J.

———, "Abraham Lincoln and the Massachusetts Whigs in 1848," *New England Quarterly*, 14 (1941), 619-32.

MacCaleb, Walter F., *The Conquest of the West*, New York, Prentice–Hall, Inc., 1947.

McCormac, Eugene I., *James K. Polk, A Political Biography*, Berkeley, The University of California Press, 1922.

McCutchen, Samuel Proctor, *Albert Gallatin Brown*, Chicago, The University of Chicago Press, 1935.

McKinley, Silas Bent, and Silas Bent, *Old Rough and Ready, The Life and Times of Zachary Taylor*, New York, The Vanguard Press, 1946.

McKitrick, Reuben, "The Public Land System of Texas, 1823-1910," *Bulletin of the University of Wisconsin*, No. 905, Madison, The University of Wisconsin, 1918.

McLaughlin, Andrew Cunningham, *Lewis Cass*, Boston, Houghton Mifflin Co., 1899.

Massachusetts Historical Society *Proceedings*, October, 1916, pp. 30-36.

Mathews, Alfred, *Ohio and Her Western Reserve*, New York, D. Appleton and Co., 1902.

Mathews, Lois K., *The Expansion of New England*, Boston, Houghton Mifflin Co., 1934.

Mearns, David C., *The Lincoln Papers*, 2 Vols., Garden City, Doubleday and Co., 1948.

Meigs, William Montgomery, *Life of Charles Jared Ingersoll*, Philadelphia and London, J. B. Lippincott Co., 1897. (Second edition, 1900.)

Merk, Frederick, *Albert Gallatin and the Oregon Problem, A Study in Anglo-American Diplomacy*, Cambridge, Harvard University Press, 1950.

Miller, Paul J., "Lincoln and the Governorship of Oregon," *Mississippi Valley Historical Review*, 23 (1936), 394 ff.

Milton, George Fort, *The Eve of Conflict: Stephen A. Douglas and the Needless War*, Boston, Houghton Mifflin Co., 1934.

Monaghan, Jay, *Lincoln Bibliography*, 1839-1909, 2 Vols., Collections of the Illinois State Historical Library, Vols. 31 and 32, Springfield, 1943.

Moses, John, *Illinois, Historical and Statistical*, 2 Vols., Chicago, Fergus Publishing Co., 1889.

Murphy, Wallace C., *County Government in Texas*, Austin, University of Texas Bulletin No. 3324, 1933.

Nevins, Allan, *The Ordeal of the Union*, 2 Vols., New York, Charles Scribner's Sons, 1947.

Newman, John B., *Texas and Mexico in 1846*, comprising the History of Both Countries, with an account of the soil, climate, and Productions of Each (with map 1840), New York, Published by J. K. Wellman. Reprinted in *The Magazine of History;* see Abbat, William.

Newton, Joseph F., *Lincoln and Herndon*, Cedar Rapids, Torch Press, 1910.

Newton, Lewis William, and Herbert Pickens Gambrill, *A Social and Political History of Texas*, Dallas, Southwest Press, 1932.

Nicolay, John G., and John Hay, *Abraham Lincoln, A History*, 10 Vols., New York, The Century Co., 1890.

Nye, Russel B., *George Bancroft, Brahmin Rebel*, New York, A. A. Knopf, 1944.

Ogg, Frederick Austin, *A Chronicle of the Ohio Valley and Beyond* (Chronicles of America, Vol. 19), New Haven, Yale University Press, 1921.

Oldroyd, Osborn H. (Compiler and Editor), *The Lincoln Memorial: Album-Immortelles*, New York, G. W. Carleton and Co., 1883.

O'Shaughnessy, Francis, "General James Shields of Illinois," *Transactions of the Illinois State Historical Society*, 1915, pp. 113-22.

Packard, Roy D., *The Lincoln of the Thirtieth Congress*, Boston, Christopher Publishing House, 1950.

Paullin, Charles O., "Abraham Lincoln in Congress, 1847-1849," *Journal of the Illinois State Historical Society,* 14 (1921), 85-89.

Pease, Theodore Calvin, and James Garfield Randall, *The Diary of Orville Hickman Browning,* 2 Vols., Springfield, Illinois State Historical Library, 1925, 1933.

———, *The Frontier State, 1818-1848,* Centennial History of Illinois, Vol. 2, Springfield, Illinois Historical Commission, 1918.

———, *Illinois Election Returns, 1818-1848,* Collections of the Illinois State Historical Society, Vol. 18, Statistical Studies, Vol. 1, Springfield, Jefferson Printing Co., 1923.

Phillips, Ulrich Bonnell, *The Life of Robert Toombs,* New York, The Macmillan Co., 1917.

———, "The Southern Whigs, 1834-1854," *Essays in American History Dedicated to Frederick Jackson Turner* (Guy Stanton Ford, Editor), pp. 203-16, New York, Henry Holt and Co., 1910.

Pooley, William Vipond, *The Settlement of Illinois from 1830 to 1850,* Bulletin of the University of Wisconsin, No. 220, The University of Wisconsin, Madison, 1908.

Poore, Ben: Perley, *Perley's Reminiscences of Sixty Years in the National Metropolis,* 2 Vols., Philadelphia, Hubbard Brothers, 1886.

"Powers of the President to Send the Armed Forces Outside the United States," Washington, United States Government Printing Office, 1951.

Pratt, Harry Edward, "Albert T. Bledsoe: Critic of Lincoln," *Transactions of the Illinois State Historical Society,* 41, pp. 153-83.

———, *Concerning Mr. Lincoln,* Springfield, Abraham Lincoln Association, 1944.

———, "Dr. Anson G. Henry, Lincoln's Physician and Friend," *The Lincoln Herald,* 45 (1943), 3-17, 31-40. (Reprinted from the *Lincoln Herald,* Knoxville, Press of Archer and Smith, 1944.)

———, *Illinois As Lincoln Knew It, A Boston Reporter's Record of a Trip in 1847,* Springfield, The Abraham Lincoln Association, 1941.

———, *The Personal Finances of Abraham Lincoln,* Springfield, The Abraham Lincoln Association, 1943.

———, "The Springfield Mechanics Union, 1839-1848," *Journal of the Illinois State Historical Society,* 34 (1941), 130-34.

Priestly, Herbert I., *The Mexican Nation: A History,* New York, The Macmillan Co., 1923.

Quaife, Milo Milton (Editor), *The Diary of James K. Polk During his Presidency, 1845 to 1849,* 4 Vols., Chicago, A. C. McClurg and Co., 1910.

Rauck, James Byrne, *Albert Gallatin Brown, Radical Southern Nationalist,* New York, D. Appleton–Century Co., 1937.

Randall, James Garfield, *Constitutional Problems Under Lincoln* (Revised Edition), Urbana, The University of Illinois Press, 1951.

———, "Has the Lincoln Theme Been Exhausted?" *American Historical Review,* 41 (1936), 270-94.

————, *Lincoln the President*, 4 Vols., New York, Dodd, Mead & Co., 1945-55.

Randall, Ruth Painter, *Mary Lincoln: Biography of a Marriage*, Boston, Little, Brown and Co., 1953.

Reeves, Jesse Siddall, *American Diplomacy under Tyler and Polk*, Baltimore, The Johns Hopkins Press, 1907.

Reynolds, John, *My Own Times; Embracing Also the History of My Life*, Chicago, Fergus Publishing Co., 1879.

Riddle, Donald W., *Lincoln Runs for Congress*, New Brunswick, Rutgers University Press, 1948.

Rippy, James Fred, *Joel R. Poinsett, Versatile American*, Durham, Duke University Press, 1935.

Rives, George Lockhart, *Mexican Diplomacy on the Eve of the War With the United States*, New York, Extract from the *American Historical Review*, 1913.

————, *The United States and Mexico, 1821-1848*, 2 Vols., New York, Charles Scribner's Sons, 1913.

Roll, Charles, *Colonel Dick Thompson, The Persistent Whig*, Indianapolis, Indiana Historical Collections, Vol. 30, Indiana Historical Bureau, 1948.

Rolston, Charles (Editor), *Biographical Dictionary of the American Congress, 1774-1903*, Washington, United States Government Printing Office, 1903.

Rose, James A., *Counties of Illinois, Their Origin and Evolution*, Compiled and published by James A. Rose, Secretary of State, Springfield, State of Illinois, 1906.

Ross, Earle D. (Editor), "A Travelogue of 1849," *Mississippi Valley Historical Review*, 27 (1940), 435-41.

Sandburg, Carl, *Lincoln Collector; the Story of Oliver R. Barrett's Great Private Collection*, New York, Harcourt, Brace, 1949.

Schlesinger, Arthur M., *Paths to the Present*, New York, The Macmillan Co., 1949.

Schouler, James, "The Whig Party in Massachusetts," *Massachusetts Historical Society Proceedings*, 50 (1916-1917), 39-53.

Scott, Franklin William, *Newspapers and Periodicals of Illinois, 1814-1879*, Collections of the Illinois State Historical Library, Vol. 6, Bibliographical Series, Vol. 1, Springfield, 1910.

Seaton, Josephine, *William Winston Seaton of the "National Intelligencer,"* Boston, J. R. Osgood and Co., 1871.

Seward, Frederick William, *William H. Seward;* an autobiography from 1801 to 1834. With a memoir of his life, and selections from his letters, New York, Derby and Miller, 1877, 1891.

————, *Reminiscences of a War-Time Statesman and Diplomat, 1830-1915*, New York and London, G. P. Putnam's Sons, 1916.

Seward, William H., *Life and Public Services of John Quincy Adams*, Auburn, N. Y., Derby, Miller & Co., 1849.

Sioussat, St. George L., *James Buchanan, Secretary of State*, New York, A. A. Knopf, 1928.

Smith, Justin H., *The Annexation of Texas* (Corrected Edition), New York, Barnes and Noble, 1941.

——, *The War With Mexico*, 2 Vols., New York, The Macmillan Co., 1919.

Smith, Theodore Clarke, *The Liberty and Free Soil Parties in the Northwest*, New York, Longmans, Green & Co., 1897.

Smith, Willard H., *Schuyler Colfax: The Changing Fortunes of a Political Idol*, Indianapolis, Indiana Historical Bureau, 1952.

Snigg, John P., "Edward Dickinson Baker — Lincoln's Forgotten Friend," *Lincoln Herald*, 53 (1941), 33-37.

Starr, John William, *Lincoln and the Railroads, a Biographical Study*, New York, Dodd, Mead & Co., 1927.

Stephens, Alexander H., *A Constitutional View of the Late War Between the States*, Philadelphia, National Publishing Co., 1868-70.

——, See Avary, Myrta Lockett (Editor).

Stephenson, Nathaniel W., *Texas and the Mexican War, A Chronicle of the Winning of the Southwest.* (Chronicles of America, Vol. 24), New Haven, Yale University Press, 1921.

Stoddard, Henry Luther, *Horace Greeley*, New York, G. P. Putnam's Sons, 1946.

Stone, Irving, *They Also Ran, The Story of the Men Who Were Defeated for the Presidency*, New York, Doubleday, Doran, and Co., Inc., 1943.

Swisher, Carl Brent, *American Constitutional Development* (Second Edition), Boston, Houghton Mifflin Co., 1954.

Sydnor, Charles S., *The Development of Southern Sectionalism 1819-1848*, Baton Rouge, Louisiana State University Press, 1950.

Tarbell, Ida M., *The Life of Abraham Lincoln*, 2 Vols., New York, McClure, Phillips Co., 1900.

Thomas, Benjamin P., *Abraham Lincoln, A Biography*, New York, A. A. Knopf, 1952.

——, *Lincoln, 1847-1853*, Springfield, The Abraham Lincoln Association, 1936.

Thorp, Willard (Editor), *The Lives of Eighteen from Princeton* (Wheeler, John A., "Joseph Henry," pp. 265-81), Princeton, Princeton University Press.

Townsend, William Henry, *Lincoln and His Wife's Home Town*, Indianapolis, Bobbs-Merrill Co., 1929.

Turner, Frederick Jackson, *The United States 1830-1850, The Nation and Its Sections*, New York, Henry Holt & Co., 1935.

Van Abele, Rudolph, *Alexander H. Stephens, A Biography*, New York, A. A. Knopf, 1946.

Van Deusen, Glyndon G., *Thurlow Weed, Wizard of the Lobby*, Boston, Little, Brown and Co., 1947.

Wallace, Joseph, *Sketch of the Life and Public Services of Edward D. Baker, U. S. Senator from Oregon*, Springfield, Illinois Journal Co., Printers, 1870.

Warren, Louis A. (Editor), *Bulletin of the Indiana National Life Foundation*, Fort Wayne, Indiana.

No. 451, "Lincoln and the General Land Office Appointment."
Nov. 29, 1937.

No. 854, "Lincoln and John Quincy Adams." Aug. 20, 1945.

No. 855, "The Spot Resolutions." Aug. 27, 1945.

No. 858, "Congressman Lincoln's Committee Work." Sept. 17, 1945.

No. 861, "Congressman Lincoln Observes Congressman Johnson." Oct. 8, 1945.

Watterson, George, *New Guide to Washington,* with new and correct map, Washington, Published by Robert Farnham, 1847.

Webb, Walter Prescott, *The Texas Rangers: A Century of Frontier Defense,* Boston, Houghton Mifflin Co., 1935.

Wentworth, John, *Reminiscences of Early Chicago,* Chicago, R. R. Donnelley and Sons Co., 1912.

————, *Congressional Reminiscences,* Fergus Historical Series, No. 24, Chicago, Fergus Publishing Co., 1882.

Wheeler, Henry G., *History of Congress, Biographical and Political,* New York, Harper & Brothers, 1848.

White, Horace, *The Life of Lyman Trumbull,* Boston, Houghton Mifflin Co., 1912.

White, Leonard D., *The Jacksonians, A Study in Administrative History 1825-1861,* New York, The Macmillan Co., 1954.

Williams, George, "A Political History of Oregon," *Oregon Historical Society Quarterly,* 2 (1901), 1-35.

Wilson, Rufus Rockwell, *Washington the Capital City, and Its Part in the History of the Nation,* 2 Vols., Philadelphia and London, J. B. Lippincott and Co., 1901.

Wiltse, Charles M., *John C. Calhoun, Nationalist, 1782-1828,* Indianapolis, Bobbs-Merrill Co., 1947.

————, *John C. Calhoun, Sectionalist, 1840-1850,* Indianapolis, Bobbs-Merrill Co., 1951.

Winthrop, Robert C., Jr., *Addresses and Speeches on Various Occasions,* 4 Vols., Boston, Little, Brown and Co., 1852-56.

————, *A Memoir of Robert C. Winthrop.* Prepared for the Massachusetts Historical Society, Boston, Little, Brown and Co., 1897.

Woodford, Frank B., *Lewis Cass, The Last Jeffersonian,* New Brunswick, Rutgers University Press, 1950.

Woodward, Walter C., *The Rise and Early History of Political Parties in Oregon, 1843-1868,* Portland, J. K. Gill and Co., 1913.

Wortham, Louis J., *A History of Texas from Wilderness to Commonwealth,* 5 Vols., Fort Worth, Wortham-Molyneaux Co., 1924.

Yoakum, H., *History of Texas from its first Settlement in 1685 to its Annexation to the United States in 1846,* 2 Vols., New York, Redfield, 1855.

INDEX